T3-BNT-997

BLACK EVANGELISTS

BLACK EVANGELISTS

THE SPREAD OF CHRISTIANITY IN UGANDA 1891–1914

M. LOUISE PIROUET

REX COLLINGS LONDON 1978

First published in Great Britain by
Rex Collings Ltd. 69 Marylebone High Street
London W1

ISBN 086036 0512

Typesetting by Malvern Typesetting Services Ltd
Printed in Great Britain by
Billing and Sons Ltd
Guildford, London and Worcester

FOR MY UGANDAN FRIENDS

Preface

In this study an attempt is made to show how Christianity, and especially Protestant Christianity, represented by the (Anglican) Church Missionary Society and the Native Anglican Church (as the Church of the Province of Uganda, Rwanda, and Burundi was then known), spread from Buganda into certain western and northern areas of the country. In this process of expansion African initiative played a considerable part, and it seems worth examining the nature and extent of this initiative, and the motives underlying the eagerness with which the people of Buganda in particular, but also other Ugandan peoples, helped to spread their newly found faith. A second purpose of this study is to examine the reactions of various peoples to the introduction of Christianity. In the Bantu areas of the south and west of Uganda rivalry between Protestants and Catholics was intense and was an important factor in the spread of Christianity, and some attention is therefore paid to the growth of the Catholic Church. The need to keep the study within reasonable limits has meant that where Protestants and Catholics impinged less on each other, as in the north and east of the country, it has not been possible to include a parallel account of Catholic expansion. Two areas outside the Bantu kingdoms have been chosen for study because of the contrast they offer, and hence the light they throw on developments in the kingdom states. These areas are Acoli in the north and Teso in the north-east, both adjacent to Bantu areas, and both largely evangelized in the first instance by Christians from the Bantu kingdoms. In the final chapter the reasons for the gradual decline of this remarkable missionary movement are considered. At a time when expatriate missionaries are considering the possibility of a moratorium on their work, such a study may perhaps be interesting and apt.

My thanks are due to many people who helped me with this work. The study originated in a Ph.D. thesis for the University of East Africa and this, in turn, grew out of a scheme for the preservation of records of the history of the church in East Africa, sponsored by the Theological Education Fund's Special Africa Project. I am particularly grateful to Professor D. H.-W. Gensichen of Heidelberg University and Dr Walter Cason of New York who administered this scheme, and who have given me much help and encouragement. To those in the Departments of Religious Studies and History at Makerere University, Kampala who supervised me I also owe a special debt of gratitude: to the Rev. Professor N. Q. King and Professor R. Beachey, and, after they had both left Uganda, to the Rev. Professor J. S. Mbiti, who succeeded Professor King as Head of the Department of Religious Studies, and Professor M. S. M. Kiwanuka of the Department of History. Among others special mention must be made of the Rev. F. B. Welbourn, Dr Tom Watson and Dr J. A. Rowe (the last mentioned kindly read through the whole typescript, making many useful suggestions); Mr Z. K. Mung'onya, Bishop K. Shalita and the Rev. T. S. M. Williams for their help with Ankole material; Mr O. W. Furley for help with Toro; Dr Michael Twaddle for Toro and Bunyoro material; Dr Okot p'Bitek and Bishop J. K. Russell for help with Acoli; and Professor Bryan Langlands for help with a number of points of historical geography. Miss José Smith, of the Department of Geography, Kingston-upon-Thames Polytechnic (and formerly of Makerere University) kindly took my inadequate and inaccurate sketch-maps, and made something of them for me, and any imperfections which may remain are mine, not hers.

In the course of doing fieldwork I acquired many debts of gratitude. First must be mentioned the informants whose names appear at the end of this book. Among them I made many friends, and the courtesy with which they invited me into their homes and offered me their hospitality as well as their knowledge made fieldwork the most pleasurable part of this study. Then, too, I must express my gratitude to the bishops and clergy of the Church of Uganda, who gave me much help and who have had more faith than I in the ultimate completion and usefulness of this study. A large thank you must be said to those who interpreted for me. They did so much more than interpret: they entered very fully into what I was doing, and went to great lengths to help me seek out knowledgeable informants and to win their confidence. The Church Missionary Society provided the car without which fieldwork could not have been done at all.

To many Catholic friends who have assisted with this study I must also express my thanks. In the period which is discussed here there was bitter rivalry between Catholics and Anglicans in Uganda. Today that has disappeared, and my time in Uganda was greatly enriched by my contacts with the Catholic church there. In particular I should like to thank Mgr B. Wamala and Mgr E. Wandera, Frs A. Seité, P. Etchevery, R. Chaput, V. Pellegrini, V. Dellagiacoma, F. Hoefnagels, and Brother Ludgers, all of whom helped me with information; the White Sisters communities at Villa Maria and Hoima and the Sacred Heart Sisters at Nkozi; and the staffs of Katigondo National Seminary and Nkozi Parish and the Mother-General of the Bannabikira who gave me access to written material. The Rev. Dr A. Shorter asked me to do a study of catechists in Uganda and allowed me to reuse the material here, and the Archivists of the White Fathers in Rome and of St Joseph's Foreign Missionary Society, Mill Hill, were generous with their help when I was working on their archives.

For the help in gaining access to written sources I also wish to thank the Librarians of the Uganda Society, the Royal Commonwealth Society, the Church Missionary Society, and Makerere University. To those in charge of the Africana and Archives Sections of the last mentioned, as well as those in the Photographic Department and Bindery, I am grateful for invaluable help in repairing and reproducing documents lent by the Church of Uganda. I was able to obtain a microfilm of the Fisher Papers through the good offices of Professor Roland Oliver and the University of London Library, and the University of Nottingham Library Xeroxed the Willis papers for Makerere.

Finally I must thank a generation of students in Mary Stuart Hall, Makerere University, whom I pestered on innumerable occasions for bits of information about their history, languages and customs, and who always, with good nature, helped me to find the answer.

M.L.P.
Department of Philosophy and Religious Studies,
University of Nairobi

Contents

List of Maps

List of Tables

A note on the spelling of proper names and vernacular terms

PLACE-NAMES

The spelling adopted for these is that in use by the Uganda Lands and Surveys Department, and found on the Ordnance Maps of Uganda.

PERSONAL NAMES

As far as possible the spelling of personal names is that used by the person himself, where this is known. Otherwise the form used is that most commonly used by his contemporaries. This is sometimes at variance with modern spellings of the same name: e.g. the Rev Andereya Dwakaikara is spelt thus, although the modern spelling of the name is Rwakaikara. This is done to save confusion when the name appears in quotations.

TITLES AND OTHER VERNACULAR TERMS

The use of these has been kept to a minimum, and the old orthography has been retained to save confusion arising from the occurrence of the terms in extracts quoted from contemporary documents where the old spelling is used.

Bantu class prefixes have also been kept to a minimum. *Ganda* is used for the singular and plural, and also for *Kiganda*, the impersonal adjectival usage. The language prefix *Lu-* or *Ru-* has been retained, as its use gave greater clarity. Similarly, *Teso* has been used for both *Itesiot* and *Ateso*.

UGANDA AND ADJACENT COUNTRIES

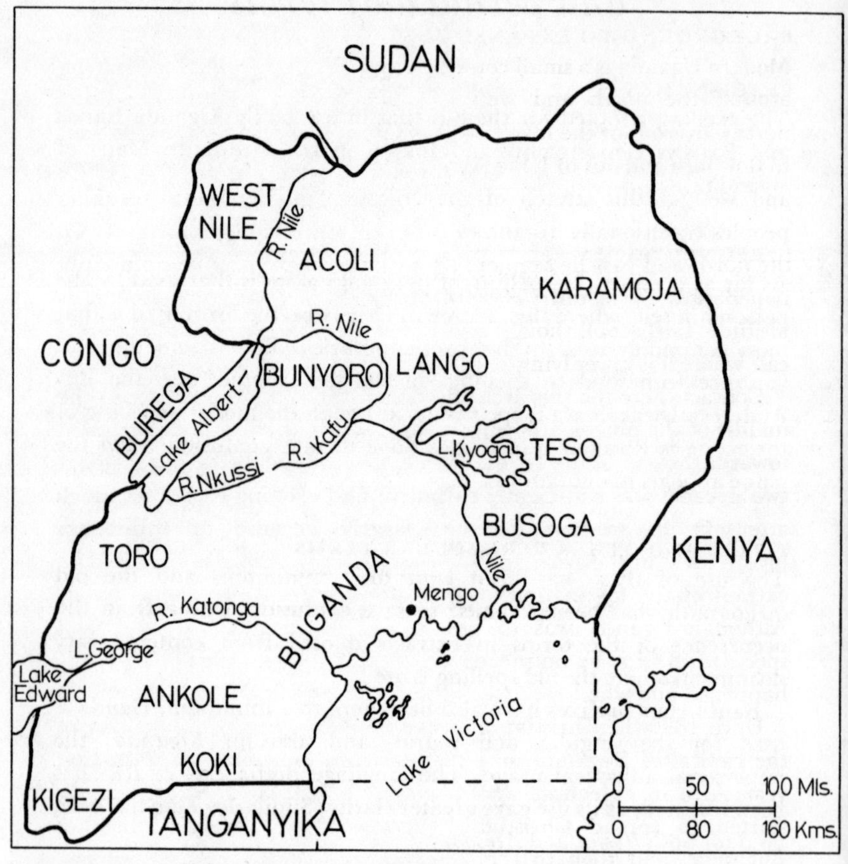

(CONGO is now (1976) ZAIRE; TANGANYIKA is TANZANIA)

Map 1

Chapter I
The Early Days of Christianity in Uganda: 1877-93

1

BACKGROUND TO EXPANSION

Modern Uganda is a small country of about 94,000 square miles lying around the north and west of Lake Victoria. The Nile flows northwards out of the lake, and then makes a great bend to the west to flow into and out of Lâke Albert (Mobutu Sese Seko). To the south and west of this stretch of the Nile live mainly Bantu-speaking peoples traditionally organized into centralized kingdom states. To the north and east lie segmentary societies whose people are mainly non-Bantu. The country is well-watered, fertile, and, by reason of its altitude, fairly cool, though it becomes hotter and drier in the north-east where it is lower lying.

Contacts between this area and the outside world began about the middle of the nineteenth century, and Christian missionaries arrived towards the end of the 1870s. The history of Uganda during the next two decades was sufficiently turbulent and exciting to attract much attention in western Europe, largely because of missionary involvement in the area, and the country and its peoples exercised an extraordinary fascination over most outsiders who came to it. Although Uganda was to be the subject of much writing and speculation, it is by no means always easy to determine what really happened and why.[1]

Until 1891 the Christian missions were confined to the vicinity of the capital of Buganda, one of the Bantu kingdom states. In that year African catechists and teachers, encouraged by the chiefs, started to spread Christianity first into the outlying areas of Buganda, and then to the neighbouring peoples and kingdoms. Writing of the immense expansion of Christianity in Uganda in the decade 1894 to 1904 Professor Roland Oliver says:

> In nearly all these vast developments, the foreign missionary expansion, both Catholic and Anglican, had followed and not preceded the expansion of the faith through indigenous channels. In most of the new districts the missionaries came to consolidate

> bands of neophytes already gathered by unordained, very often unbaptized, African enthusiasts, who had been in contact with Christian teachings at the older centres.[2]

He further remarks:

> Of the African evangelists, the most rightly celebrated was the saintly Apolo Kivebulaya . . . Tomasi Semfuma, who worked in Koki, and afterwards alone in Bunyoro, and the Firipo and Andereya who converted the King and the Prime Minister of Ankole, appear but briefly in Tucker's pages; and they must be typical of many more who have received less than their fair share of fame.[3]

This expansion, the rapid increase in the number of Christian adherents, and the importance of the part played by African Christians is unique in East Africa, and an important part of the region's history. One reason for its neglect by most historians is perhaps that those who described it at the time saw it almost entirely as a spiritual phenomenon; today we are in a better position to discern other features and put it into a historical context.

Before 1890, however, expansion was out of the question. In the first place, foreign missionaries were very few in number; and whilst it is true that expansion, when it occurred, owed as much to African converts as to European missionaries, the latter were obviously essential as teachers at this early stage, as the constant African demands for more of them show (a few years later expansion might well have continued regardless of the missionaries' presence or absence). Missionaries of the Church Missionary Society (CMS), which represented the evangelical wing of the Anglican church, arrived in June 1877. Less than two years later, in February 1879, they were joined by priests of the White Fathers Mission (the Roman Catholic *Société des Missionaires de Nôtre-Dame d'Afrique*, then basically French). Until 1890 the existence of both missions was precarious, and the missionaries were, like all other foreigners in Buganda, confined to the immediate vicinity of the capital.[4] The missionaries were not even able to occupy the country continuously. The Rev. C. T. Wilson of the CMS was alone for a year in 1877–8, and was out of the country for several months during this year; and in 1886–7 A. M. Mackay was also on his own. At the end of 1890, however, Bishop Tucker arrived with reinforcements, and by 1894 there were a dozen CMS missionaries in the country. Even this was achieved at great cost in men: between 1877 and 1894 seven of those destined for Uganda died before arrival, four were murdered, six either failed to reach their destinations or were forced to leave because of ill-health, and in 1890 Mackay died south of the lake—a total of eighteen.[5] The White Fathers fared little better, and there was a period between 1882 and 1884 when they too had no missionaries in the country.

Secondly this period was marked by active persecution, political unrest, and religious dissension. When in 1884 *Kabaka* Mwanga succeeded his father Mutesa, he was faced with three factions, and although these were basically political, the arrival in Buganda of new religious groups and the circumstances of their introduction meant that political parties became identified with different religious alignments, and as usual when politics and religion reinforce one another, the bitterness so distilled was of great intensity. The first faction was that of the older generation of chiefs, who had held power under *Kabaka* Mutesa, and who did not want to lose it. They were upholders of the *status quo* and of the traditional religion, in connection with which some of them performed ritual functions. Secondly, there was the younger generation, who aspired to power and whose best chance of acquiring it was at the beginning of a new reign, but this group was divided along religious lines. There was a Muslim party, consisting of Swahili traders from Zanzibar and Ganda who had embraced Islam. The good will of the Swahili traders was essential to Mwanga, since they were his source of firearms. Others of the younger generation were converts to Christianity. Some who had originally been interested in Islam turned instead to the Christian missions when these arrived, and their reason for doing so may partly have been that they saw Christianity as the cultural expression of a society more technologically advanced that that represented by the Swahili traders.[6] The *Kabaka,* therefore, found himself faced by three factions which had acquired religious connotations, instead of by the two competing generation groups which a new *Kabaka* normally expected to find.[7]

The persecutions which took place in 1885–7 and which were directed against the Christians, occurred partly for political reasons, and partly because of personal anger and frustration on the part of the *Kabaka.* The names of fifty martyrs, both Catholic and Protestant, are known, and many others also perished.[8] Very shortly after these executions, Mwanga turned back to the younger generation and tried, by courting their favour, to build up from among them a party who would owe their positions and therefore their loyalty to him alone, so offsetting the power of the older chiefs.[9] He founded three new chieftaincies of a kind called *bitongole* to which men were appointed directly by the *Kabaka*, and which were independent of the territorial chieftaincies. One of these he gave to a Muslim leader, one to Apolo Kagwa, a leading Protestant whom he had beaten up at the time of the persecutions, and the third to Honorat Nyonyintono, a leading Catholic whom he had ordered to be castrated.[10] The new chiefs built up large, armed followings and harried the older chiefs. By 1888 *Kabaka* Mwanga realized that these new chieftaincies constituted a serious political danger, and the chiefs and their followers found themselves threatened. But it was already too late to curtail their powers: rather than lose what they had gained, the Muslims and Christians made an alliance and combined to depose Mwanga and seize the power for themselves. The Muslims were the stronger group, and suspicion and jealousy over the disposition of chieftaincies soon brought about the break-up of the coalition. The Christian Ganda were driven into exile and took refuge on the borders of the neighbouring kingdom of Ankole, whilst the missionaries and a few of their converts went to the southern end of the lake. In Ankole the exiles were able to re-arm themselves, and were joined by many others who were not Christian converts at all, but who thought they would prefer the rule of the Christian exiles to that of the Muslim faction. In 1889, therefore, aided by these and by others who joined Mwanga, the Christian party fought its way back to power, defeated the Muslims, and shared out the offices of state among themselves. Mwanga was reinstated to legitimize the regime, but the real power now lay with the Christian chiefs.

The rivalry and suspicion which had broken up the previous alliance between the Muslims and the Christians now threatened the Catholic-Protestant alliance. It has generally been assumed that Catholic and Protestant converts were bitterly opposed to each other from the outset, as the missionaries were, but there seem to be good grounds for supposing that this was not the case. There is evidence from Ganda chroniclers that at the time of the persecutions, the Christians saw themselves as belonging to different branches of one religion, and were well disposed towards one another.[11] Bitterness between Ganda Catholics and Protestants, although latent during 1887–8, and becoming more marked during the exile of 1888–9 and a period spent crowded together on Bulingugwe Island mustering strength enough to oust the Muslims from power,[12] only became fully developed when the Christian leaders found themselves in power. There was then intense rivalry over its division, and the *Kabaka* no longer had the supreme authority to allocate positions of importance.[13] The death had occurred in battle of Honorat Nyonyintono, foremost Christian leader during the exile, and the wisest and most respected of the prominent Christians,[14] and he was succeeded by leaders less diplomatic than he. Apolo Kagwa, a Protestant, came to the fore in his place, but his ascendancy rested on his achievements in war rather than in peace. Stanislaus Mugwanya, who replaced Nyonyintono as leader of the Catholics, was also a more intransigent leader than his predecessor.[15] Catholics and Protestants came to form two bitterly opposed factions, and with religious affiliation the badge of party membership, the scene was set for a fierce struggle to gain adherents and win converts. In this struggle the chiefs played a leading part.

The chain of events through which the Christians came to power has often been referred to as the Christian revolution. It has been pointed out that in gaining control over the political structure, the Christians had gained control over one only of two structures of vital importance in Ganda society. The other was the clan structure, and this also claimed a strong allegiance, and became a focus for the discontents which arose against those in control of the political structure.[16] But in some respects the Muslims were more 'revolutionary' than the Christians. Circumcision, which the Muslims demanded, was more repugnant to the Ganda than anything demanded by the Christians; there were far more Swahili traders in Buganda than there were Christian missionaries, so that the Islamic foreign presence was perhaps more threatening; and some Muslims began to demand outward signs of conformity to Islam from the population in general in a way which the Christians did not—all this helped to alienate the people. It may be that because the Christians allowed a greater degree of accommodation to traditional structures, some people who were uncommitted to either immigrant religion (and such formed, of course, all but a tiny minority of the population) found the Christian party preferable, and so swelled its numbers that it was able to establish itself in power.[17] The Christians reinstated Mwanga, albeit with his powers curtailed, acknowledging in doing so the strength of previous loyalties. A further fact which may have helped to make the Christians acceptable was the powerlessness of the missionaries during the crises which occurred between 1885 and 1889. During these years Christian groupings had grown up on traditional Ganda patterns, small cells forming in and around the households of men in positions of traditional authority. Nuwa Walukaga, the *Kabaka's* blacksmith, martyred in 1886, and

Matthew Kisule, the royal gunsmith, were leaders of two such groups. Cells like this, formed on already existing models of chiefly clientage, had begun to develop a Christian life-style of their own, and were able to function more or less independently of the missionaries if need be. Up to the time of the 'revolution' such house-churches were the most important focuses of Christianity. So whilst there were aspects of Ganda life which Christianity was bound to call in question, it did so from within Ganda structures of society, and may have been less foreign dominated at this stage than Islam.[18]

The period from 1888 to 1889 saw a number of major changes, both in Ganda life and politics, and in the style of Ganda Christianity. Not all these changes were directly remarked upon by missionary observers, though pointers to them can be found in their writings. One reason for the missionaries' failure to notice the change is that there was an almost complete changeover in mission personnel during the crucial years. In the CMS the break occurred in 1887. Only one missionary, the Rev. R. P. Ashe, worked in Uganda both before and after that date, and he for only two brief periods after 1887. In the White Fathers Mission the break occurred in 1890. The only Catholic missionaries to work in Uganda both before and after that date were Brother Amans and Fr Denoit, and both remained in the country for only brief periods (see Tables I and II). The year 1890 saw the beginnings in both missions of a big influx of new missionaries, among whom were the leaders of the future.[19] Not least among the changes affecting the growth of Christianity was this changeover of mission personnel, which involved the arrival of new men who had not experienced for themselves the pre-revolutionary situation. The newcomers' knowledge was based on mission literature which had highlighted the heroism of the martyrs and missionaries of the previous years. They were unable to remark on subtle but important changes because they had not witnessed them.

What were these changes? In the earlier period Christianity had challenged Ganda life from within Ganda society; after the revolution 'Christianity in Uganda had both absorbed some of the traditional, *and been absorbed by it*.'[20] In gaining control of the political power structures, the Christian leaders found themselves dominated by this source of power. This absorption by the traditional structures had probably begun in 1887, when Mwanga's desire for the support of a group loyal to himself alone had led him to create the new *bitongole* chieftaincies already mentioned, parcelling the leadership out among the different groups. The revolution, occurring almost immediately afterwards, made Christianity the 'established church' of the Ganda people[21] before its leaven had had time to work on the old society, and before the reorientation demanded by Christianity had had time to be fully discovered by the converts. Christianity became one more element in the ferment of change already at work in Ganda society, and its progress became determined by Ganda developments.

The first and most obvious result of the acceptance of Christianity as the new 'established' religion was that a man could only hope for advancement in the political sphere if he threw in his lot with one of the Christian groups. To be a Muslim was to be an also-ran, and to remain a pagan was to renounce all hope of political advancement.[22] And since political advancement was the aim of all ambitious Ganda, this had far-reaching consequences. It meant, first of all, that many people were initiated into Christianity not primarily because they were interested in the Christian gospel, but because they wanted political advancement, or simply wished to show themselves as progressives. Yet it must be added that a surprising number of such converts afterwards entered into a fuller understanding of and commitment to their newly professed faith. Secondly, it meant that chiefs often insisted on their clients joining the same religious group as they themselves belonged to. A chief's strength depended to a considerable extent on the size and loyalty of his clientele, and chiefs therefore sought to bind their followers to them by making sure that they were of the same religious affiliation. Thirdly, chiefs gave every encouragement to their followers to become catechists, and senior chiefs encouraged their subordinates to ask for catechists who would teach their people. And fourthly, when questions of territorial expansion arose, the senior chiefs saw these in terms of an extension of Ganda influence and of Christian influence, and made little distinction between the two. This must not be taken to mean that the spiritual dimension was entirely swamped by considerations of personal ambition and political gain, but rather that political and religious motives had become interwoven. It has been claimed that the traditional divinities of the Ganda 'were of use in so far as they protected the *Kabaka* with the ancient glory of Buganda'.[23] Much the same might be said of the role Christianity came to play, and in this process Christianity suffered, though this was not apparent as yet.[24]

We must now examine the state of Christianity immediately after the Christians came to power. Even before his arrival, the new Anglican bishop, the Right Rev. A. R. Tucker, had decided from accounts he had received that Christianity there, 'in spite of adverse

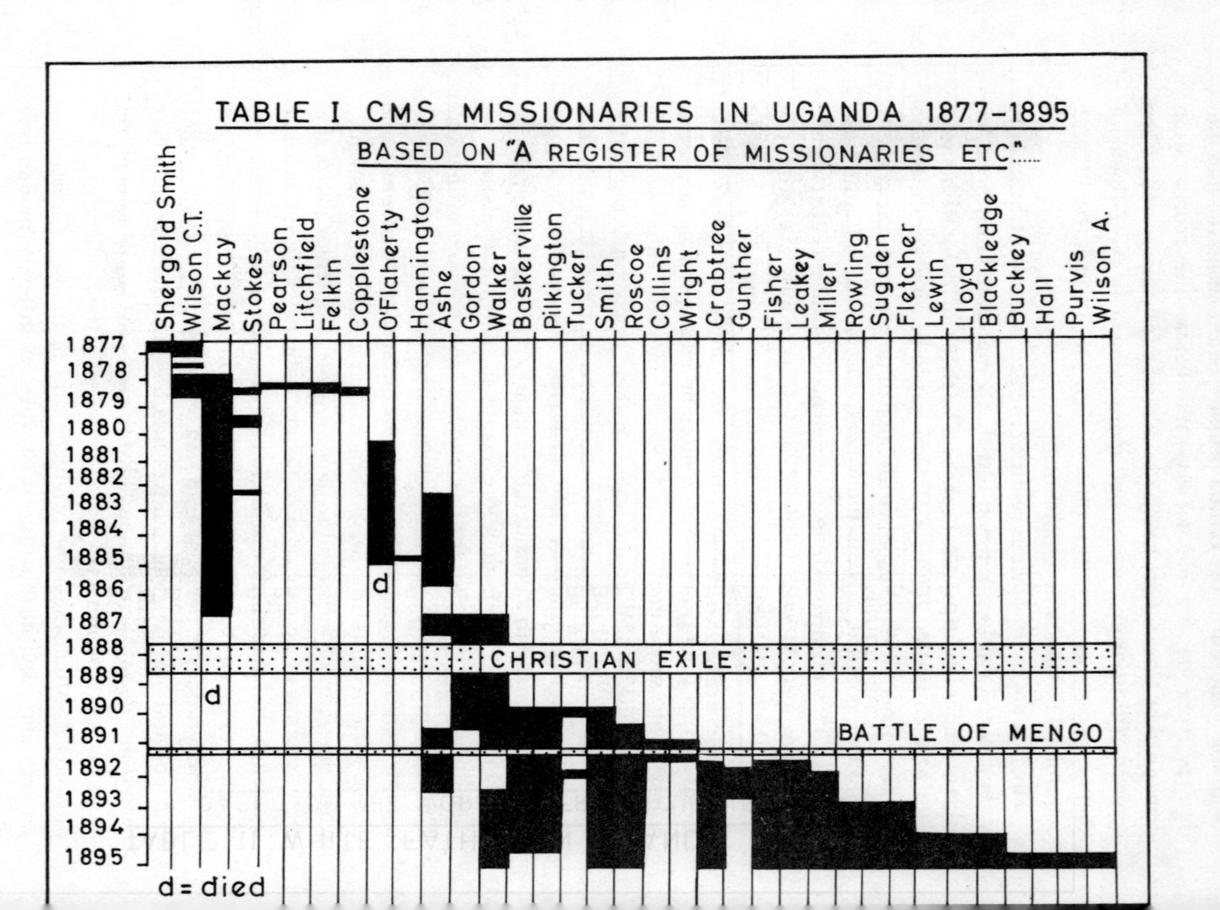
TABLE I CMS MISSIONARIES IN UGANDA 1877–1895
BASED ON "A REGISTER OF MISSIONARIES ETC".....
Shergold Smith
Wilson C.T.
Mackay
Stokes
Pearson
Litchfield
Felkin
Copplestone
O'Flaherty
Hannington
Ashe
Gordon
Walker
Baskerville
Pilkington
Tucker
Smith
Roscoe
Collins
Wright
Crabtree
Gunther
Fisher
Leakey
Miller
Rowling
Sugden
Fletcher
Lewin
Lloyd
Blackledge
Buckley
Hall
Purvis
Wilson A.
1877
1878
1879
1880
1881
1882
1883
1884
1885
1886
1887
1888
1889
1890
1891
1892
1893
1894
1895
CHRISTIAN EXILE
BATTLE OF MENGO
d
d
d = died

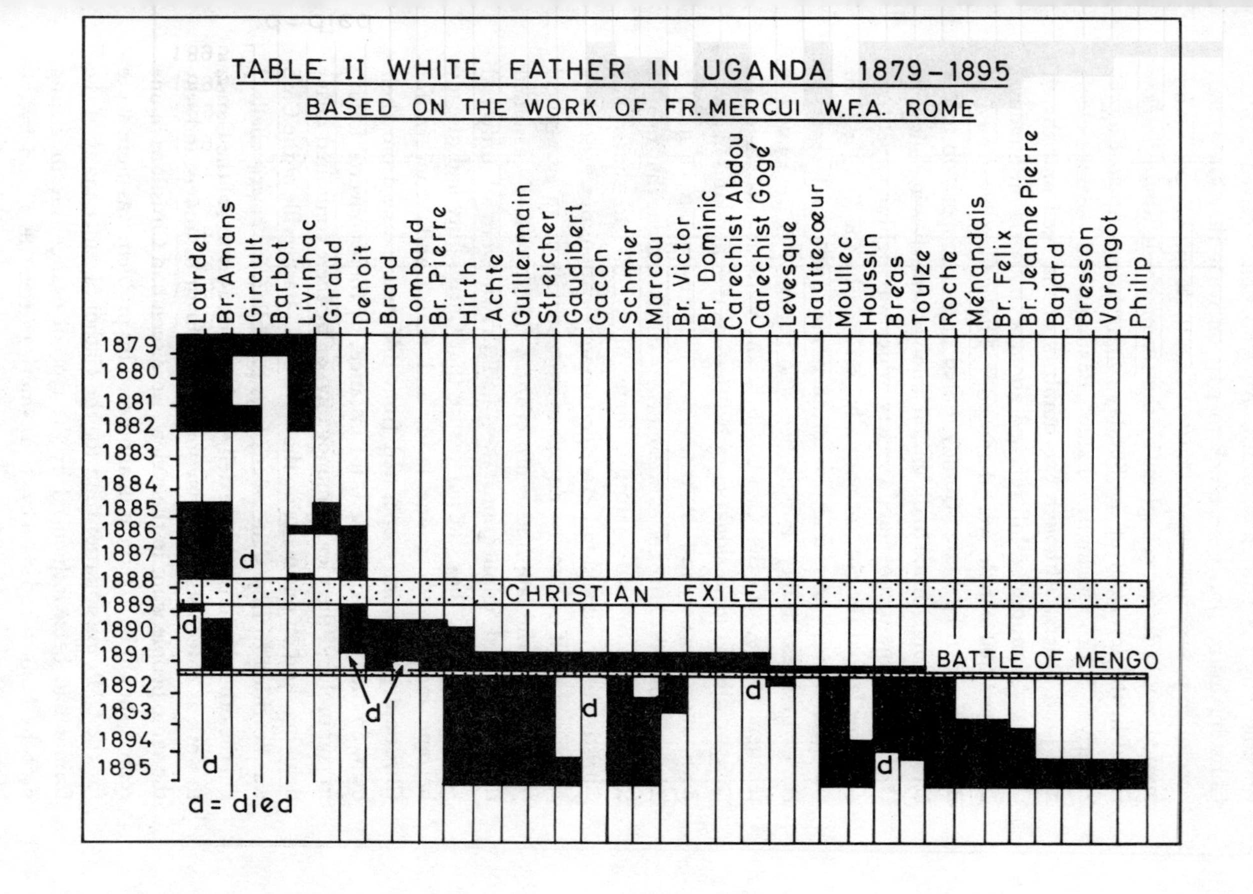

TABLE II WHITE FATHER IN UGANDA 1879 – 1895
BASED ON THE WORK OF FR. MERCUI W.F.A. ROME
Lourdel
Br. Amans
Girault
Barbot
Livinhac
Giraud
Denoit
Brard
Lombard
Br. Pierre
Hirth
Achte
Guillermain
Streicher
Gaudibert
Gacon
Schmier
Marcou
Br. Victor
Br. Dominic
Carechist Abdou
Carechist Gogé
Levesque
Hauttecœur
Moullec
Houssin
Bréas
Toulze
Roche
Ménandais
Br. Felix
Br. Jeanne Pierre
Bajard
Bresson
Varangot
Philip
1879
1880
1881
1882
1883
1884
1885
1886
1887
1888
1889
1890
1891
1892
1893
1894
1895
CHRISTIAN EXILE
BATTLE OF MENGO
d = died

circumstances, was fast becoming a living power in the political and social life of the people'. On arrival he found the political situation volcanic but the church vigorous. All who had received a little Christian instruction were quick to pass on what they knew, and needed no prompting from the missionaries to do so. Any prompting needed would have been given by the senior chiefs whom Tucker found in the forefront of the Sunday congregation: Apolo Kagwa, Zakariya Kizito Kisingiri, Paulo Bakungu—all senior chiefs now—and others. Although the numbers in the reed and thatch church on Namirembe hill reached about a thousand on Sundays, only about 200 people were baptized.[25] The leaders were men of initiative and tried faith, strongly united in their opposition to the Catholics, though prone to dissension among themselves in politics in the habitual manner of Ganda society, which was highly competitive, and now lacked the control normally exercised by the *Kabaka.*[26] In the missionaries' letters and journals there are constant references to the earnestness, ability, intelligence, and potential of the Ganda as teachers. Moreover, the Ganda Christians were at this stage the companions of the missionaries rather than their dependants in a way not found elsewhere in East Africa, nor, in later years, in Uganda.[27] The missionaries at times expressed their bewilderment that men of such intelligence and maturity, many of whom had shared the Christian exile, should fail to see certain implications of Christianity which were self-evident to European missionaries of an evangelical persuasion in the late nineteenth century. They too easily assumed that the moral implications they had drawn were of universal validity. Besides, they did not realize that Christianity had already become indigenized at one level, and that Ganda concern for Christianity sometimes operated from different causes from their own. So they were distressed, for instance, by their converts' failure to comprehend the idea of monogamy, or by their continued heavy drinking, and on one occasion the Rev. G. K. Baskerville of the CMS was horrified to find some of his boys gambling for cowrie shells.[28] On the other hand they were delighted at the eagerness of the Ganda to work as catechists, and they found it difficult to understand why the same people who, in their view, were such bad Christians in one respect should be so fervent in another. This problem was more acute for the CMS missionaries than for the Catholics, since many of the former had been influenced by the type of evangelistic preaching used by Moody and Sankey, two American revivalists, and by the 'Keswick Movement'.[29] As a result they tended to judge a man's spirituality by the degree of evangelistic fervour he showed, and by the extent to which he had renounced 'worldly' things, and for the CMS these were two different manifestations of the same kind of Christian commitment, which they could not envisage in separation from each other. Whilst the Catholic missionaries adopted the same attitude as the Anglicans towards polygamy, they did not expect people to give up what the CMS missionaries described as 'worldly pleasures', and were more willing than the CMS to wait until their converts worked out the implications of Christianity for themselves. Yet in spite of these strictures, J. V. Taylor is surely right in considering the church of this period to have reached a remarkable degree of maturity.[30] A comparison with other areas of East Africa confirms this view, as does the initiative taken by Ugandan Christians in spreading Christianity during the next few years.[31]

2

THE INDIGENOUS MISSIONARY MOVEMENT BEGUN

We must now go back to December 1890 and trace the beginnings of the indigenous missionary movement. When Bishop Tucker arrived in the country he brought with him George Pilkington, F. C. Smith, and the Rev. George Baskerville. Already in the country were the Revs. C. T. Gordon and R. H. Walker, and the Rev. R. P. Ashe returned to Uganda after a three-year absence. The number of CMS missionaries was therefore almost doubled, and here was one reason why expansion now became a possibility. Plans for establishing work in Busoga and Buddu were discussed immediately. On 8 January Baskerville recorded in his journal that the people of Busoga were asking for teachers ('Is this country to be lost to Protestant England?' he asked), and that in Buddu, under Nikodemo Sebwato, then the county chief and a strong Protestant, the people were asking for catechists. Bishop Tucker, who had been impressed by the enquiring spirit of the Ganda, and the way which those who could read took it for granted that they should teach those who wanted to learn, quickly acted on their potential as teachers and catechists. On 6 January 1891 he wrote:

> I hope to license four or five young men as lay workers or evangelists before I leave for the coast. My object . . . is to form a band of young men who shall be trained for itinerating work, with the ultimate object, if the Lord so direct, of the fittest being ordained for the work of the ministry.[32]

These first six catechists were commissioned on 31 January, and their training, which was to follow, was entrusted to Walker.[33]

Whilst these six were being trained, and before they could be allocated, we find the first reference to the Anglican church sending out catechists on her own initiative. Baskerville, in his journal for 2 February 1891, notes that the native church was sending teachers into a neighbouring district where they had heard of a number of people wanting to learn. Unfortunately he does not tell us who was sent or where, nor can we learn anything more of this first mission of the church in Uganda.

Just before Easter 1891 Walker set out for Buddu to open mission work there at the request of Nikodemo Sebwato, taking with him two of the recently commissioned catechists, Mika Sematimba and Yohanna Mwira, whose training was now completed.[34] Walker returned temporarily to Mengo in July and told the other CMS missionaries of the openings in Buddu. He had been entirely supported by Sebwato; and a sub-chief, Zakariya (probably Zakariya Kizito Kisingiri), was also asking for catechists, and promising to feed and house them. It was decided to call a meeting of the Church Council, and at this Sematimba and Mwira spoke of what they had been doing in Buddu, and the meeting discussed plans for future expansion. Baskerville described the meeting:

> We also asked the elders to bring us a list of Xtian chiefs who are willing to undertake the entire support of English missionaries, i.e. build a house for them and their boys with a regular supply of native food. We believe there are many such. We also arranged with regard to native effort that any who feel called shall come forward and offer themselves to the Church Council—if it is decided for them to work in Buganda proper the chiefs shall support them; if in the neighbouring dependencies, the Church Fund shall as far as possible maintain them, the C.M.S. being responsible for any going to foreign parts. In such case it is understood that they will only be provided with cloth to wear, food to eat, and a house to live in.[35]

The immediate upshot was that three men offered to go to Nassa south of the lake, where the work among the Sukuma was less encouraging than that among the Ganda. The leader of this group was Nathanieli Mudeka, who, we are told, might have been a chief but allowed the chieftaincy to pass to his brother in order that he might give his time to teaching, or, at any rate, let it be known that if the chieftaincy were offered to him he would not accept it.[36] Mudeka had been south of the lake during the exile of 1888–9, and when leaving, he had promised the people that if the opportunity arose, he would return.[37] With him went two young men, Simeoni Kalikuzinga and Bartolomayo Mudiru, the former of whom had also been in Sukuma country during the exile.[38] They were followed by others, and in 1898 Tucker wrote:

> On Sunday November 7, I confirmed twenty-six candidates . . . of these, two were Baganda women, wives of teachers, who, at considerable self-sacrifice, had left their homes in Buganda for this missionary enterprise south of the lake. Baganda as evangelists have done what no European missionary has ever had it in his power to do—they have shewn the Wasukuma that the gospel of Christ is for the black man as well as for the white, and that it is possible for the black man to live a life of self-sacrifice and self-denial. The Baganda have been a great object lesson to the Wasukuma.[39]

One of the main interests of the work of these catechists is that things were just as Tucker said: there appears to have been no question of political motivation in this case.

Just as Walker had taken Ganda catechists with him when he went to Buddu, so Smith and Gordon took some with them when they went to Busoga in March 1891, but they had a less happy experience. The Ganda had held some kind of an ascendancy over the Soga, and had frequently raided them for tribute in the past.[40] Smith and Gordon were received with caution by the Soga, and it was not long before there was trouble. The Ganda catechists, considering themselves superior to the Soga, refused to do any manual work, presumably expecting the Soga to do it all for them. Three weeks later, Smith, who had been ill, returned to Mengo (Gordon had already returned) and told of an open rift between the Soga chief, Wakoli, and the Ganda catechists. Wakoli had an inveterate hatred for the catechists and had refused to feed them any longer, and was even putting difficulties in the way of their buying food. The missionaries considered sending one of their earliest converts, Sembera Mackay, there, because he might be more acceptable to the people, being a Soga himself.[41] During the next year or so CMS missionaries worked in Busoga for short periods, and a few Ganda catechists hung on in spite of difficulties, but nothing very effective was accomplished.

Meanwhile the White Fathers were reinforced in 1890 by Frs Brard and Lombard, Brother Pierre, and Mgr Hirth, consecrated in that year as Vicar Apostolic. In 1891 a further group of eleven missionaries arrived, made up of seven priests (one being Fr, later Bishop, Streicher, whose years as Vicar Apostolic saw a steady progress in the development of indigenous priests as well as religious brothers and sisters in Uganda), two lay brothers, and two doctor-catechists of West African origin, Abdou and Gogé. These reinforcements, and the freedom of movement in the country which resulted from the revolution, enabled the White Fathers to expand their work too. In Busoga the mission they attempted to establish lasted, like its Anglican counterpart, only a short time (from March to October 1891), whilst a mission started at the same time in Kyagwe came to an end even sooner in July.[42] In Buddu, however, greater permanence was achieved, and this mission is interesting since it saw the first use of Ganda catechists by the Catholics. The missionaries, Frs Streicher and Gaçon and Brother Victor, arrived at Kiwala, some miles from the later centre of Villa Maria, on 19 March, and on 8 April they sent a catechist to the neighbouring small principality of Koki. Towards the end of April two men from Kiziba (now in Tanzania) arrived at the mission, and Fr Streicher began to give them Christian instruction with a view to sending them back to their own country as catechists. A little later a veritable army of 107 catechists was sent out into the country around the mission.[43] The placing of the Protestant and Catholic mission stations shews that religious competition was acting as a spur to the missionaries to speed up evangelism. Baskerville's question, quoted earlier, 'Is this country to be lost to Protestant England?' suggests that the religious competition may also have been flavoured by nationalism. Among the Ganda Christians competition was equally fierce, religion in this case being reinforced by local politics. In a county ruled by a Protestant chief as Buddu was, an army of over a hundred Catholic catechists was probably wise tactics. In the main, however, the Catholics were in the stronger position since the *Kabaka* inclined to them, and the Ganda were always sensitive to his lead.

Towards the end of 1891 the political situation in Buganda grew steadily worse, and the country was constantly on the brink of war. The trouble brought CMS work in Busoga to an end for the time being, and both missions withdrew from there. Fighting broke out between Catholics and Protestants on 24 January 1892,[44] and in the Battle of Mengo the Protestants were victorious, thanks to the intervention of Captain Lugard of the Imperial British East Africa Company, recently arrived in the country. But their victory was less than complete because the *Kabaka* fled with the Catholics. After he had been persuaded to return, there was a redistribution of chieftaincies, and as a result the south and west of the country went to the Catholics by agreement, and the east and north to the Protestants. An agreement made a year later was slightly more generous to the Catholics and sandwiched the Muslims between the two Christian groups.[45]

In spite of the upheavals caused by these attempts to divide the country between the different religious groups, Christian expansion continued. Neither Protestants nor Catholics were prepared to accept the territorial division permanently, and each side was more eager than ever to increase its own political security by winning religious adherents. After the Battle of Mengo the White Fathers temporarily withdrew to Buhaya, and on returning to Buddu, their first work was to entrench themselves firmly there, and then try to regain a foothold at the capital. At the end of March 1892 Frs Brard and Roche returned to Rubaga, leaving Frs Streicher, Lesveque, and Toulze in Buddu. These latter moved the mission to the headquarters of Alexis Sebowa, now county chief in Sebwato's place. Sebowa himself gave a site for the mission, and supported it strongly. This marked the real beginning of the mission at Villa Maria, as the place was now named. The White Fathers opened two further stations in Buddu to strengthen their position. Both were re-sited quite soon after they were founded, and were finally established at Bikira and at Bumangi in the Sesse Islands which lie off the coast of Buddu. It was some time before anything could be done to re-establish Catholic work in Busoga, since that was a natural extension of the area which had been allocated to the Protestants.[46]

The Catholics were far from satisfied with their position. At the time of the Battle of Mengo they had been more numerous than the Protestants, and the *Kabaka's* inclination to Catholicism, though regrettably half-hearted, had given them a further advantage. They (correctly) attributed the Protestant victory to Lugard's intervention, and resented being confined to Buddu and the south-west. And since Lugard was a representative of British imperial interests, and he had supported the Protestants, the Catholics found themselves willy-nilly cast in the role of opponents to the Protectorate which was provisionally declared in 1893, and ratified the following year. The agreements of 1892 and 1893 resulted in Mwanga being more or less under the thumb of the British and of the senior Protestant chiefs, who were in the majority.

The political position of the Catholics meant that two kinds of people were found among their converts. Firstly there were those who were genuinely Christian and Catholic by persuasion—the political opportunists tended to become Protestants, though not all Protestants were mere opportunists. Secondly there were political malcontents, and this group included men who did not want to accept the terms the Ganda had made with the British, and who remained at heart committed to the old regime, though not so entirely as to remain pagans, which would have deprived them of political power in any case. Among such was Gabrieli Kintu, who later fought alongside Mwanga when the latter rose in arms against the British and against the Ganda who had made terms with them. But Catholic chiefs also had a place in the new establishment, even if a less advantageous one than the Protestants. Their personal interests dictated loyalty to the British and to the Ganda settlement, and many of their Catholic clients sided with them and against Mwanga. To such chiefs, men like Kintu proved an embarrassment.[47] It was to be at least a decade before either Catholics or Protestants were finally convinced that the others were there to stay, and that they could not be reduced to powerlessness either by force or by guile. Although the Protestants controlled a majority of the senior chieftaincies, the Catholics never lost their overall numerical advantage, and this indicates that there was greater opposition to the Protestant ascendancy than has sometimes been realized. The peasants were not as subservient to their chiefs, or as easily influenced by them, as the missions sometimes thought.

In spite of the Protestant victory of 1892, the instability of the country caused a setback to their work. The promising beginning in Buddu under the patronage of Nikodemo Sebwato and Zakariya Kizito Kisingiri had come to nothing. It was possible, however, to restart the mission in Busoga, and in June 1892 F. C. Smith returned there. But in September he had to be recalled to Mengo to escort Dr Gaskoin Wright to the coast because Wright was too ill to travel alone. Two or three catechists were to remain in Buddu, now under the Catholic chief, Sebowa, and one of these was Yohanna Mwira.[48]

On 13 May 1892 the Church Council discussed the need for work among women:

> We are to discuss the advisability of appointing female elders for the better instruction of women—there are some three or four eminently qualified to give Scripture instruction, and in the absence of lady missionaries, it is impossible for us to do what should be done for the women . . . I feel confident that the church cannot be firm and strong unless the women are taught to be good

> Christian wives and mothers, and this can scarcely be done until we have lady missionaries to teach them.[49]

In 1893 Tucker found that this resolution had been acted upon, and that the wives of some of the Church Council members were teaching classes of women and girls.[59]

A Church Council meeting held a month later on 22 June 1892 was concerned for the people of Kiziba. There is no indication that the CMS missionaries knew of Streicher's plan to train two Ziba as catechists, nor, indeed, do we know if he was able to carry out this plan. But the CMS would certainly know of the Catholic mission that had been established at Kashozi in neighbouring Buhaya, and they may have wanted to establish Protestant catechists to limit Catholic expansion.[51] Why should the Mengo Church Council have developed an interest in Buziba at this juncture? It was probably Ashe who awakened their interest. In January 1892 he had travelled back to Uganda through Kiziba, and had visited Mutatembwa, the Ziba chief, in the company of Captain Langheld, the German officer in charge of the area. On his way to Masaka a few days later

> The chief of the Kiziba side of the Kagera came to say he would like to see me . . . so I turned aside and went down to his village. He was quite a young fellow, son of Mutatembwa, and expressed himself as anxious to learn the white man's wisdom and religion. The Baganda had frequently visited him – in fact all this country had formerly been regular raiding ground for these people.[52]

It was decided to send three men in response to this request, and Baskerville noted:

> They are not sent by us, but by the native church, and we are in no way responsible for them. Of course, though, we have warned the Christians of how responsible a mission theirs is. They are to take plenty of reading sheets with them and their main work will be to teach reading, and by the time several can read, it is hoped others will go and further instruct them.[53]

The catechists departed a few days later.[54] But neither written records nor oral evidence is able to throw any light on the subsequent history of this mission.[55]

Later in 1892 there was concern among the CMS missionaries that those who had been appointed lay-evangelists and those on the Church Council should accept a greater measure of responsiblity in the church. The church elders were appointed to read the daily services in turn to give them practice for the time when some of them might be ordained.[56] They were also encouraged to take more responsiblity for teaching, 'on the ground that if they wish to see a great work done here and in the near countries it must be done by them and not by the white men who can only hope to set the work going and then leave it to the native.'[57] But when a day or two later the Church Council was found to be acting responsibly and on their own initiative by stopping people from coming to receive Holy Communion whom they felt should not do so, the missionaries were indignant. They had a talk with the elders which they felt did a lot of good, and would stop them from being so independent in future. J. V. Taylor has drawn attention to the bewilderment they must have felt over the missionaries' inconsistent attitudes.[58]

In January 1893 the Catholics also took the first step towards the establishment of an ordained Ugandan ministry when a junior seminary was opened at Villa Maria under the directorship of Fr Marcou. Its establishment was an act of considerable boldness, for the only Catholic missionaries in East Africa who had so far ventured on seminary training, the Holy Ghost Fathers at Bagamoyo, had quickly decided that the time was not yet ripe. It had seemed to them that the educational requirements were too high as yet, and that it was impossible to expect first generation Christians to practise celibacy. This decision had been reached in 1877, and no further efforts had been made to achieve an indigenous clergy. Instead catechists had been trained. Had the White Fathers' venture also proved a failure, the consequences might have been serious.[59] It was important that one of the first entrants to the seminary, Basil Lumu, persevered to ordination although it took him twenty years to do so.[60] The strong support of leading chiefs such as Alexis Sebowa and Stanislaus Mugwanya must have been a further help, and the vision and faith of Mgr Streicher was of immense importance. He was in charge of the seminary from 1893 until he became Vicar Apostolic of Nyanza in 1896.

It was easier for the CMS to take the first step on the road to the establishment of an indigenous priesthood, not only because they did not demand celibacy, but also because they did not require of Africans the same educational standards as were required of Europeans. In adopting a policy of ordaining men with only a little formal education in the vernacular they were departing from an earlier policy of the mission in West Africa. There a high level of education had been provided in the Grammar Schools of Lagos and Freetown, and at Fourah Bay Institution, where, by the 1840s, men were studying Hebrew and Greek as part of their ordination course, just as they would have done in an English university. By 1890 seventy-six West Africans had been ordained, and of these at least seventy per cent had had a grammar school education, and sixty per cent had been through Fourah Bay. From 1875 Fourah Bay was affiliated to Durham University so that students might sit for degrees. Among the West African clergy there were eight Durham and one Cambridge graduates, whilst a number who had studied before 1875 at Fourah Bay must be considered of graduate standard.[61] In East Africa the bishop was faced with an entirely different situation from that in the west, since in Uganda he found that a Christian community had grown up and reached some degree of maturity before it had been possible to establish any regular education at all, and the first men whom he ordained were already among its recognized leaders.[62] However, the CMS in Uganda neither continued to ordain men of this type, nor did they establish proper theological education.

In 1893, then, when Bishop Tucker paid his second visit to Uganda, his first concern was with the vast increase in the numbers of catechumens and baptized Christians, and with providing shepherds for the rapidly increasing flock. The first seven men ordained as deacons were chosen by the bishop and the missionaries from a list of fourteen men submitted by the Church Council, and those chosen were given five months of intensive training before their ordination on Trinity Sunday.[63]

Of equal importance was the extension of work into new areas of Buganda, in each case at the request of a Christian chief. Nikodemo Sebwato, one of those chosen for ordination, had been appointed county chief of Kyagwe, an area to the east of the capital. Through the Church Council he asked for missionaries to be sent to his area, just as he had previously done when he had been county chief of Buddu. The bishop decided that Baskerville should open this station, assisted by the Rev. W. A. Crabtree who had formerly worked in Freretown, Mombasa, and who had now come to work in Uganda. The bishop himself selected the site at Ziba, about thirty-five miles east of Mengo, and not far from Sebwato's headquarters. It was arranged that Yonosani Kaidzi should join Crabtree and Baskerville after his ordination.[64]

Baskerville's journal for 1893 shows the extent to which the evangelization of Buganda came to depend upon the Christian chiefs. Sebwato's sub-chiefs were either men who had already been baptized, or else men who were catechumens, or 'readers' as they were called. These men built little chapels and collected their clients together for Christian instruction. For instance, in February Baskerville reported:

> We have been to see the two nearest chiefs . . . [They] are going to bridge the marshes between here and the other places so that we can easily go and visit them. What we hope to do is to go on Sunday afternoons to various chiefs and hold services, each of us going to a different place.[65]

On 7 March he wrote:

> Last Sunday I went in the afternoon to a small neighbouring chief to hold a service at his place. We had twenty people present. He talks of building a small church so that all his people can meet regularly each week.[66]

Christian chiefs did not stop at this, but felt themselves responsible for teaching their people to read.[67] Wherever the missionaries went, they noticed in the congregation people carrying the little bags in which it was customary to keep their reading books. In August, however, when many of the chiefs were called away to fight, it was difficult to carry on this type of work because the people depended so greatly on the leadership of the chiefs that when they were away, nothing was done.[68]

3

THE FIRST TRAINED CATECHISTS AND CLERGY

The six Anglican lay-evangelists commissioned in 1891 were Henry Wright Duta Kitakule, Sembera Mackay, Yohanna Mwira, Mika Sematimba, Paulo Bakunga, and Zakariya Kizito Kisingiri. They were an outstanding group of men, and it is worth looking at them a little more closely. All of them were among the early converts of the Anglican mission, and were thus Christians of some years' standing. All were tried leaders, and all had already been helping with the work of teaching catechumens. Four of them, Paulo Bakunga, Henry Wright Duta Kitakule, Zakariya Kisingiri, and Sembera Mackay had been members of the first Church Council formed during the persecutions of 1885-7. In 1888, when most of the Christians took refuge in Ankole, Sembera Mackay had gone with Alexander Mackay to Usambiro south of the lake, and had helped him with translation work. All the others had been among the Christian exiles in Ankole, and Bakunga, Duta, Kizito, and Sematimba had been among the Protestant leaders there. Professor Low notes that the group which had been exiled in Ankole came to form a kind of Christian élite by reason of the subsequent Christian victory over the Muslims. From this group were drawn almost all of those who later held important chieftaincies, as well as nearly all of the early Anglican clergy.[69]

They were not, however, quite the group of *young* men which Bishop Tucker had envisaged. Most of them were considerably older and more experienced than later generations of catechists. Yohanna Mwira was the oldest of the group: the Rev. R. H. Walker estimated that he must have been about fifty since he had been born in the reign of *Kabaka* Suna.[70] Paulo Bakunga was probably about forty and Kizito about thirty-seven at the time when they were commissioned.[71] Mika Sematimba was about twenty-seven, and since the other two were Church Council members, they can hardly have been younger than he.[72] Most of them were, therefore, old enough to command respect in a society where age is associated with wisdom.

Mika Sematimba, Sembera Mackay, and Paulo Bakunga did not go on to be ordained. Sembera Mackay was killed in the Battle of Mengo in January 1892, and was deeply mourned. Pilkington wrote to his mother the next day: 'He is a far greater loss than almost any I can think of to our work here; he was respected by both parties, and his humble, useful, consistent life has been, and will be, an eloquent sermon on the grace of God.'[73] Mika Sematimba, on the advice of the missionaries, accepted a chieftaincy. 'Unless a chief he has no voice at court, and we feel the opinion of such men is of great advantage to the cause.'[74] Walker later took him to England in 1893, where he greatly impressed the mission supporters who met him, but on his return home, he put on European airs, and gradually lost touch with his fellow Ugandans.[75] Paulo Bakunga also became a chief—first county chief of Kyadondo, and then county chief of Singo—and was one of the signatories to the (B)Uganda Agreement of 1900. Walker considered that his reason for accepting such a chieftaincy was that he wanted to use his position for the spread of the gospel, and thought him to be 'not so much a man of great ability as a man who has a sincere wish to live acceptably in the sight of his master'.[76]

The other three men were among the first group ordained deacon by Bishop Tucker in 1893.[77] Yohanno Mwira was, as we have seen, an older man. He was a man of quiet influence and commanded considerable respect. Before the religious wars he had held a sub-chieftaincy in Buddu, and he was with Walker when the latter went to open a mission there in 1891. He also worked for a while in Busoga before ordination. In 1893 he had been sent to help Fisher open a mission station at Mityana, and his final place of service from 1904 to 1914 was Mengo.[78]

Henry Wright Duta Kitakule was the most intellectually able of this group. He and Pilkington worked together on translation, and he taught church classes at Mengo. Pilkington, the best scholar among the CMS missionaries, had a deep respect for his co-worker's ability.[79] He might, Pilkington thought, have been *Katikiro* (chief minister), had he wished, but preferred to be a 'simple teacher'.[80] Duta worked at Mengo until his death in 1913, and was a great friend of Apolo Kagwa who became *Katikiro*. Through this friendship he had a measure of political influence which he wielded with some astuteness (there is little evidence to support Pilkington's statement that he could himself have been Katikiro had he wished, but the remark serves to indicate the missionary's opinion of him).

Of the six men, Zakariya Kizito Kisingiri achieved the highest political position. Unlike Sematimba and Bakunga, who, because they became chiefs were not ordained, Kizito became one of the greatest chiefs and was at the same time ordained. Only three other men ever held both the secular and the religious office at the same time, one of whom was Nikodemo Sebwato, who was ordained at the same time as Kizito. Kizito was county chief of Bulemezi, and then, in 1897, when Mwanga was deposed and replaced by his infant son, Kizito became one of the three regents. Because of their chiefly status these men were made 'perpetual deacons'.[81] Two other senior chiefs were also ordained perpetual deacons in 1896, but then the experiment was dropped.[82] No attempt seems to have been made to revive in these men the ancient concept of the diaconate: they seem rather to have been made second class clergy.

Two events at the close of 1893 and the beginning of 1894 had a profound effect on the growth of the indigenous missionary movement in the Anglican church in Uganda. The first was a spiritual revival led by Pilkington.

Something must be said here about revivalism which has been a recurring feature of the Anglican church in Uganda. It is impossible to define revivalism exactly, and the following characterization is made from a psychological rather than a theological standpoint. Although the Anglican church in general includes Christians of widely differing view points, the Church Missionary Society, and especially that part of it found in East Africa, represents the evangelical wing of Anglicanism. Its members, as well as distrusting ritual, set less store by the sacraments, the apostolic succession in the episcopacy, and other apparent corner-stones of Anglicanism than do the Anglo-Catholics or even the more 'central' members of the church. They sometimes appear to have more in common with evangelicals of other churches than with many members of their own church.

Evangelicals have always been characterized by a horror of what they describe as 'nominal' Christianity; that is, people whom they believe to be Christians in name only. For evangelicals, the distinguishing mark of a true, as opposed to a nominal Christian, is not good works or habits of devotion, but the ability to look back to some definite moment in life when the person became overwhelmingly aware of himself as a sinner and of God's complete and undeserved forgiveness. If this conversion was genuine, the evangelical expects it to have been followed by a continuing assurance of forgiveness and a fervent desire to help others to share his experience. A good life and habits of devotion are seen as by-products of this experience, whose appearance after conversion is to be taken for granted. A gradual loss of assurance of salvation, or a decline in evangelistic fervour—these have always been difficult facts for an evangelical to accommodate in his thinking, and there has been a tendency for some less realistic groups to hive off into perfectionism and deny that post-baptismal sin occurs at all. But the inescapable fact is that many an evangelical finds himself at times growing less fervent, and becoming aware that although he once rejoiced in an assurance of forgiveness, this may fade when he finds himself falling into the same sins as beset him before conversion. For some evangelicals the best way to deal with this situation is by attempting to recapture something akin to the original conversion experience, and this is termed 'revival'. It has already been remarked that many CMS missionaries of the period under discussion were affected by the Moody and Sankey Revival, and by the Keswick Movement which stemmed from it. Although at first sight poles apart, the Keswick conventions seem to have fulfilled for many evangelicals the same function in the religious life as the keeping of Lent and Advent for those of a more Catholic outlook, namely, providing a periodic opportunity for the re-examination and rededication of life.

When faced in the mission field with the task of converting people straight out of non-Christian societies, evangelical missionaries quickly came to realize that in spite of all they did to ensure that no one was baptized who had not undergone an evangelical conversion experience, it did not follow that the converts always lived the sort of Christian lives which the missionaries hoped for. J. V. Taylor suggests that in missionary areas there was less difference than might be expected between what Catholic and Protestant missionaries came to look for in their converts, both recognizing that baptism was only a beginning. But whereas the Catholic missionary sought to encourage the work of grace by inculcating habits of devotion and attendance at confession and mass, the evangelical missionary, when his converts' or his own original fervour seemed to be declining, longed and prayed for revival, and taught his converts to do the same.[83]

Revivals were experienced in Uganda in 1893/4 and again in 1906, but the impetus of these revivals did not last for very long. A revival which began in the 1930s, the only revival most modern East Africans know about, had a longer-lasting effect, though by now it is largely institutionalized. It stemmed from African rather than European initiative, and hence came to speak in a more African idiom—which has meant that it has often posed great difficulties for Europeans who have tried to identify themselves with it. Another reason for its continuing momentum may lie in the fact that it has evolved a method for frequent release of conscience through public confession of sin at the fellowship meetings which are characteristic of the movement. Since few non-Catholic Christians make a practice of going to confession and hearing a priest pronounce absolution, a substitute is often sought. This was found by members of the revival movement of the 1930s known today as the East African Revival, and it dealt at one stroke with the problem of sin in the believer and with the need for repeated experiences of reviving grace which for Catholics came through the reception of the sacraments. This continuation through the fellowship meeting did not result from the earlier revivals, and it may be that much of the spiritual energy generated by these was dissipated into political channels.[84]

By the end of 1893, then, the CMS missionaries were far from satisfied with the state of the church—they felt it lacked spiritual life. Since the revolution of 1889 too many of its adherents had become Christians because that was now the safest and most profitable thing to do. There were too many of them for the missionaries to be able to give the kind of individual care and attention that had been possible in the early days when Christian enquirers were only a handful.[85] At the beginning of December Pilkington came back from a holiday on the island of Kome telling of a great spiritual experience he had undergone. What happened is best described by Baskerville in his journal:

> Pilkington came back yesterday from Kome about 5.30; he came over to dinner with us at Roscoe's, and told us of the glorious times he had had on Kome. He told us, too, how he had definitely, while away, received by faith the baptism of the Holy Ghost, and manifestations of his power had followed. People were testifying to the saving power of Christ including Christians of some standing, I mean some who had been baptized but who had as yet not really accepted Christ.[75]

Unhampered as they were at that time by the demands of institutions or timetables, the missionaries were able to embark on a series of special services the very next morning, to which the people flocked. These lasted for three days, and for many hundreds of church members this was a time of spiritual reawakening, and of a new committal of themselves to Christian service.[87]

The second event occurred in March when Pilkington visited a newly opened mission at Mityana, where a young missionary, A. B. Fisher, had developed a system of sending out catechists which impressed Pilkington by its good organization. Fisher described this in a letter dated 1 January 1894:

> Soon it became evident that as most of the gardens were from two to four miles away, it would be impossible to get the people to attend classes here daily. We therefore devised the scheme of building reading-houses, or as the natives call them, Synagogi . . . The small chiefs, in whose gardens they are built, will be responsible—(i) for cleaning and keeping them in repair; (ii) selling books; (iii) gathering the people to daily classes; (iv) and, if possible, to bring them in here on Sundays to church. After Sunday morning service, a short prayer meeting and conference is held at my house for chiefs of synagogues and teachers, when reports of progress are given in, and etc., and the whole work brought to God in prayer. We have sent out fourteen boys to teach reading in the gardens where we found no one knowing how to read, seven of whom are baptized, and the others are converted boys reading for baptism. Every week all the synagogues within three hours' march are visited by myself and the other five teachers here, three of whom have been sent me by the Church Council . . . The average daily attendance at the synagogues is twenty, and the average here eighty, making a total of 480 people attending daily classes in connection with our work here.[88]

The three teachers sent by the Church Council were perhaps some of the first fruits of the revival, for one of its main results was that Christians began to volunteer to go as catechists, and this was strongly encouraged by the missionaries, and seen as a proof of the genuineness of the converts' new spiritual experience. Pilkington proposed that their work should everywhere be organized along Fisher's lines. By the end of March over thirty men had volunteered to go as catechists, and special commissioning services were held for them at Mengo.[89] On Easter Sunday, when thirteen men had been commissioned, a great collection both in cash (cowrie shells) and in kind had been offered for their support, and Pilkington had been the preacher. Three of the men had been sent to the Bavuma Islands, and the remainder had been sent in pairs to the Sesse Islands. Each pair included one older man and one younger.[90] By August the number of volunteers had risen further, and Roscoe wrote of nearly a hundred catechists supported by the local church being sent out. It was hoped that when a second group had been trained, these would relieve the first group, who would then have a further spell of training. The areas of Buganda in which catechists were working were under the supervision of missionaries. Some catechists were working outside Buganda, two at Nassa in Usukuma, twelve in different parts of Busoga, three in Koki, and two in Ankole.[91] The missionary outreach of the Anglican church in Uganda had truly begun.

At about the same time very similar developments were taking place in the Catholic church. In some cases the sending of Catholic catechists was a counter-measure to Anglican expansion. The despatch of Anglican catechists to Koki, for instance, led Mgr Hirth, during a visitation to Bikira in July 1894, to write the following comments:

> La plus grande oeuvre et la plus pressée en ce moment est celle des catéchistes à l'étranger; malheureusement sur ce point nous ne pouvons qu'être en retard toujours sur les hérétiques . . . L'entrée des protestants au Koki est tout un evénement pour cette station de Bikira . . .
>
> Pour préparer le terrain aux missionaries il faut exciter sans relâche les Bagandas à aller faire amitié avec les chefs de ce pays, et à les catéchiser . . . On fera en sorte que des maintenant chaque village paien, ou même déjà hérétique, soit assigné à un chef muganda, catholique et voisin si possible; celui-ci dura user de toutes sortes d'industries pour y faire pénétrer la foi . . .[92]

Mgr Hirth went on to propose that catechists should also be sent to the villages of all the chiefs in Buddu itself, and also to Kiziba across the border in German territory 'car les Bagandas seuls peuvent ouvrir ce pays à Dieu'.[93] Competition between the two missions was leading to an intensification of effort in evangelism. Less than a year later Mgr Guillermain, who was made Vicar-Apostolic of the northern part of the Vicariate when this was divided from the area south of the lake, reported that all the missionaries were convinced of the necessity for indigenous catechists. These were needed to work in Buganda itself around existing missions, and also for work further afield which would open up the way for missionary priests. But the White Fathers were hampered by a lack of funds and could not provide the catechists with the basic necessities of life. Apparently Protestant catechists were far more numerous than Catholic.[94]

A further insight into the work of Catholic catechists at about this time comes from the diary of the Nsambya mission. By 1895 there was no longer any attempt to keep to the religious spheres which had been agreed under Lugard and Portal, and which the missions had considered to be only a temporary expedient. In 1894, as we shall see, Protestant catechists were sent to Toro, formerly considered a Catholic sphere, and in 1895 the English-speaking Mill Hill Fathers arrived to work in the eastern part of the country which had formerly been considered a Protestant sphere. They were given Nsambya Hill, only a couple of miles from Rubaga, as their headquarters. From April 1896 onwards the mission diary records contacts made with groups of Catholics and their catechists in the part of the country now allocated to the new mission. Most of the catechists had been sent out by Mgr Guillermain, and by the end of April contact had been made with ten different groups of Catholics in Busoga. By July the Mill Hill Mission was itself sending out catechists. In August there was still mention of Catholics in Protestant areas with whom contact was being made for the first time, and one of these groups was being taught by a man not yet baptized—it seems as though this catechist was self-appointed. Quite a number of those being taught by the Catholic catechists had formerly been Protestants; and had no Catholic mission returned to the area, possibly they would have remained Protestants.[95] Whilst many Ganda followed the lead of their chiefs—and the influence of the chiefs was very considerable—the Nsambya diary is a useful corrective to the idea that the people had no mind of their own. A Protestant or Catholic chief could not make his clients do just as he wished, even when those who joined the opposite religious group knew that they ran the risk of being turned off their land. The reports of evictions for religious reasons are innumerable in both Protestant and Catholic sources.

Before we turn to examine the motives which led people to work as catechists, one further point concerning the Anglicans needs to be made. It has already been noticed that when catechists first went out there was a special commissioning service, and that a collection was taken up for their support. Each month a special missionary meeting was held at Mengo, and was attended by hundreds of people. Catechists who had temporarily returned to the capital had an opportunity to report on their work, collections were taken, interest in the work was maintained, and a sense of responsibility was fostered in those who sent the catechists.[96] News about them was also given prominence in the *Church Missionary Intelligencer*, a magazine published in England for the information of CMS supporters, and this is an indication of how important the mission felt the catechists' work to be. But in later years much of this died out. It became routine to send out catechists, and both the early enthusiasm of the supporters, and the interest shown in their work were allowed to fade. The *Rapports annuels* of the White Fathers, at least until the mid 1920s, show a more sustained interest in and appreciation of the part played by these men than does the literature of either of the other missions. This probably owed much to the drive of Mgr Streicher.

4

MOTIVATION FOR MISSION

What were the factors responsible for the acceptance and spread of Christianity in the period under discussion? And what were the motives that led to so many offering to work as catechists? Firstly, we must notice the validity of the spiritual motivation. No Christian reading the story of the Uganda Martyrs, or of men such as Apolo Kivebulaya, Yohana Kitagana, Placidi Mutyabi, or Sira Dongo can fail to see in these men the working of the Spirit. But it would be futile to deny that there were other factors involved. We need to remember that the motives of converts and catechists were as mixed as those of Christians of all nationalities have always been, right back to apostolic times;[97] and, on the other hand, that in seeking to analyse social and political factors which may have predisposed people to accept Christianity or work as catechists, it may be argued that we are explaining little, but pushing the question one stage further back, and highlighting the fact that at a critical moment in her history, a whole complex of factors came together to dispose the people of Uganda to move in a particular direction.

Firstly, as had been pointed out by several writers, Ganda society in the nineteenth century was in a state of flux, and there was some undermining of belief in the efficacy of the traditional religion.[98] Christianity was not the first new religion to reach the *Kabaka's* court: Islam had already made some impact, and the *Kabaka* had received some instruction and had led Muslim prayers for a time. In 1876, however, Islam had suffered a setback, and some two hundred of its adherents had been martyred when a clash occurred between loyalty and obedience to the *Kabaka,* and the new demands of obedience to Islam. But in spite of this, Islam was stronger than Christianity at the beginning of the period of warfare which broke out in 1888.[99] The earlier arrival of Islam and the royal patronage it at first received probably made it easier to accept the presence of another immigrant religion, especially another religion 'of the Book'.[100] Reading, quite apart from religion, soon drew the fascinated attention of many of the most intelligent courtiers.

The enormous popularity of reading and writing (and the intimate connexion between these and Christianity) was certainly another factor leading to the success achieved by the missions. So closely linked was Protestant Christianity with learning to read that catechumens were generally known as *basomi,* readers, and in the Anglican church the verb *to read* came to be synonymous with *to receive Christian instruction.* M. C. Fallers remarks on the avidity with which the Ganda took to reading and writing: 'It could almost be said that Buganda society needed writing and was standing ready to receive it when the first Arabs and Europeans arrived'.[101] Among the early Anglican missionaries were Felkin, Ashe, Baskerville, Tucker and Roscoe—all writers; and Pilkington, Mackay, Gordon and Ashe were translators and linguists. They conveyed to their converts something of their respect for letters, so that the Ganda language is, apart from Swahili, the only East African language with a considerable literature of its own.[102] To be able to read and write quickly became a necessity for anyone aspiring to become other than the most junior of chiefs, and to possess a book and a Christian name was to show oneself a progressive.

But the question remains why literacy in Buganda (and later in the other kingdom states of Uganda—though to a lesser degree) was espoused so readily, and why such a flood of writing resulted from it. The vast majority of writings by the Ganda are concerned in one way or another with politics—political tracts, histories, even religious writings, all centre around this theme. One of the earliest uses of literacy was for sending notes to the missionaries from the royal enclosure at the time of the persecutions telling them the political news.[103] Literacy was also, of course, used in administration, both in church and state. Most of the older Anglican parishes possess large numbers of minutes books in which copious records of committee meetings of various sorts were made, usually in the vernacular.[104] It has been noticed that increasingly complex socio-political administration often precedes the emergence of a new script.[105] Whilst the Ganda did not invent a new script, the enthusiasm with which they adopted the script brought by the missions and the uses to which they put it suggest that in Buganda we have an example of this increasing complexity, and that here lies at least part of the explanation for the rapid adoption of literacy.

The success with which certain aspects of the Christian faith and of church organization came to be expressed in Ganda forms further facilitated the acceptance of Christianity. At the time of the religious wars Christianity seemed more willing to make concessions to Ganda society than Islam, and this contributed to the Christian victory. Certain Christian beliefs came to be expressed in linguistic terms which were readily understood. An example of this can be found in a description by Simeoni Kalikuzinga of how he first heard of Christianity some time in the 1880s. He describes a conversation with his friend Nathanieli Mudeka:

> Then he asked me, 'Do you know God?' and I said, 'How could I?' Then he said, 'There is a God who created man; he created us. But our forefather Adam committed a crime and was condemned to death—that is why we all die—but afterwards God became merciful and he sent his son, Jesus Christ, who came to die for the people, so that he might shew them that he was to die as all men die, and all the suffering which would have fallen on them would fall on him, but that in the end he was going to rise from the dead, that people might see that there will be resurrection from the dead.'[106]

Anyone acquainted with the multitude of traditional stories of Africa describing the genesis of customs or phenomena will see at once how the teaching of St Paul in I Corinthians 15: 21-22 ('For since by man came death, by man came also the resurrection from the dead. For as in Adam all die, even so in Christ shall all be made alive') has been re-expressed in the form of one of these stories, and so stated in a way which puts the teaching beyond all questioning. A further example of the way in which Christian ideas were adopted into Ganda thinking can be found in the following extract from a letter:

> When I came to the *kibuga* [capital] and was staying at Rubaga, I met our beloved Mr Pilkington and he told me about the Saviour . . . Slowly I understood that there was nothing greater than God. So I came to know my Saviour who died for me and I gave my allegiance to him [Luganda: *nemusenga*]. Daily I ask him to abide with me so that the one from whom I have transferred myself [the Luganda verb is the derived *senguka*] may never again count me among his subjects.[107]

The use of *senga,* to give one's allegiance to, is entirely felicitous. Every Muganda had to *senga* a chief, and he was free to choose whom he would *senga.* Thus the act of repentance and conversion was placed within a readily understandable Ganda context.

It is interesting to note the way in which these and other Ganda modes of expression arose. For the first fourteen years of the CMS's existence in Uganda, most of the teaching of reading had been in Swahili, and the only Bible in use among the Ganda Christians had been the Swahili Bible, except for a gospel or two and the Acts of the Apostles. Pilkington wrote of the work he did in translating the Bible, saying that over the years a Luganda version had already been hammered out by the Ganda themselves, and that it was this that had been the basis for his version:

> There was never anyone who more than I entered into other men's labours. I found several men, H. W. Duta far ahead of them all, with a good knowledge of the whole New Testament; they knew Swahili and were thoroughly practised in translating from Swahili into Luganda; there were none of the ordinary difficulties of searching for words to translate the important terms and phrases of the Gospel; these were not only at hand, but so far stereotyped by extensive use, that any radical changes, had I wished to make them, could hardly have been justifiable. This fact made the work possible, and it also makes me hope that the translation (thanks not to me but to my predecessors), is a better one than a first translation into a new language can generally be; it has been, really, beaten out during many years by the best brains among the Waganda themselves, with the help of Mackay, Ashe, Gordon, Walker, and the others who have been here.[108]

Pilkington's hope has been justified, and the Luganda Bible has needed little revision down to the present.

But of all the factors other than the spiritual, the political was the most important. This applies to the spread of Christianity both within Buganda and beyond it. Although it involves taking a look into the present as well as into the past, it is legitimate to spend some time examining the reasons why Christianity was able to attract and retain the loyalty of many Ganda leaders. It was a rare phenomenon in Africa for Christianity to achieve success among the leaders of a traditional regime, and yet it was characteristic of the Christian impact throughout the interlacustrine region of Uganda.

First, however, that statement must be modified, although as it stands it is a commonplace of Ugandan history. Christianity made very little headway at all among the older generation of leaders who were in power when the missions first arrived. In Buganda none of those in high office under *Kabaka* Mutesa was converted to Christianity, though there were some palace officials of lesser importance who became Christians. The Christians came to power through a revolution which swept away the older generation of senior office holders. *Kabaka* Mwanga, not a Christian, eventually could brook no longer the curtailment of his traditional powers which these men forced on him, and his rebellion led to his downfall and replacement by an infant who was brought up as a Christian. By the time he attained his majority, the old structures had been drastically modified by colonial rule. Everywhere else in the Bantu kingdoms Christianity succeeded partly because it had to deal with new rulers or with colonial appointees, and because, as in Buganda, traditional political structures were remodelled. Newly appointed chiefs or aspirants to chiefly office were perhaps more open to Christianity in Buganda than in some African societies because they did not succeed to important ritual functions. These were the prerogative of others.

The next point which must be made concerns Buganda only. A process was going on there by which power was becoming increasingly centralized, and positions of power more and more open to men whom the *Kabaka* had singled out for their abilities instead of being tied down to a hereditary system. The kingdom, when Christianity arrived, was not extensive, but concentrated and centralized to a degree unique among the interlacustrine kingdoms, and administered through not one, but two, systems of chiefs, the second of which, the *bakungu* and *batongole* chiefs, formed an efficient, largely non-hereditary corps, directly responsible to the *Kabaka*. This group of chiefs formed the basis of the system of county chiefs of the colonial era, and to this group the royal pages aspired to belong. Their power was enhanced by the Christian revolution of 1888-9 at the expense of the power of the second group, the *bataka* (clan heads) who were closely concerned with aspects of the traditional religion. The *bakungu* were opportunist and progressive, and were appointed on merit, and on whether they could attract the favourable attention of the *Kabaka*, whereas the clan heads were the conservative guardians of the traditional religion. Their powers were eroded both by the widespread acceptance of Christianity in Buganda, and by the Uganda Agreement made with the Protectorate government in 1900. The more deeply Christianity became entrenched, the more the powers of the clan heads declined, whilst those of the county chiefs increased. Christianity therefore became a factor in the rivalry between these groups of chiefs. In 1892 and 1893 certain county chieftaincies became associated with either the Catholic or the Protestant form of Christianity, or with Islam, and factional religious rivalry gave a further incentive to the scramble for converts. Part of the *Kabaka's* dilemma which he himself initiated when he allowed the missionaries into his country and kept them near the court, lay in the fact that as *Kabaka* he was *Ssabataka* (head of the clan heads) as well as being the one who appointed the *bakungu* and *batongole* chiefs.[109]

Secondly, throughout the Bantu kingdoms, rulers and chiefs were able to use the churches, especially the Anglican church, to modify the actions of the colonial government, or against some neighbouring or rival kingdom. A notable occasion was that of the drawing up of the 1900 Agreement when the intervention of Archdeacon Walker and Bishop Tucker ensured the Ganda better terms than they would otherwise have obtained,[110] and others were when Byakweyamba, a county chief in Toro, succeeded in getting Tucker to intervene on his behalf when he was being preyed upon by the Sudanese garrisons left by Lugard,[111] or when Bunyoro tried to gain a greater measure of freedom from Ganda domination.[112]

In this connection it must be remembered that the Anglican missionaries were members of an established church whose head was also the head of state, and when they found themselves working in areas with an apparently familiar monarchical system, they not unnaturally set about trying to reproduce something of what they knew in their homeland. Whereas the British administrators tended to undervalue and play down the power of the hereditary rulers and their chiefs (in spite of their commitment to indirect rule), the missionaries tended to do the opposite. It was only later, and then gradually and imperceptibly, that it became clear that Christianity would not do for the traditional kingdoms what their leaders had hoped. The final disillusionment did not come until after 1967, when the monarchies were abolished under a new constitution. The issue was further clouded by the fact that in the Bantu kingdoms the Anglican church achieved a semi-established position, and, as the converts failed to understand the true concern of the church, so the missionaries failed to enunciate that aim clearly, because of their vested interests in the traditional power structures. Their attempts to Christianize the monarchies blinded them to an understanding of the true nature and sanctions of these institutions, and, more seriously, their preoccupation with the Bantu kingdoms, and especially with Buganda, blinded them to the importance and potential of the non-Bantu areas of Buganda.[113]

By a happy accident the Catholic church was saved from the unfortunate involvements of the Anglican church. However, it was something of an accident, and had the Catholics been able to win the allegiance of the traditional rulers, they would have exploited the situation just as readily as the Anglicans did. To establish Catholic kingdoms was part of the White Fathers' clearly expressed policy.[114] But the Anglicans were successful in winning over the traditional monarchs and the majority of the senior chiefs. Nor did the Catholics think this a *happy* accident at the time: they bitterly regretted their misfortune. It is not clear that even today they realize that the Anglican success was eventually to turn out to the Catholic advantage. Nor did their work suffer to the same extent from being Buganda-centred. The Verona Fathers in Northern Uganda thought of that area as the goal towards which they had been working for half a century, and since the rest of their work was to the north they were never tempted as were the Anglicans (and the Mill Hill Fathers) to make comparisons between the Bantu and the non-Bantu, and consider the latter inferior.

When we come to consider the conditions which favoured the quick spread of Christianity both within Buganda and beyond it, it is first of all noticeable that the very political unrest which had confined the missionaries prior to 1891 was afterwards a factor in the spread and acceptance of Christianity. The wars themselves and the attempt to create Catholic and Protestant areas of the country involved large movements of people, and helped to break down old ties and loyalties, whilst the political implications of the religious factions meant that numbers of people were brought into contact with the new religion much more quickly than was otherwise likely to have been the case.[115] Baskerville's journal for 1892–3 shows this process at work in Kyagwe. This formerly Catholic area was allotted to the Protestants by Lugard, and everywhere that Baskerville travelled, he found small groups of catechumens grouped about the person of one or other of Nikodemo Sebwato's sub-chiefs. Almost all of these were either Protestant Christians, or were catechumens. The Nsambya diary shows that there were also small groups of Catholics in the area. Without the missionaries' knowledge, Christianity had spread out into the countryside through the dispersal of the population, and in some cases the small groups had had no contact at all with the mission. One of the most interesting stories is that of a small group of Protestant Christians from the Catholic county of Buddu who went across the border into German East Africa and founded cells of Protestant Christians long before the arrival of any Protestant missionaries from Europe.[116]

It must be emphasized again that political as well as spiritual motives were often present when chiefs requested catechists, and in the decision of the Mengo Church Council to meet these requests. After 1892, when the Protestant chiefs were in the ascendancy because they had been the victors in the Battle of Mengo, the pace of evangelism was largely determined by these chiefs, some of whom sat on the Church Council. Because they were still numerically weaker than the Catholics, they needed to secure their position, and they were able to use the political initiative they had gained to send catechists to neighbouring areas. The rulers of these neighbouring kingdoms always quickly requested European missionaries, but these were not often immediately available, for the mission's resources were always stretched to the utmost in spite of urgent and frequent appeals to the home base for more men. Within a year or two a Catholic mission was bound to follow the establishment of the CMS unless the Catholics wanted to lose all chance of getting a foothold in the area. They too found it difficult to meet all the demands made on them. Moreover those missionaries who wanted to meet urgent requests to extend into new areas had to contend with opposition from other missionaries who said, with some justification, that there were not enough people to meet all the needs of the work already started, and no new demands should be met until the existing work was properly staffed. In the case of the CMS, Archdeacon Walker was the leader of this group, and was influential because of his position as mission secretary. But he was offset by the bishop. Walker became reactionary and pro-Ganda, and, like many CMS missionaries, under-estimated the importance of work outside

Buganda and the Bantu kingdoms.[117] Those who advocated expansion usually won the day.

Lastly we must look at the reasons for the desire to extend Christianity from Buganda into the neighbouring areas. The places to which Ganda catechists went were, with the exception of Sukuma country, places in which Buganda had political interests. She was at this time at the height of her power, and her ambition was to extend her territorial supremacy. She was involved in a life or death struggle with Bunyoro, and was finally victorious, partly because she was successful in winning over the British to her point of view about the Nyoro. She had raided into Toro and Ankole, and tried—though not with lasting success—to exert her influence when succession disputes arose. She considered she had achieved a measure of supremacy over Busoga and Buziba, and had certainly established a pattern of raiding for tribute. When we come to examine in detail the beginnings of evangelism in Toro, Bunyoro and Ankole it will be found that in each case evangelistic motives became entangled with a desire to increase the influence of Buganda, and that the peoples of these areas came to fear this. The influence of the senior chiefs on the decisions of the Church Council; the important role of Zakariya Kizito Kisingiri, especially in the case of Toro, and of Apolo Kagwa on whom the CMS missionaries came to rely to an extraordinary degree; the readiness of the missionaries to equate Ganda influence with Christian influence; their consequent pleasure whenever literate Ganda (to be literate meant to be baptized) were appointed to chieftaincies in other areas, and their willingness to use their influence to see that this happened; all these together created a situation in which it was almost impossible for the Ganda not to use the Anglican mission to further their expansionist ends. Christian expansion would probably have been slower if it had not been for this motivation, but political motivation was only part of the total picture, and did not render valueless all that was done. The claims made by Apolo Kagwa and the regents in 1898 that Busoga, Toro, Ankole, and Bunyoro should pay tribute to Buganda show the lines along which the Ganda were thinking.[118] These claims astonished the British in spite of an earlier recognition that Busoga had owed tribute to Mwanga, and reveal the extent of Ganda misunderstanding of what Protectorate government was going to mean to them. The extent of the government's misunderstanding of Ganda aims is seen in their readiness to go on using Ganda as chiefs and political agents outside Buganda; and the extent of most missionaries' misunderstanding is seen in their surprise at the fear of

Ganda domination which quickly appeared in the Western Kingdoms. But just as the misunderstanding over the relationship of Christianity to the institutions of the traditional kingdoms has never been stated explicitly, so also this situation in which the Ganda came to see themselves as favoured politically and by the churches has not been made explicit either.

The group of men commissioned as Anglican lay-evangelists in 1891 were outstanding, as were a number of the early clergy, four of whom also held important secular positions. The fact that a lead was given by men of their standing made it easier for others to follow and had an effect on the way the movement to work as catechists spread so widely. Nevertheless it was the rank and file who followed, not men of equal standing. From 1893 onwards the division between the secular and the spiritual leadership became more marked,[119] and it was perhaps partly because of the experience of the 1891 group that it did so. Two out of three of the lay-evangelists of this group felt that they could not be chiefs and also be ordained. The experiment of ordaining senior chiefs was not repeated. For men in their position it was inevitable that politics should claim a very large share of their attention. This was, in fact, also true of the missionaries, though on occasion many of them strenuously denied it, insisting that they had come only to preach the gospel. They did not understand the involvement of the Ganda Christians in politics. Baskerville, in 1891, noticed that all the lay-evangelists had other responsibilities in addition to their teaching:

> The native Christians, though in many cases the most earnest men, are not yet, I fancy, prepared to give up their whole time to mission work, and we have no men who can be relied upon for definite service at a fixed station. If they have no chieftainship, they still have gardens, and they must visit these from time to time. e.g. Henry Duta has two large gardens widely separated, Sembera has one near here and another four days off. I mention these men as being those spoken of as rejecting chieftainships; true, they are men of sterling Christian character but they must look to their possessions—they are ever striving to advance Christ's cause but cannot settle down to any one station.[120]

From this Baskerville appears to conclude, not that a new pattern of Christian service might be worked out in these men, but that their dedication, in some way that he cannot quite grasp, must be incomplete. Walker stated the Ganda viewpoint accurately enough, but showed no more sympathy with it than Baskerville:

> We press on our people that we do not care for them to have political power, and that we would just as well see all our people holding only gardens and no chieftainship. They say many of us are ready to do this *but others feel that they are Baganda as well as Xns,* and they have gained their country in fair fight with from the Mohammedans [and] they do not want it to be handed over to the Catholics.[121]

The missionaries were, in fact, not at all consistent on the subject of chieftainships, as their advice to Mika Sematimba shows.

When we come to examine in detail the different areas to which Christian catechists were sent, we shall come across other motives which operated in certain circumstances, but one further general point needs to be made here. A young man who had learned to read naturally wished to find some outlet for his newly acquired skill, and to work for a time as a catechist was one of the few uses he could find for it. Only a few men could become chiefs or be absorbed in other capacities into the service of the traditional or colonial administrations. Those who could get such jobs usually took them. For the rest, the only outlet lay in teaching, and, as this was long before the days of secular education, that meant being a catechist. Few Anglicans considered this a life-long calling. For some it was the first step towards a chieftaincy; others might hope to climb the ladder towards eventual ordination; for many it was a temporary occupation before marriage. It held little in the way of material reward, but in those days it still carried some *kitiïbwa* (glory, status, kudos), and this was of enormous importance.[122]

In the chapters which follow it will become clearer that people's motives were not purely political or self-seeking in the evangelistic enterprises they undertook. The contemporary missionaries, however, tended to view their motives as largely spiritual (Walker, always pessimistic, being something of an exception); and what follows is an attempt to redress the balance, and to show that, like all human motivation, that of the Ganda was mixed.

Chapter II

Toro

1

THE KINGDOM RE-ESTABLISHED

A modern map of Uganda shows the central and western areas of the country roughly divided into three: Bunyoro, Toro and Ankole, all more or less equal in size, and known, until 1967, as the Western Kingdoms. But this neat division into three was a British creation. In 1890 the main centre of power was Bunyoro, resurgent after a long period of decline, and extending further south than the present-day district of that name. Ankole was a second and also growing centre of power to the south, and neither Toro nor Ankole in the 1890s coincided territorially with the modern districts of these names, both being smaller. The political structure of these areas was different from that of Buganda, though the British did not always realize this, and tried to impose on them the same modifications as they had imposed on Buganda. Their lack of success they attributed to the relative backwardness of the Western Kingdoms instead of to its true cause, a different original structure.

Nowhere in the Western Kingdoms had population density assisted the growth of a centralized administration to such a degree as in Buganda. In the west we find extension rather than concentration, and delegation of power rather than direct administration. At one time the main centre of power of the empire of Bunyoro-Kitara had lain in the area of Buyaga and Bugangaizi and western Mubende; that is, where the majority of the tombs of the *Bakama* are to be found. It is claimed that in the past Bunyoro's rule had stretched from the Ituri Forest in the Congo into western Kenya, and from Buhaya to Lake Rudolf. This was too vast an area to be administered directly, so members of the royal Bito clan were sent to take charge of outlying areas, and their rulership became hereditary. With the gradual weakening of Bunyoro the contacts between these areas and the centre of power became increasingly tenuous. Buganda may have hived off early and developed on her own lines. There the royal Bito clan and the cattle-keeping Hima element completely merged with the agriculturalist people (if this is a correct understanding of the

BUNYORO AND HER NEIGHBOURS IN THE TIME OF KABAREGA

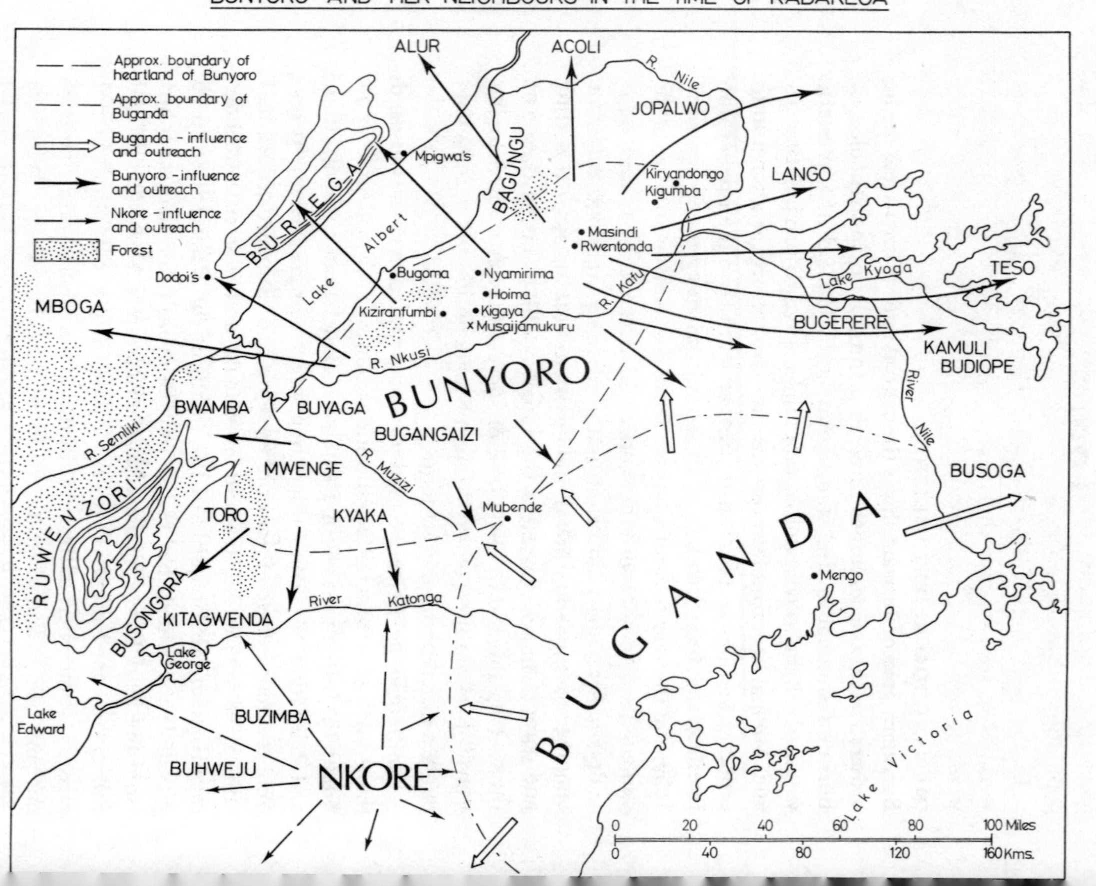

origin of Buganda), whereas in what is now Toro and Bunyoro only limited merging had taken place, and further south, almost none. In much of the west rainfall is less plentiful than in Buganda, millet rather than bananas the staple crop of the agriculturalists, and the pastoralist Hima grazed their herds over wide areas, so that the population was much more thinly spread.

In the west, both fissiparous and clustering tendencies were at work. Map 1 shows how the semi-independent principalities which were numerous in the area grouped themselves around more powerful nuclei—Koki looking towards Buganda; Buzimba, Buhweju, Igara, Bunyaruguru, Busongora, and Kitagwenda being brought into the orbit of Ankole (though the attachments of Buzimba, Busongora, and Kitagwenda were loose and they were also within the orbit of Bunyoro); Kyaka, Mwenge, Bwamba, Burega, and Mboga had firm attachments to Bunyoro in the nineteenth century; and Toro, which was only a small area prior to British interference, had been trying to become a centre of power since 1830, but had been severely punished for this presumption under the rising power of Kabalega in Bunyoro.

Practically all the peoples of the Western Kingdoms spoke one language with only slight dialectal differences, and in spite of raiding and competing for power, cultural affinities were strong. Between these areas and Buganda the cultural differences were greater, but none of the western rulers was above accepting aid from Buganda against a neighbour upon occasion. The British intrusion into the area caused the situation to congeal, and the colonialists' handling of Toro and Bunyoro made it particularly difficult for these two kingdoms to readjust themselves.

The looser pattern of rule in the west, the multiplicity of small principalities which the British tidied up into three kingdoms, and their treatment of the traditional rulers and assumptions about the nature of their power had an effect upon the spread of Christianity, and hence must be looked at at some length.

Tradition has it that in 1830 Kaboyo, son of Kyebambe III Nyamutukura, *Mukama* of Bunyoro, was sent by his father to collect tribute from Toro and Busongora over which he had some authority.[1] He grew to love the country of Toro, and the people asked him to become their ruler. So instead of returning to his father with the tribute he acceded to their wishes, and settled at Mukoli, not far south of the River Muzizi. He then moved further south to Rwamukora near Rusekere, but here the cows died, so he moved to Butiti. This was very presumptuous, since in Mwenge, where Butiti is, lay some of the best royal grazing grounds. Kyebambe sent arms against Kaboyo, but later was reconciled to him, and to mark this reconciliation sent him a royal drum and other regalia.[2] Kaboyo's death was followed by a war of succession between three of his sons, Kazana Ruhaga, Nyaika Kasunga, and Kato Rukidi. Kazana first became *Mukama*, but Nyaika seized power and killed him. Kato Rukidi then made a bid for power with the aid of Ankole, but this failed. Later, with the aid of Buganda, he was more successful, and Nyaika was forced to flee to Mboga. Mboga, beyond the Semliki River, was inhabited by a group of Hima people who owed some allegiance to Bunyoro. News reached here that after setting up Kato Rukidi as *Mukama,* the Ganda had returned home. So Nyaika collected his followers, returned to Toro, and succeeded in killing his brother and establishing himself as *Mukama*.

During the reign of Nyaika, Bunyoro's power, which had been declining, began to revive under *Mukama* Kabalega, and an army was sent against Toro. By this time Nyaika had established himself at Burahya in Toro, and Kabalega's raid was primarily made in retaliation for a raid made by Nyaika into Mwenge. Much damage was inflicted on Toro and many cattle were captured, but Nyaika himself escaped. His death two years later was followed by further succession quarrels between his sons. Kabalega took advantage of this moment of weakness to send an expedition against Toro under Mutebere. Oliimi Mukabirere, the successful contender for the position of *Mukama,* was captured and taken to Bunyoro, where he died in exile. Two other Bito, Mukarusa and Nyamuyonjo, tried to establish themselves in power, but they too were captured and taken prisoner to Bunyoro. In all this fighting and confusion the country and people of Toro suffered considerably. Nyaika's other sons were scattered. One, Karema, was taken to Bunyoro; the mother fled south with three others. She was sheltered on the way by the Konjo at Nyagwaki, a people who live on the lower slopes of the Ruwenzori. She made her way to the court of Ntare V, *Mugabe* of Ankole, but Kabalega sent orders that the three children with her were to be killed. Ntare succeeded in having two killed, but the mother escaped with the third, Kasagama, and took him to Buganda.

Here they found shelter with a Bito of the royal line of Toro named Byakweyamba. He had been captured by the armies of *Kabaka* Mutesa I and had been placed in the royal household as a *mugalagala* (page), and having won Mutesa's favour, had been awarded with a minor chieftaincy entitled *Kitanda* and had been given land in Buddu. There he came into contact with Christianity and was instructed by a Ganda teacher, Petero Nsubuga, who stayed in his household. When he was baptized in 1886 he took the name of Yafeti (Japhet). Kasagama began to learn to read when staying in Byakweyamba's household.[3]

Byakweyamba, Kasagama, and their story were known to Zakariya Kizito Kisingiri, at that time a sub-chief under the *Pokino* of Buddu, the county chief in whose territory Byakweyamba held his lands.[4] When Lugard arrived in Uganda as the first representative of the Imperial British East Africa Company, he first marched against the Muslim party which was receiving help from Kabalega in Bunyoro, and then turned south to journey through Buddu, Ankole, and Toro to Kavalli's to bring out the Sudanese troops left behind there when Stanley had 'rescued' Emin Pasha. Lugard had by this time been persuaded that Kabalega was an implacable enemy, and the Ganda were delighted at this since it meant that they could count on British aid against Bunyoro. When Lugard passed through Buddu, Kisingiri put into operation a plan he and Apolo Kagwa had already thought out, seeing in it a chance of extending Protestant Buganda's power and influence in the west at the expense of Kabalega and Bunyoro.[5] Kisingiri carefully prepared the ground by bringing gifts to Lugard, and then presented Kasagama and Byakweyamba to him, introducing them as members of the royal house of Bunyoro. He said they would be willing to accompany Lugard to the west and raise Toro to his support against the tyrannies of Kabalega, and they had the advantage of being staunch Protestants. 'All this reads like the veriest fiction,' remarked Lugard, 'which I could possibly have invented to fit in with my wishes . . .'[6] At first Lugard was under the impression that neither of these men was the prince of Toro, but that they would introduce this prince to him when they reached Ankole, and there is no note in Lugard's diary of when he came to realize that Kasagama himself was the claimant to the throne of Toro. On 11 August 1891, having passed through Ankole, Lugard halted between the Sebwe and Mubuku rivers. It was decided to build a fort there—not too far north of the fort built to protect the Salt Lake at Katwe—and that Kasagama should make his capital there and give the people of Toro a chance to acknowledge him. Five days later a treaty was drawn up and signed between Lugard and Kasagama. In this, Kasagama agreed to place Toro and all its dependencies entirely under the rule of the IBEAC; he acknowledged that he had been established in the kingship by the British, and in return it was understood that he was to have the protection of the Company. For the time being his rule was confined to what Lugard described as

'Toro proper', by which Busongora, Kitagwenda, Butuku, Mboga, and Kyaka were specifically excluded. Included, however, were Mwenge and Kitagweta (now part of Kyaka), which had never previously been under the rule of Toro.[7] It is in fact claimed that 'Toro proper' applied only to a fairly small area lying between Kabarole and Ruwenzori, though even before Kasagama's instalment by Lugard the term had begun to denote a rather wider area than this.[8]

This arrangement pleased everybody but Kabalega. It pleased Lugard that a British appointee had been put in a key position for stopping the passage of arms from the south to Bunyoro; it pleased Kasagama that he was thus able to gain a throne which apart from some such miracle could never have been his; it pleased Byakweyamba that he was able to regain a position he had lost, and he also had private ambitions not yet disclosed of making himself *Mukama* of Mwenge;[9] and finally it pleased Kisingiri and Kagwa that they had achieved a diplomatic triumph which would greatly enhance their personal standing and add considerably to the extent of Buganda's influence, as well as gain support for the Protestant party. If the British saw Kasagama as their appointee, there is no doubt that Kisingiri and Kagwa saw him as their protégé, and as an ally of Buganda against Bunyoro. That Lugard would not go on to wipe out Kabalega's power immediately was something none of them could have envisaged; nor could they have foreseen the price which Kasagama, Byakweyamba, and the people of Toro would have to pay over the next few years to keep what had been gained. The treaty went on to forbid slavery (no British-made treaty would have dared to omit an anti-slavery clause at this time, whether it was meaningful or not); the sole right to ivory was ceded to the Company; and the passage and holding of unregistered firearms was forbidden, these last two clauses being the ones Lugard was really interested in.[10]

Once established in Toro, Kasagama's problem was to exert his authority. In Toro proper the people apparently acknowledged him gladly, and Kabalega had dealt with the problem of rival claimants for him by killing all his brothers save one, Karema, who was still in Bunyoro. But the confederacy with Kasagama at its head, which was what Lugard had envisaged, was foreign to traditional thinking, and Kasagama had to rule areas which had never before been ruled by Toro. Johnston wrote of Toro as constituted by the British: 'It really consists of a number of little principalities, which at the beginning of the British Protectorate were confederated and made to recognize as supreme chief the king of Toro Proper, this being a small country on the east of the Ruwenzori range.'[11] When by later agreements Kasagama's rule was extended, his problem became more acute, for the British expected him to rule in the manner of a *Kabaka* of Buganda—and indeed this was the only pattern of rule he knew; but we have already seen that the concentrated pattern of rule evolved in Buganda was foreign to the west of Uganda, and there was no infrastructure to sustain it. His difficulties were further intensified because strife arose between him and Byakweyamba, who had conceived the idea of setting himself up independently in Mwenge. In view of all these difficulties it is not surprising that Kasagama was not satisfied until his suzerainty was clarified in 1906, and no coronation rituals were performed until after this was done.[12] Lugard's idea of efficient rule, 'appointing chiefs of districts, and a law and tribunal where justice could be got and complaints heard and grievances redressed', must have made very little sense in a society where rulership was more readily assessed in terms of successful raids and the numbers of chiefdoms willing to pay tribute.[13]

As soon as Lugard left, the Sudanese garrisons on the Toro/Bunyoro border, which were supposed to be for his protection, began to prey on Toro for food. They had no other way of getting it than by seizing it, and Lugard had had no objection to their harrying the people of Bunyoro. In 1893 Bishop Tucker came to know of what was happening, and wrote to inform the Commissioner. This gave Macdonald an added reason for ordering the withdrawal of the garrisons when the British government declared itself unwilling to accept any responsibilities outside Buganda. Captain Owen, sent to carry out the evacuation, realized that to withdraw them altogether would be to invite raids from Bunyoro. Although the evacuation was not so complete as was originally planned, Kabalega's forces descended on Toro, driving Kasagama into the Ruwenzori, and forcing Byakweyamba into the forests. They were pushing through to Busongora—from time to time subject to tribute-collecting forays—when Colvile was sent to attack Bunyoro in 1894. From then on, Kabalega's whole attention was fixed on defending himself against the British and the Ganda who were determined on his total overthrow, and Toro was left in peace. Kasagama was reinstated and a second treaty was made. This enlarged his borders to the modern boundaries, and made him head of a larger confederacy, in return for which he was to pay an annual tax in ivory.[14]

The threat of Kabalega and of the Sudanese garrisons was thus removed; but Kasagama was still left with the difficult task of trying to rule this confederacy. Parts of it had been further impoverished by the raids from Bunyoro, and parts of it did not want him as overlord. There was an additional complication in the shape of the British resident officer now placed in Toro, and there was a good deal of friction between him and Kasagama during the next few years. It is improbable that Kasagama had much idea of what was involved in signing a treaty, and still less of what the British would expect him to do in order to keep it. From Kasagama's point of view there was nothing unusual in someone being established as *Mukama* with outside help. It had happened repeatedly in the history of the Bantu kingdoms that a claimant to the throne established himself with the help of one of the neighbouring peoples—it had happened in the wars preceding Nyaika's accession in Toro only a few years before. This had made little difference to the way the ruler wielded his power subsequently. He did not thereby become the puppet of, or even limited by, those who had helped him, though he might feel an obligation to reciprocate help should the need arise. This is not to suggest that Kasagama made no attempt to adjust to the situation created by the imposition of British overrule. He made great efforts, but he did not always do so in the way the British thought he should. Complaints made against him of dealing illicitly in arms (a main part of the reason for the treaty was to prevent arms reaching Kabalega); of 'stealing women'; and of acting without reference to the British administration were complaints made against actions which, within the traditional framework, were perfectly allowable ways of enhancing his power. In the matter of gun-running it was mere misfortune that he should have been found out, and in 'stealing women' he was exercising a traditional prerogative.[15]

3

THE ARRIVAL OF CATECHISTS AND MISSIONARIES

It was during this difficult period that Christianity first impinged on Toro. When Yafeti Byakweyamba had returned home he had taken with him a number of Ganda followers, and in 1892 the Rev. R. P. Ashe sent him some copies of the *Mateka* (a first reading book, containing, among other things, the Ten Commandments, from which it got its name). These were seized by the Sudanese garrisons and destroyed.[16] Soon after this, Byakweyamba and his followers were routed by forces from Bunyoro and driven into the forest. When

Owen restored Kasagama in 1894, Byakweyamba sent to Buganda to ask for catechists. He may have hoped that if they came the British would feel more responsible for defending Toro from Bunyoro. The request arrived at a propitious moment. The Mengo church had just been revitalized by the revival of 1893/4, and there was great eagerness to share in the work of evangelism. Petero Nsubuga, who had once taught Byakweyamba in Buganda, and Mako Lweimbazi responded to the request, and left for Toro about June 1894, taking with them two companions, Nuwa Nakiwafu, later to become well-known as a clergyman, and Tito Wakibingi.[17] Byakweyamba had by this time been given the chieftaincy of Mwenge and was established at Butiti, whilst Kasagama had his capital at Kabarole, Fort Gerry (now Fort Portal). Nsubuga stayed at Butiti and probably spent much of his time teaching the Baganda there, and Lweimbazi taught at Kabarole, where he started to build a small church outside Kasagama's enclosure.[18]

By the settlements of 1892 and 1893 it had been accepted at least temporarily that the Catholics should be allowed to extend towards the west and the Protestants to the north and east, and Toro was thought to be within the Catholic sphere. In 1894 permission was granted for a Catholic mission in Toro,[19] but it was nearly a year before Frs Achte and Toulze could be spared from elsewhere to open this mission.[20] Since the area was known to be within the Catholic sphere, Bishop Tucker had some hesitations about Anglican work being started there. He got round the difficulty by allowing the Mengo Church Council to send the catechists and bear the cost: a largely African body could hardly be ordered to refuse the request of a fellow African, and no white missionaries were to be sent.[21] It seems not to have been known to the CMS that the White Fathers had concrete plans about Toro, and the Catholic missionaries were surprised, on arrival, to find themselves forestalled by Anglican catechists. Kasagama was committed as a Protestant and he did not want his kingdom to be torn by religious strife as Buganda had been, so he gave his full backing to the Protestant catechists, and obstructed the Catholic mission in every way that he dared, hoping they would be sufficiently discouraged to leave.[22] With his backing the Protestants had already achieved some success at court by the time the Catholics arrived—Achte described the influence of Apolo Kivebulaya in particular. He had arrived in Toro in 1895, was privileged to sit on the same mat as the king, and had persuaded him to give up beer and the playing of *mweso* (often a gambling game, and therefore frowned on by the Protestant missionaries). The

Catholics arrived before any baptisms had taken place, but the men appointed to chieftaincies dared not oppose Kasagama by accepting Catholic catechists. Even though Achte made blood-brotherhood with Kagoro, a chief in Mwenge, and Bishop Streicher did the same with a chief in Kitagweta, catechists sent to these chiefs were not accepted by them.[23] Kasagama made it clear that loyalty to him meant being a Protestant, and so used religion to strengthen his position.

In 1895 Lweimbazi and Nsubuga returned to Buganda, and recruited further catechists for work in Toro. Those who volunteered were Sedulaka Zabunamakwata and Apolo Kivebulaya, whose influence Achte was to comment on, and who later became widely known for his saintliness and apostolic zeal.[24] He had connexions with Toro for early in 1894 he had accompanied Owen's expedition to restore Kasagama. He perhaps went as a porter or camp servant. Soon after his baptism in 1895 he asked to become a catechist. Ham Mukasa, later to become county chief of Kyagwe, in whose household he stayed, stood as his sponsor when he offered to go to Toro. He had occasionally been sent to teach children in the villages round the capital and had not been very successful. The children had teased him because of his quaint dress and manner. In Toro, however, things went better, and he felt that God was good to him in giving him joy in teaching and preaching. Achte judged him to be a somewhat insignificant person who would never have risen to a position in his own country.[25] This simplicity, which was one of his most marked characteristics, stands in striking contrast to the complexity and astuteness of many of the Ganda leaders. He was a man of endearing childlikeness, and in spite of a liking for smart clothes (of which in fact he had few enough), there was an almost Franciscan love of poverty and humility which is a far cry from the Ganda love of wealth and status. It is difficult to imagine that he would have made much of an impression in Buganda, but by being always ready to go to some new and remote place, he found a milieu in which his spiritual genius was able to flower, and make him an inspiration to many.

When Kivebulaya and Zabunamakwata arrived in Toro they found the people building a little church about 30 feet long outside the *Mukama's* palace, and fifty or so people were learning to read. Kasagama himself was the most eager among them, and the new catechists entered on their work with enthusiasm. It was temporarily halted by a crisis in relations between Kasagama and Captain Ashburnham, the British resident officer. Ashburnham heard in

November 1895 that Kasagama was in collusion with a caravan taking gunpowder to Bunyoro. The Sudanese troops were ordered to search his enclosure, but Kasagama himself had fled to the mountains. When the surrounding homesteads were also raided, people and catechists fled across the Mpanga river. Several were caught and arrested, including Kivebulaya, and when he complained that the troops had looted 4,000 cowrie shells which were mission property, Ashburnham disbelieved him and sent him off in the chain gang to Kampala. Fr Achte tried to intervene on Kasagama's behalf, but the *Mukama* too was sent under arrest to Kampala. There charges were brought against him of allowing slavery, conniving in gunpowder-running, and not paying the ivory tax in full. He pleaded his cause before the Commissioner, and thanks to Bishop Tucker's intervention on his behalf, was cleared. Kivebulaya was released without any charge being laid against him. Ashburnham's handling of the situation was judged to have been high handed, and he was replaced.[26]

Once in Kampala, Kasagama was persuaded to stay for a while in order to receive further religious instruction, and he was then baptized with the name Daudi (David) in Namirembe Cathedral in the presence of the Commissioner. This was an event of some strategic importance for the Protestants. Zakariya Kizito Kisingiri, who had effected the introduction of Kasagama to Lugard, was one of his god-parents,[27] and the others were the county chief, Samwili Mukasa, and his wife.[28] A fortnight later the Bishop himself set out with the Rev. A. B. Fisher to open a CMS mission station, and Apolo Kivebulaya and reinforcements of Ganda teachers followed them.[29]

By this time the attempt to keep to separate 'spheres' had been abandoned by the missions. Neither had ever agreed to abide by in indefinitely, and in 1895 the Mill Hill Fathers had arrived to work in Eastern Uganda, formerly a Protestant sphere, and all pretence of avoiding competition was dropped.[30] The administration in Toro tried to allow both denominations an equal opportunity, and defended this as religious liberty. But in the political situation in Toro no such thing as religious liberty could exist, and both the missions knew it, though both invoked it when it suited them to. In 1896 Achte noted that two chiefs who had intended to become Catholics had been given Bibles and asked (i.e. ordered) to go to the Protestant church by Kasagama. One had sent a daughter and another a relative to the Catholic mission for instruction, but they themselves chose to play it safe.[31] Achte noted a little later that Kasagama 'ne veut pas deux partis dans son pays'.[32] When a chief named Kayibare decided to become a Catholic, he was accused by the *Mukama* of disloyalty. Although Achte said his only disloyalty was to align himself with the Catholics, he knew quite well that a chief who did so probably was disaffected, and that the chiefs most likely to accept Catholic catechists were those who did not like Kasagama, and he acted accordingly. A certain Kalijyangire claimed to have intercepted Kasagama's men trading ivory for guns, and demonstrated his dislike for the *Mukama* by seizing the ivory and sending it to the British administrator, thus incurring the *Mukama's* displeasure. Achte promptly approached him, and within a few days he had agreed to allow Catholic catechists to work in his domains.[33] Shortly after this Achte asked permission to visit Busongora where all the chiefs were known to be hostile to Kasagama. The Catholics had little choice but to resort to such tactics, and religious liberty was non-existent.

Achte was so disturbed at the ascendancy of the Protestants that at the beginning of 1896 he wrote repeatedly to his superiors about the situation. He noted that Protestant catechists were well received because the people thought they were sent by the powerful Apolo Kagwa; and so in a sense they were, for Kagwa was a power to be reckoned with on the Mengo Church Council. When catechists went to Mboga across the Semliki, Achte connected this with Kasagama's ambitions, and was almost certainly right in doing so. Fr Toulze expressed equal concern at the Protestant involvement in politics which gave them this advantage. By April Achte was recommending the establishment of a Catholic council of great chiefs, to be presided over by the Vicar Apostolic or the Superior of the mission at Rubaga, which should assume the responsibility of sending out Catholic catechists, but the suggestion was never taken up.[34] After a while the tensions eased a little.

4

EARLY CMS EXPANSION IN TORO

Soon after Fisher arrived in Toro the first group of people was baptized. This group of fifteen included the woman whom Kasagama chose as his 'ring' wife, the one married in church. The queen mother, several other women who had been his wives, and some palace servants made up the group. No chief would as yet commit himself. These baptisms were a necessary piece of

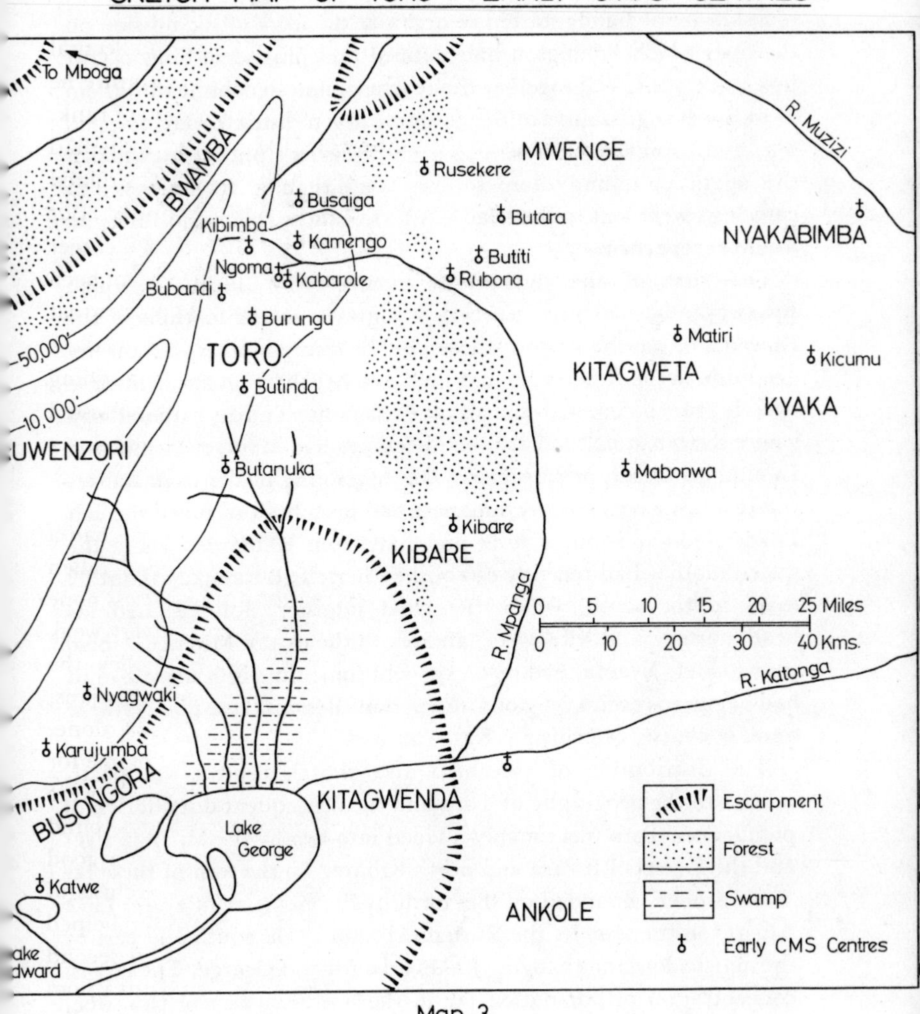
SKETCH MAP OF TORO - EARLY C.M.S. CENTRES
To Mboga
BWAMBA
MWENGE
R. Muzizi
Rusekere
Busaiga
Butara
Kibimba
Kamengo
NYAKABIMBA
Butiti
Ngoma
Kabarole
Rubona
Bubandi
Burungu
Matiri
50,000'
TORO
Kicumu
KITAGWETA
Butinda
10,000'
KYAKA
RUWENZORI
Butanuka
Mabonwa
Kibare
KIBARE
R. Mpanga
0 5 10 15 20 25 Miles
0 10 20 30 40 Kms.
R. Katonga
Nyagwaki
Karujumba
BUSONGORA
KITAGWENDA
Escarpment
Lake George
Forest
Katwe
Swamp
ANKOLE
Lake Edward
Early CMS Centres

Map 3

consolidation for the Protestants. During Kasagama's absence in Kampala the Catholics had naturally seized the opportunity to win over some influential persons, including the queen mother and Kagoro, Byakweyamba's deputy. The latter had previously made blood-brotherhood with Achte, and he now accepted a medal as a sign of Catholic allegiance, but when Byakweyamba returned with Kasagama, Kagoro and the catechist were sent away.[35]

Fisher immediately started to organize the work of the mission on the lines which Pilkington had noticed and praised in Singo: 'Our first work was to call together the teachers, and to consult with them as to the evangelization of the country. Seven districts were mapped out, and two evangelists sent to each'.[36] Fisher's phraseology makes the operation sound more sophisticated than it really was, but catechists were sent to the headquarters of those chiefs and Bito who would accept them.

The first of the outstations opened was Butiti to which Byakweyamba had just returned. Nyagwaki, in the foothills of the Ruwenzori, was the second, chosen by the queen mother to show her gratitude to the Konjo who had sheltered her there on her flight into Ankole years before with the infant Kasagama. Thirdly came Mboga where the *Mukama,* Tabaro, had been persuaded by Kasagama and Lweimbazi to accept catechists. The remaining places were Katwe, where a fort garrisoned by Sudanese had been built to guard the Salt Lake; Ngoma, about a mile and half from Kabarole, where the queen mother had recently established herself; Butanuka, about 20 miles to the south, where the chief minister, Rusoke, had his headquarters; and Kitagweta, an area to the east of Mwenge, whose young chief, Nyama, had recently spent some time in Kampala, and had begun to receive religious instruction. Besides these places, there were, of course, catechists at Kabarole itself.[37]

The distribution of catechists and church centres was partly related to the geography of Toro and the consequent distribution of population. Toro was roughly divided into two by the Mpanga river and the forests of Itwara and north Kibare. To the west of these lay 'Toro proper', bounded on the north by the escarpment above Lake Albert, on the west by the Ruwenzori, and to the south and east by the marshy lowlands fringing Lakes Edward and George. The largest concentration of population lay in the northern part of this area, north of the Rwimi. Before the modern counties were demarcated, three senior chiefs, entitled by Kasagama *Kaima, Mukwenda,* and *Kago* (their titles borrowed from Ganda usage), had their lands in this area, and a large number of little churches spread out from

Butanuka and Kabarole, and later from Burungu and Butinda. To the east of the Mpanga lay Mwenge, Kitagweta, Nyakabimba, and Kyaka, the best grazing lands: but except around Butiti the population was sparse. Butiti became the only other European-staffed CMS centre in Toro, and quite a number of church centres grew up around it. Elsewhere church centres were few in number. Somewhat inaccessible from Kabarole were the parts of Kibare south of the forest, and Kitagwenda, still further cut off by the Katonga river. In the north-west, Bwamba was still more isolated, the road to it running, at that time, over the Bwamba Pass, almost due west of Kabarole. In these more isolated areas very few Protestant church centres were established. The geography of Toro explains why there had been a number of independent principalities here previously, why Kasagama had so much difficulty in welding this diverse area into one, and why the missionaries were unable to provide adequate supervision for catechists in the more distant regions.

One of the catechists who arrived with Fisher in 1896 was Nuwa Nakiwafu, who had temporarily returned to Buganda, but now came back to Toro for a second tour of service. He was one of the outstanding early Ganda converts. His father was a Muchwezi priest at Mwanga's court, and Nakiwafu's conversion involved a particularly sharp break with the old way of life. The missionaries found him a spiritually minded man who was very conscientious in his work.[38] He became a favourite with Kasagama and with a high-ranking Toro woman named Hana Kageye. These two taught him Rutoro which he learned to speak well.[39] He and Tito Wakibingi were posted to Kabarole.[40] Another whose doings are known to us was Apolo Kivebulaya, who was sent to Nyagwaki, where he slowly won the confidence of the Konjo people. A few of them came seriously to 'read' for baptism, and many more just to listen to his teaching.[41] But after only a few months he was relocated to Mboga with Sedulaka Zabunamakwata. The catechists there had been unable to cope with an increasingly difficult situation, so they were replaced by the two best men available. The people of Mboga were undoubtedly the gainers, though not before Kivebulaya and Zabunamakwata had overcome considerable opposition. What happened at Nyagwaki we are left to guess, with only the baptism register to help us. From the record there we learn that one person was baptized in 1896, and no one else until 1900, when four names are found. There were few men with Kivebulaya's apostolic zeal and gift for making himself loved by all.

At Butiti progress was made, and a group of sixteen men and two women was baptized in October 1896. Several of them were Ganda who had come to Toro with Byakweyamba, and this was true of the next group also. It seems as though the catechists concentrated their attention on their fellow Ganda. Some of the Ganda had been there for years, and had fought against the Nyoro forces in 1892. Although they had been defeated, they had won renown for their exploits then. One of the women baptized was Byakweyamba's wife. In 1897 a further group of twelve was baptized by Zakariya Kizito Kisingiri, now a deacon, who visited Toro on a semi-pastoral, semi-diplomatic mission.[42] After this, the church at Butiti ceased to develop for some time. Byakweyamba found himself frustrated in his desire to become an independent ruler in Mwenge, and had quarrelled with Kasagama and with Ashburnham who disapproved of his ambitions. His physical disabilities would probably have rendered him unacceptable as *Mukama* in any case, and these troubled him increasingly. In 1897 he returned to his lands in Buddu and there committed suicide. He took many of his Ganda followers with him, and left a young nephew, Kagwahabi, to act as his deputy. Because this boy was too young to rule, Byakweyamba was temporarily replaced by Kyerre, but the disruption which followed the chief's suicide resulted in his headquarters falling into ruin, and the church work became disorganized without a patron.[43]

Soon after Kasagama's return, the White Fathers urged the administration to get the *Mukama* to proclaim religious liberty. The gains they had made during his absence could hardly be maintained otherwise. Kasagama naturally procrastinated about making a pronouncement which was tantamount to giving his chiefs permission to join the opposition, and he took steps to minimize the effect of what he was forced to do. This included threatening his pages that they would be severely beaten if they took advantage of the freedom offered them. He also made ostentatious gifts to the Protestant church at a ceremony in which he took care to involve his chiefs with him, and he tried to get the White Fathers mission closed. The vigour of his actions suggests that there was support for the opposition, and that he felt himself to be insecure. His absence in Kampala and the bad relations which existed between him and the administrators Ashburnham and Sitwell were situations the opposition were able to exploit. In August 1896 he became so alarmed by Sitwell's antagonism to him that he considered fleeing to Buganda, hoping to win the support of Bishop Tucker as on a previous occasion.[44] Sitwell, for his part, wanted to depose him and have Toro incorporated into Buganda.[45] In these circumstances a number of chiefs risked declaring themselves Catholics as soon as he was finally made to declare religious liberty. Achte had few illusions about the value of some of these professions ('Catholique de nom, car c'est le type du vrai sauvage' was his description of one such). He probably understood the politico-religious situation better than anyone else, and he can hardly be blamed for exploiting it whenever possible, and with considerable success. The Catholic mission, unable to work through the chiefs, built up a reputation for themselves for caring for the sick and destitute, and won a large peasant following.[46]

The Protestants, who were riding on the crest of the wave, showed little concern about the Catholic opposition, and the missionaries were sometimes naive about the motives for conversion. They came to lean increasingly on the support of the *Mukama* and those chiefs who followed him into the Protestant church. But the ups and downs of the embryonic Christian communities in Toro show that it was not sufficient to have the support of a chief and to send a catechist to work in his domain. The quality of the chief and of the catechist were equally important. Whilst some catechists were zealous and faithful, others displayed the arrogance which was soon to make the Ganda unacceptable throughout the Western Kingdoms. The political situation could militate for or against Protestant or Catholic Christianity, and create a climate of opinion favourable to its initial acceptance or rejection; but after that came the slow discovery of what the newly accepted faith meant and demanded, and this was beyond the reach of politics. Political alignments might saddle a church with numerous adherents who made little progress in the faith, and in Toro circumstances dictated that more of these were found among the Protestants than among the Catholics, though there were a good many in both churches. The political opportunists became Protestants; the disgruntled, Catholics. It is surprising that so many who were baptized for motives which were largely other than religious, later on entered into a genuine understanding and acceptance of Christianity.

5

1895-1905 THE CHURCH ESTABLISHED

After 1895 Toro became more stable and the missions were able to establish themselves and diversify their activities. In 1897 Mwanga rose in arms against the British, and Kasagama surprised the

Protectorate administration by remaining 'loyal'. Had they understood that his baptism as a Protestant was a virtual declaration of his acceptance of the need to accommodate himself to British rule, they would have been less surprised. He owed his whole position to the British, and to the Ganda hierarchy of Christian chiefs in whose interests it was to collaborate with the British in suppressing Mwanga's revolt. Kasagama's 'loyalty' greatly improved his standing with the British, and Bagge, who replaced Sitwell, initiated an era of much improved relationships between the *Mukama* and the administration.[47]

One consequence of this was that he gained a firmer hold over his chiefs. This was reflected in the number of those who asked for baptism in the Anglican church. In 1898 Tucker noted that their numbers had greatly increased, and he contrasted the mission's popularity with its precarious position in 1896 when no chief had been willing to follow Kasagama's lead. By 1898 the potential opposition was melting away: 'Several chiefs who have for some time been nominal Roman Catholics, have given up their empty profession, and with numbers of their followers have cast in their lot with us'.[48] There was to be a good deal of defection from one side to the other, and, *pace* the Bishop, there were plenty whose adherence to the Anglican church was purely nominal.

Tucker decided, as a result of his visit to Toro, that the work of the CMS there must no longer be considered an outpost of the work in Buganda but an independent work meriting an equal priority of staffing, and this he brought to the notice of the home committee of the mission.[49] A larger matter was here at stake than was realized at the time, and the bishop's decision was never fully implemented. Archdeacon Walker was the leader of those in the mission who always put the needs of Buganda first. He considered the Ganda superior to other people, and wanted to see Ganda influence spread throughout Uganda because he equated it with Christian influence. He could not understand why others feared Ganda aggressiveness. He and others extended this to the question of language, and whilst there was much good sense in what this group said about the desirability of having one language for the whole country, they failed to understand that for political reasons that language could not be Luganda.

In 1895, in spite of opposition, the bishop took immediate action to improve the staffing position in Toro. The Rev. T. R. Buckley was for some time the only European missionary there: Callis, a young recruit, had died after only six months, and both Lloyd and Fisher went on leave.[50] Roscoe was therefore sent to take charge of the work, and the Rev. C. T. Ecob and Mr (later the Rev.) H. E. Maddox followed shortly, the latter to have special responsibility for translation work. In 1899 the Rev. Asa Nkangali, a deacon, arrived to strengthen the mission further. Walker disapproved of all this and wrote to the CMS headquarters in Britain complaining about Maddox in particular: there was far too much work at Mengo for him to be spared, according to the Archdeacon.[51]

Roscoe was disappointed with Toro at first: 'I expected to find the Christians more advanced than they are and hoped to be able to start at once to train some for teaching. I found, however, that all needed general training, and it makes us dependent upon the Baganda as leaders'.[52] In Buganda the first converts had lived in close and intimate contact with a group of devoted missionaries over a period of years, and at a time of crisis in which all had shared. The missionaries had given them individual teaching and had made friends in a way that was never to be repeated. The very organization which made possible the wide and rapid spread of Christianity also made less possible the meeting in depth which had taken place in the early years. However, Roscoe hoped that within a few months some Toro Christians would be able to take charge of the smaller centres, and some he considered promising teachers.

Towards the end of the year further progress was made in the church. A meeting of all communicant members was held, and these elected a church council for Toro. Locating and disciplining teacher-catechists became one of its chief concerns.[53] The members of the council included secular as well as religious leaders. Mikaeri Lusoke, entitled *Kimbugwe,* held his lands in Busongora. He was the *Mukama's* treasurer and was responsible for the pages in training at court. He was a quiet, thoughtful man who did not act until he had carefully weighed the possible consequences of his actions. Later he became chief minister under Kasagama's successor.[54] Samwiri Kwitakulimuki was senior chief of Kibare, and he started by being an enthusiastic Christian. Later he wanted to divorce his wife and marry again, and since he could not do so as a Christian, he became a Muslim.[55] Nasanieri Mugurusi was Kasagama's chief minister, and remained in office for over thirty years. He had been baptized by Callis, the young missionary who died soon after his arrival. Those to be baptized were drawn up on one side of the Mpanga river, and they passed right through the water to join the Christians who were waiting for them on the other side. The ceremony made a lasting impression on all who saw it or took part in it. After baptism, Mugurusi went to Mboga as a catechist for a while. In about 1906 he was made county chief of Kitagwenda and did much to establish the Anglican church there—prior to this the Catholics had had a monopoly in the area. He was a strong and courageous man—more impulsive than Mikaeri Lusoke. The missionaries recorded how he meted out summary punishment to those who failed to attend church classes. He was always one to take up new ideas. Unlike most of the chiefs, he did not belong to the aristocratic Hima group.[56] Petero Tigwezire started by being a catechist in Bwamba and later in Mwenge, but he was quickly appointed to a senior chieftaincy in Bwamba, was transferred to Kibare, and later still to Mwenge. He had a reputation for being merciful to the poor, and for looking after widows and orphans, and at one time he wanted to be ordained, but he would not promise to give up all beer-drinking, which apparently made him unacceptable. This did little to detract from the high regard in which he was held by Toro Christians. He is sometimes spoken of as bringing light to the people at a time when many were being baptized simply to please the *Mukama,* and he is remembered as one of those who did most for the furtherance of Protestant Christianity in Toro.[57] Gaburieri Kiza was a less important chief. In 1902 he was one of the first catechists to go from Toro to Ankole, where the missionaries found him much better than most of the Ganda they were being sent at that time, and they put this down in part to his belonging to the chiefly class and so commanding respect. The distinction between Hima and Iru was more marked and more important in Ankole than in Toro. Like Tigwezire he had wanted to be ordained, but he had been turned down for the same reason. Later he became somewhat inflexible, and an over-stern disciplinarian. He held sub-chieftaincies in Burahya and Kibare.[58] Musa Katuramu held a sub-chieftaincy in Busongora, and started by being an enthusiastic Christian, but later lapsed. Eriya Buligwanga was a Ganda who was appointed to a sub-chieftaincy in Toro. Ibulayimu Bugelamule was also a Ganda, a teacher, and when he left in 1900 his place on the church council was taken by Apolo Kivebulaya. The composition of the council reflects the close connexion between the Anglican church and the Toro Kingdom Government.[59]

Bishop Tucker had been led to believe that Luganda was widely understood, and that this would speed up evangelism. Luganda was known at court, and Kasagama's long sojourn in Buganda influenced him to model his kingdom on the Ganda pattern, that being the only one he knew. He gave his chiefs Ganda titles, though they did not always fulfil the same functions as their Ganda counterparts. But Maddox soon realized that most people did not understand Luganda, and made a start on translation into Rutoro. By April 1899 the *Mateka* had been completed and work had begun on the gospels. The following year Tucker gave formal permission for the use of the local vernacular in teaching for baptism and confirmation as soon as the necessary books could be made available.[60]

In both Toro and Ankole there was, for a short period, a desire to emulate the Ganda, even to the extent of using their language, whilst copying Ganda customs was considered progressive. Naturally this was encouraged by the Ganda. Hence Walker's remark, 'The Waganda Christians do not think that the people of Toro who learn to read will care to be taught in their own language'.[61] This was quickly seen to be wishful thinking on the part of the Ganda. The purpose of Zakariya Kizito Kisingiri's visit in 1897 had been partly to try and persuade Kasagama that he should place himself under Ganda rule, and to offer him a position akin to that of the *Kamswaga* of Koki, whose forebears had been rulers of an independent principality, but who was reduced to the position of a county chief in the Ganda kingdom. The notion was rejected firmly, and perhaps marked the beginnings of the desire later shown by the Toro to be free altogether of Ganda influence.[62] There was a not altogether groundless fear that in subtle ways the Ganda were trying to gain an ascendancy over them, and suspicion fell on catechists as well as chiefs.[63] Maddox noted in 1899, 'The Baganda are jealous of their advancement, and are undoubtedly influenced by this feeling. It has existed for ages, but as long as the Batoro were insignificant there was nothing to call it out'.[64] Lloyd wrote more explicitly of the situation in Bunyoro a little later: 'A very strong idea of the Baganda is, that once get the Banyoro to speak Luganda, and they are morally putting themselves under the rule of [B]Uganda'. The *Bakama* of Toro and Bunyoro wrote jointly to request the use of Runyoro/Rutoro. This question of language was linked with the possibility of making the church in Toro independent of the Mengo Church Council, and some of the missionaries, led by Walker, protested against this, and deplored Kasagama's desire to be free of the influence of Buganda. At about the same time a number of Ganda chiefs from around Butiti were sent away, together with Ganda settlers in the area.[65] Some of the feeling against the Ganda does indeed seem somewhat chauvinistic, but on the other hand it marked a growth in self-confidence among the people of Toro which was welcome.

By the end of 1899 Toro was recovering from Nyoro attacks, from a period of bad relations with the British, and from communal fines. Cultivation was on the increase around Fort Portal, roads were being built, and a flourishing market and trading centre was growing up in the town. But according to Maddox, conditions in the church were far from satisfactory. The congregation at Kabarole was reported to be small, apart from the *Mukama's* retinue, and Maddox said there was 'gross sin' among the Christians, indolence in learning to read (i.e. attending baptism classes), and base motives for baptism. He thought this was due to a shortage of missionaries, a lack of elementary teaching in the local dialect, and the difficulty of visiting outstations frequently enough.[66] He might perhaps have added that the Anglican church had spread itself too widely too fast. Besides these difficulties, Roscoe, the one experienced missionary, had had to leave, and Ecob, who had replaced him, did not get on well with the catechists. In 1900 he had to be moved. Fisher succeeded him, and immediately the numbers of those asking for baptism and confirmation increased.[67] The happier situation is reflected in the baptism statistics. The relationship between a missionary and the catechists on whom he so greatly relied was of prime importance.

In August 1900 a special meeting of the church council was held at which the *Mukama* and the *Nyina Omukama* (queen mother) were both present. It was unanimously agreed 'to take the responsibility of Apolo Kivebulaya's support should the Bishop be pleased to ordain him as the first deacon of Toro'.[68] The minutes also record the sending out of the first trained Toro catechists. From the minutes of this and subsequent years it can be seen that a fair proportion of catechists worked for a considerable length of time. Among the earliest catechists to be commissioned were Paulo Byabusakuzi, still at work in 1971, and Andereya Sere and Yosiya Kamuhiigi, who became the first Toro Anglican priests.[69]

In 1901 the training of women church workers became a possibility with the arrival of two women missionaries, Ruth Hurditch and Edith Pike. Up until World War I women played a significant role in church life in Toro. During their period of training the women attended classes twice daily, studying Old Testament history and various books of the New Testament. They were questioned at the end of their training.[70] In February 1902 the first ten women were sent out to church centres, and two more taught at Kabarole. Thirteen more were licensed by the end of the year. Among these women was Ketura Balya, wife of Aberi Balya, the first Anglican to be consecrated bishop in East Africa; Zipora Kamuhiigi and Lea

Sere, whose husbands were ordained in 1907; and Miriya Tigwezire and Loi Kiza, whose husbands were chiefs and sat on the Church Council. Damari, the *Mukama*'s wife, was another of those trained, and she helped teach catechumens at Kabarole. Hana Kageye, whose husband had held high rank under the *Mukama* Nyaika,[71] and who had shared the exile of some of the royal clan in Ankole, returned there in 1902 to help teach the women at the court of the *Mugabe* of Ankole. Later she helped in the girls' boarding school in Toro, looking after the general welfare of the pupils, and teaching them sewing, knitting and traditional handicrafts. Ruth Komuntale, the *Mukama*'s daughter, later became a pupil in this school under Hana Kageye's care.[72] The recollections of those women still alive, and the missionaries' letters and record book show that much care was lavished on the training of these women, and this seems to have been the secret of their success. Many of the women worked for years.

The first informal training of girls by the White Sisters began in Buganda in the same year, 1902, and in 1903 two of these novice-catechists, or 'rèligieuses indigènes' as they soon began to be called, started work in Toro. They taught catechism to children, and helped to prepare them for first communion. They also took care of the altar linen.[73] In 1903 they were teaching 80 to 100 children who lived at the mission for a while before receiving their first communion.[74] These two may have been the Elisabela and Sesilya mentioned as being there in 1910. Elisabela was referred to as 'la fameuse institutrice', and Sesilya joined the noviciate of the Bannabikira (Daughters of the Virgin) in 1910.[75] The White Sisters themselves arrived in Toro in 1912, and the first foundation of Bannabikira was opened in 1919.[76] By this time women were playing a less important role in the Anglican church, and not until after independence was a further effort made to train Anglican women as church workers.[77]

In 1903 a further milestone in the history of the Anglican church was passed when a mission hospital was opened. From the beginning missionaries had given informal medical treatment, and had remarked on the high incidence of scabies and chest conditions. These probably resulted in part from the unsettled conditions prevailing in the 1890s which had led people to huddle together in flimsy huts: when they might have to flee to the mountains because of armed raids, what incentive was there to build anything more than a rough shelter?[78] The high rainfall of Toro meant mud and dirt, and the cold of the nights meant that people crowded around smoky fires for warmth. Such conditions were ideal for the spread of scabies and chest complaints. As soon as conditions became more stable, it was noticed that people began to build better houses for themselves. But plenty of scope for a medical mission remained.

Yet some CMS missionaries were opposed to the opening of a hospital. They were only interested in medical work in so far as it offered opportunities for evangelism. Other missionaries argued that the need of the people warranted medical work and that such work should not be seen only as a means to an end. Only Maddox saw a little further: 'Healing of sickness is so much the most prominent idea in this people's notion of religion that it is humanly speaking unreasonable to expect them to give up what they believe to be efficacious while offering them nothing in return. It is not surprising to find many of them holding on to two religions.'[79]

So 1903 saw the arrival of Dr Ashton Bond. To begin with the people were slow to accept new ideas about health care, but Kasagama led the way by allowing himself to be operated on under anaesthetic.[80] He was also instrumental in getting people to accept smallpox vaccination. By 1905 the hospital's thirty-four beds were barely sufficient, and patients often had to sleep on the floor, whilst seventy to eighty out-patients were treated daily. Until a small fee was introduced numbers had been even higher. Danieri, one of the *Mukama*'s household servants, took a daily service for the patients. By 1908 it had become necessary to build an additional men's ward. Western ideas of medicine slowly began to be understood: when Nasanaeri Mugurusi was seriously ill in 1908, he sent a sample of his blood to the hospital in a basin to be microscopically examined to see if he was bewitched. Later he sent down all his cooking utensils to ask if they had caused his illness—both actions suggest a blending of old and new ideas about the cause of disease.[81]

6

OUTSTATIONS AND CATECHISTS

Several times a year Dr Bond would set out on a medical safari to one area of Toro or another, stopping at each church centre on his route. The people would come to the centre both to attend his clinic and for a church service. The letters describing these safaris are among the sources of information about the development of CMS outstations.

Visiting and supervising catechists in Toro was difficult because of the large area served and the nature of the terrain with its forests, its innumerable fast-flowing rivers, and its hills and mountains. For a few years from 1902 onwards a CMS missionary was resident at Butiti and had charge of the eastern part of Toro, and in 1907 the Rev. Andereya Sere was appointed to Butiti and assumed much of this responsibility. In 1904 the White Fathers also opened a second mission at Butiti, and this became their base for work in eastern Toro. Protestant catechists were more numerous than Catholic catechists, but suffered from being constantly moved around. Some were moved almost every year. For both churches the information about catechists is incomplete, and one therefore hesitates to make comparisons, but the records suggest that a greater proportion of the Catholic catechists gave long service than was the case among the Anglicans, that they were moved about a good deal less frequently, and that they received more supervision and help from the missionaries. Even remote areas were visited twice a year by the White Fathers, whereas the CMS missionaries managed to visit these areas only once in two years on average.[82] It was easier for the celibate Catholic priest to go off on safari than for the married CMS missionary; the Catholics had more missionaries and more mission stations; and the Catholics placed greater emphasis on the reception of the sacraments, and hence the priests were under a greater obligation to visit outstations. The Anglicans, on the other hand, developed parishes staffed by Africans faster than the Catholics, but these were staffed by only one clergyman, whereas a Catholic mission always had at least two priests, often three. Both the CMS and the White Fathers expected their catechists to come in to the central mission from time to time, and both ran conferences or retreats for the catechists. None of the missionaries felt the catechists received enough help and supervision.[83]

The first CMS outstation we will look at is Butiti. The church here declined after the death of Byakweyamba, and as many of the Christians were Ganda, numbers were seriously depleted when these left.[84] There were no baptisms in 1898 and this year and the following one the catechists were said to have made no attempt to learn Rutoro and were 'conspicuous for their laziness'. Ecob was in charge there in 1899 and 1900, and things did not improve: it has already been noted that he could not get on with the catechists, and had to be transferred for that reason.[85] However, in 1900 a change for the better occurred. This was in part due to the arrival of a new catechist and his wife, Yakobo Kiwunyabuganga and Dulukasi. They were both trained catechists, and Dulukasi organized the women into doing systematic visiting, and persuaded the chief's wife to teach one of the church classes.[86] Then in March Apolo Kivebulaya, now ordained deacon, arrived to help. He and Yakobo went round visiting the people, and many promised to come to church. Apolo describes how the two of them worried as to whether the people would keep their promises, but they did, and in August Fisher was able to record that the congregation had more than doubled, and that hundreds had begun to attend catechism classes.[87] Apolo had been able to introduce reading sheets in Runyoro/Rutoro, and probably the newly completed translation of St Matthew's Gospel which he and Maddox had been working on, and for the first time the Toro people around Butiti were taught in their own language.[88] In 1901 there was a record number of 75 baptisms. By the following year almost all the Ganda had left the area, and all the catechists were from Toro. The Rev. A. L. Kitching arrived in 1902, and Apolo was moved to Kitagwenda, but the work in Mwenge continued to spread and there was soon a total of sixteen outstations.[89] In 1904 under the Rev. T. B. Johnson, Butiti became the headquarters of the CMS for eastern Toro, and began to keep its own register of baptisms.[90] When the Bonds arrived on a medical safari in 1905, nearly 500 people came for treatment, a far larger group than had been treated anywhere else in eastern Toro, and an indication of growing confidence among the people of Butiti.[91] The Rev. Andereya Sere came to Butiti in 1907. He had been baptized here in 1897 by Zakariya Kizito Kisingiri, and he came to Butiti at the request of the people there. As a young man he had lived in the chief's enclosure at Butiti, and had later worked in the households of Kitching and Johnson, both of whom thought highly of him. He was a quiet, thoughtful man who always took the trouble to talk with the parents of children brought to him for baptism, and who did not act until he had thought over a matter carefully. The people of Butiti helped him to build a new church on the hilltop where Callis had been buried, and they responded to his quiet and encouraging leadership.[92] Lea, his wife, had been trained at Kabarole by Miss Pike, receiving her 'letter' in 1905, and she took a lead in work among the women.[93]

Butanuka was the headquarters of Yosua Lusoke, chief minister of Toro until 1899. He had first gone to church for the purpose of scoffing rather than listening, but he had been moved by a sermon given by Lloyd, and his attitude changed completely. When Lloyd later visited him at Butanuka, where two catechists were working, the missionary noted, 'Nothing seems to please him more than to sit with his Testament in his hand reading the gospels to his people as they gather round him'. A church was built at Butanuka, able to hold about 120 people, and Lusoke was baptized on 16 September

1898.[94] But during the next two years there were only seven further baptisms and a considerable opposition to Christianity showed itself in the area. A Ganda catechist, Yasoni Kironde, found a congregation of some thirty baptized Christians and catechumens coming to church on Sundays, but stated that most of them were women and children with hardly a 'bearded man' among them. One man forbade the catechists ever to come near his house again, and some of the opposition which Yasoni commented on arose because he was a Ganda.[95] He stayed only a few months, and by 1902 the situation had improved. Three women catechists, Eseri Nyakabwa, Samari Lutahya, and Julia Kibate, were at work, and there were nineteen baptisms. In 1903 Lusoke himself acted as a catechist, and in this year the number of baptisms reached a peak and numbered thirty-four.[96] The Bonds visited the place in 1909 on their way to Lake Katwe. Tito Balikurungi was then the catechist, but it was Lusoke who called the people together for the Sunday service. Erisabeti and another woman were helping with church work also, and perhaps partly because of the doctor's presence in the area, the little reed church was packed with people.[97]

Ngoma,[98] the home of Vikitoliya Kahinju, the *Nyina Omukama* (queen mother) was only two miles distant from Kabarole, and benefited from its proximity to the mission headquarters, and from the *Nyina Omukama*'s active support. Vikitoliya had been baptized on 8 May 1896, her name being the first in the Baptism Register, and a number of women from her enclosure were among the first to be trained by Miss Pike and Miss Hurditch. She was strict in seeing that all the girls in her enclosure attended church classes: 'A list is made of all her dependents around here, and if any damsel is found careless or neglectful of church, or lacking in perseverance with her daily reading, report has it of the *Namasole* [this is the queen mother's title in Luganda, still the court language] that she administered a smacking with her own hands.'[99] On her estates the *Nyina Omukama* built a large church where the congregations were sometimes larger than those at Kabarole (the Bonds estimated that there were 450 people present when they visited in May 1905), and Holy Communion was celebrated at Kabarole and Ngoma on alternate Sundays.[100] For herself Vikitoliya built a two-storeyed house, the only one in Toro other than Kasagama's own. It was quite elaborately furnished, and the walls were hung with coloured cloth, but perhaps the builders lacked skill, for it collapsed.[101] Sedulaka Zabunamakwata was among the catechists at Ngoma in 1903, and among the women catechists was Mirika Kabahita, a close relation of the *Nyina Omukama,* and Ketura Balya who worked there both before and after her marriage to Aberi Balya, later to become a bishop.[102]

Rubona, which lay to the west of Butiti, was another early church centre. This was the headquarters of Zedekiya Nkojo, a member of the royal Bito clan, and a brother of Kasagama. Bishop Tucker gave a dramatic account of his conversion:

> He is a most interesting man; in features he is intellectual looking—his expression being bright and attractive. In stature he is small, but his bearing is distinctly that of a chief or man of rank. The story of his conversion is a very interesting one. Until he had heard the gospel his life was a very wild and unrestrained one—drunkenness and debauchery were its main features. But Christ found him, and he was arrested in his wild and mad career almost with the same suddenness as Saul of Tarsus. It has not been merely a change in the outward life . . . it has also been a great inward and spiritual change. A love of God's word and work, a love for God's people and a zeal in his service are the distinguishing marks of the new life. He has learnt to read and is very interested in getting others taught. He has built a church and maintains a teacher.[103]

But about a year later Yasoni Kironde arrived at Rubona and had a very different story to tell. He found that the church had fallen down, and said that although some 70 people came to services, none of them were proper Christians. He described Nkojo as 'a very weak man. He called himself a Christian but he did not obey the promptings of his conscience. He did not care for other Christians, and his mind was not on religion, though in that he was not alone, for very few of them were really in earnest'.[104] He laid the blame for all this on Nkojo, but he goes on to relate two facts which were perhaps more to blame. Early in 1901 Fisher had travelled round Toro and had marked out 165 church sites. This met with a good deal of opposition from landowners, who accused the catechists of having come to 'eat up' the country. That Kironde, a Ganda, helped to demarcate the sites must have made matters worse.[105] The second matter he records was even more serious. The three catechists whom he had replaced at Rubona had all been sent away for immorality and fined.[106] People voiced their anger over this to Kironde: 'You Baganda lie to us, you say those who are readers do not commit sin, and yet those fellows the other day, was not their conduct abominable, and probably you will do just the same, do you not want to tempt our women just as they did?'Well, we are not going to agree to our women reading, perhaps we may agree to our boys coming'.[107] Kironde accused the Toro of making excuses! However, he did something to restore confidence, for the congregation increased to about 100 during his three months stay. Baptisms of people from Rubona were not separately recorded until 1907. In that year nine people were baptized and the following year thirty, but Kironde's account shows that there were baptized Christians in the area years before this.[108] In 1909 the Bonds reported that they 'had a crowd of people for service and dispensary in the afternoon, notwithstanding heavy rain, and the fact that the message we had sent on to them beforehand had not been delivered'. The catechists, who included Paulo Byabusakuzi and his wife Sofu, and Rebecca Ikanga, all of whom were outstanding, gave the visitors a great welcome.[109]

In the old principality of Busongora in the extreme south of Toro there were three small centres, Katwe, Karujumba and Nyagwaki. Despite promising beginnings, the church here did not develop well. The area was so isolated that it was seldom visited by missionaries. By 1909 the people were suffering from a disease they called *muhinyo*, at first thought to be brucellosis, but later diagnosed as sleeping sickness. All but one catechist, Firipo Kato, had succumbed to the disease. The Katwe area was evacuated because of the disease in 1913. Rather better progress was made in the eastern counties of Kitagweta, Nyakabimba, and Kyaka, though sometimes a place would suffer a setback when the initial ardour of a newly converted chief wore off. In Kitagwenda and Kibare work was late in starting, and the CMS found it particularly difficult to get a foothold in Kitagwenda, where the Catholics were firmly entrenched. As always, the CMS leaned heavily on the chief for support, and if he was indifferent, or had become a Catholic or a Muslim, they were somewhat nonplussed.[110]

The missions became less dependent on the chiefs after the Toro Agreement had been signed as it then became possible to obtain land for church use by registering plots with the administration. The Catholics benefited more from this than the Anglicans as they had fewer chiefs among their adherents. The people had to give their assent before a plot could be registered, and as happened at Rubona, there was sometimes trouble, but once the matter had been sorted out the catechist was able to work with more freedom, since the plot owned by the church included land which he could cultivate to support himself, and he no longer had to depend on the chief for food supplies. The Catholic catechist, paid by the mission, probably had rather more freedom than his Protestant counterpart. The latter usually lived close to the chief and remained to some extent subservient to him. Neither mission appreciated that it might be advantageous to be free of the chief, and both of them overrated the influence a chief was able to exert over his clients. Although the majority of the chiefs were Protestants, Catholics came to outnumber Protestants in almost every area of the country.[111] Yet the Protestants continued to hang on to an imagined political advantage, and the Catholics continued to expend energy in trying to break the near-monopoly of the Protestants, neither group recognizing the advantages to be gained in freeing themselves from local politics.

7

KASAGAMA AND THE ANGLICAN CHURCH IN TORO

Shortly after his conversion, Kasagama found himself faced with insistent demands that as *Mukama* he should return to traditional ways. This is typified in the story of Bagaya, his sister, who returned from Bunyoro and became the *Bàtebe* (royal sister), a position of much influence. She was horrified by the extent to which Ganda ways of doing things had been introduced, and the manner in which Christianity had modified traditional custom. The story goes that after refusing to be greeted in Luganda and protesting at other instances of Ganda influence, she precipitated a crisis by taking exception to food cooked in Ganda style, and publicly flung a dish of it at the cook on an occasion when many chiefs were present. She found sympathy among the chiefs for her attitude. Bagaya helped to stir up discontent at the presence of Ganda catechists. At first Kasagama had no child by his 'ring' wife, and she pestered him to follow Toro custom and take another wife, and whilst he never did so officially, the pressure of custom, coupled no doubt with his own inclinations, made her demands impossible to resist. The same thing happened over the matter of beer-drinking, which the missionaries deplored. With Bagaya at his side and the chiefs only too happy to see royal beer-drinks reintroduced, Kasagama found himself unable to stand out against the practice any longer. Bagaya herself was eventually baptized and took the name Maliza, and in doing so she in her turn yielded to pressures too great to be withstood.[112]

In 1908 the first *empango* (coronation anniversary ceremony) was celebrated since Kasagama's accession. In 1891 the country had been too disturbed and his own position too precarious for the usual rituals to be carried out in full. Besides, the regalia had been lost or destroyed during the wars against Bunyoro.[113] In 1908 the situation had so changed that Kasagama decided the time was ripe to revive the ceremony. His position was secure, and the holding of the *empango* was in part an assertion of this growing confidence. He was, for instance, sufficiently sure of himself to appoint a Catholic to a senior chieftaincy, and a new agreement made in 1906 had clarified and ratified his position as far as the Protectorate government was concerned.[114] Bagaya and the other women of the court were surely behind the holding of the ceremony—the *Nyina Omukama* had personally remade the *kondo* (headdress adorned with parrot feathers, beadwork and a colobus monkey-skin beard). This was worn by certain chiefs as well as by the *Mukama*.[115] The holding of the *empango* at this juncture must also be seen in the context of the unrest which had occurred throughout Western Uganda in 1906 and 1907 because of the presence of the Ganda. This culminated in a rising against them in Bunyoro in 1907. At the same time the Anglican church in both Toro and Bunyoro had achieved something of a victory in getting agreement for the whole Bible to be translated into Runyoro/Rutoro, and in getting the Bunyoro Church Council freed from dependence on Mengo.[116] In Toro the first two local clergy had been ordained in the same year, whilst in Bunyoro three had been chosen for theological training. Events in church and state were closely related, and the time seemed ripe for some symbolic assertion of Toro's identity which would also serve to make her position more secure still by means of ritual sanctions.

What took place in 1908 illustrates the close link between Kasagama and the Anglican church, and was an attempt to fuse traditional ways and Christianity. Since Kasagama had not previously been crowned, this was not strictly speaking an anniversary at all, and a suitable date for it had to be chosen. Kasagama had always celebrated the anniversary of his baptism publicly, and this was the occasion that he chose for the *empango*. Rumours that something was afoot reached the mission, but they knew nothing definite until two days before when they received an invitation to see him crowned, and were told that an old ceremony was to be revived.[117] The Rev. G. Blackledge described the next move:

> On Sunday March 14 Nasanieri Katikiro, Nasanieri Kimbugwe, and Nicodemu Kasuju came to my house with a request from the

> King that I should place the crown upon his head at the ceremony on Mondy. It is looked upon as a great honour, this, as in the old days the crowning was performed by some high priest of the ancient religion, but now the Christian king wanted a Christian priest to place the crown upon his head.[118]

Not many of the traditional ceremonies were enacted, since Kasagama did not want any 'heathen rituals', but certain of them were retained, as well as a tea-party being held for European guests. Blackledge noted an important aspect of the occasion when he wrote:

> The value of such a ceremony and pageant to the Batoro is very great, for in these days when the real power and authority are vested in the government, the native king naturally takes a subordinate place, but last Monday the people were able to honour their king and the assembled thousands and the gifts which were brought, all formed an eloquent testimony to their loyalty to the royal house of Toro.[119]

However, to the people of Toro this was more than a mere 'ceremony and pageant', and the integration of Christianity at this *empango* suggests that it was impinging on the lives of the people at a fairly deep level.[120]

But in spite of the speech made by Kasagama on this ceremonial occasion in which he spoke of his joy at the return of the past glories of his kingdom, in fact they could not be restored, either with or without the church's aid. There would always be a conflict between the *Mukama* and his chiefs over the distribution of power, and the British administration would always be on the side of those who appeared to want a more democratic sharing of power. Although in the early days of British rule, the *Mukama* and his chiefs were able to wield a good deal more power and influence in a quiet way than the British always realized, the time would come when they would appear, not only to the British, but also to many of their subjects, as reactionary; and whilst they had, in the first place, been the means whereby the forces of modernization were able to begin to work by providing a link with the past, they eventually became the means of slowing down modernization. The kingdoms of Uganda accepted some of the technical advances of the West and used them to enhance and support traditional structures of society. By becoming too closely identified with the traditional regimes and not sufficiently aware of the shifting balances of power, the Anglican church found it difficult to adjust to the new situation when the too-rigid traditional structures were at last seen to be eroded at base. Like the traditional regimes, the Anglican church gradually changed from being an instrument of progress until she was in danger of becoming the opposite. To Anglicans, who were wedded to the idea of a state church with a monarch at its head, the alliance formed with the monarchies of Uganda seemed particularly attractive, and Anglican preconceptions helped to blind people to the strength of other forces at work. But all this lay far in the future.

However, even before the end of Kasagama's reign his loss of power had begun to become apparent, and a rather sad picture of him was drawn by Bishop Gresford Jones in about 1926:

> To the artistic mind of Bishop Tucker this Mukama was always 'king' of Toro. To our administration at Fort Portal he is the presiding chief of the district. King, Mukama or chief, he is an attractive young fellow with an estimable wife. He speaks some English, but there is something pathetic about the barrenness of their life. Escaped from savagery and heathenism, they still seem unable to enter the fields of education and the higher interests of life.[121]

After the adventures and glories of the early days, no wonder Kasagama found life empty under an administration which considered him merely a provincial chief, and a bishop who looked on him as 'an attractive young fellow' (he was about fifty years of age at this time, and was to die two years later). Doubtless he would have described his escape from 'savagery' into the colonial doldrums of the 1920s in rather different terms. For so many people of his generation, life, which had begun at the end of the nineteenth century as a stirring adventure, full of possibilities, ended in the dullness of the inter-war years. This is why biographical accounts of many early leaders devote twenty or so pages to the years before 1900, while two or three pages are sufficient to cover all of interest that remained.[122]

The Anglican church in Toro continued to suffer its ups and downs, and was to some extent a disappointment to the high hopes first entertained of it. The faith started to spread widely before it had taken root deeply, and from the beginning many people professed Christianity as a way of showing their loyalty to the *Mukama*. Although Christians went from Toro to Ankole, Bunyoro and Mboga as catechists, there was never the same evangelistic interest and fervour as marked Buganda in the first half of the 1890s. Perhaps the message preached was too often negative—salvation *from* sin—and offered too little that was positive in return.[123] It was a little too easy to make a profession of Christianity in Toro, and a little too dull to carry one's profession through.

Catholic Christians did not suffer quite the same disillusion as did the Protestants. Because they failed to win political power, their expectations were different, and there is no doubt that they benefited from their failure eventually. The Catholics laid more stress on attendance at mass, and various forms of lay associations were introduced, designed at covering the whole community, which were aimed at fostering Christian devotion. But lay Catholics found little outlet for initiative. Yet if for some Christians in Toro, both Anglican and Catholic, Christianity was superficial because it had been too easily accepted, this is by no means the whole of the picture. The success or failure of evangelism in Toro must not only be judged by those Christians whom the missionaries saw as failures (and the judgement of local people did not always coincide with that of the missionaries), but also by those for whom baptism came to mean much more than a mere assent to the fashion of the times, and who lived out their faith in such a way that it could clearly be seen that they had found a new and satisfying way of life. In spite of the lack of apparent reward, many catechists who have served the church long and faithfully must be counted among these, as well as clergy and lay folk among whom one finds remarkable examples of dedication and perseverance.[124]

TABLE III
SOME ANGLICAN WOMEN CATECHISTS

KEY

* Married name: if nothing is entered in this column it is likely that the woman was married before being trained as a catechist, or that she was widowed.

If the name or space in this column is underlined, it indicates that the husband has been mentioned as an outstanding Christian leader.

[1] Has been mentioned as an outstanding catechist.

[2] Husband a catechist or clergyman.

[3] Husband a chief.

[4] Last date recorded in the record book of women teachers kept by Miss Pike. The person so indicated may have worked as a catechist after this. (For 1902 all catechists have been listed. Thereafter only those who taught for some years are listed. In later years an increasing number taught for a short period only, but the information on many is incomplete).

Name	Married name*	Last known date of teaching	Remarks
Licensed February 1902			
Ketura Byanga[1]	Balya[2]	1922	
Juliya Kabyanga	Kibate	1905	
Sara Mukabasamba		1902	
Erisaba Mukabadoka	Rwabudongo[3]	1907	
Maliza Kaboinuha[1]		1920	retired in this year
Loi Nyamazi	Bakaija[2]	1909	
Mirika Kabahita		1916	retired in this year
Basemase Wenkere	Musana	1915	died in this year
Hana Kageye[1]		1914[4]	still working in girls' school at this date
Mai Gatooma		1912	
Eseri Timbigamba[1]	Nyakabwa		still active in 1966
Samari Lutahya[1]		1914	went to live in Ankole in this year
Licensed June 1902			
Laheri Biryetega	[2]	1918[4]	is mentioned as working in Hoima at this date with husband
Mirika Kwitakulimuki	[3]	1903	husband became Muslim

TABLE III (cntd)

Name	Married name*	Last known date of teaching	Remarks
Liriya Lusongoza		1909	head of a group of women preachers
Damari Omugo[1]		1905	fell ill in this year
Miriya Tigwezire	________[3]	1906	too busy at home to teach
Licensed December 1902			
Erisabeti Kabagenyi		1919	
Ludia Kajumbukire		1907	
Zipora Kamuhiigi	________[2]	1928	died in this year
Beteseba Mungi		1914	
Rebeka Ikanga		1914	
Eseri Kaikara	Bitalitegere	1916	died in this year
Miriya Mutazinda	________[2]	1922[4]	went with husband to work in Kabale
Yunia Kyakana	Bateka	1908	
Licensed July 1903			
Yayeri Zabunamakwata	________[2]	1922	
Ada Wenkere		1909	left teaching when she married
Eseza Nkojo	[3]	1909	
Samari Ndahura		1903	husband ill
Laheri Muhindo	[3]	1908	died soon after this
Loi Kiza	________[3]	1904	
Yunia Kisoro[1]	[2]	1922[4]	still active in 1966
Sofu Byabusakuzi	________[2]	1922[4]	
Licensed February 1904			
Damari Ngaju		1914[4]	from Mboga
Susana Mukabahaguzi	Kato	1908	
Licensed July 1904			
Tezera Ntonde		1909	
Eseri Kajumbukire	[2]	1922[4]	
Miriya Kabyanga		1908	died in Ankole
Kezia Bitanirhirwe	[2]	1915	
Miriya Bamuturaki	[2]	1914	husband left work
Liriya Bamanya		1914[4]	
Licensed January 1905			
Yayeri Bisambu	[1] [2]	1922[4]	
Erisabeti Duhabya		1919	from Mboga; died in this year

TABLE III (cntd)

Name	Married name*	Last known date of teaching	Remarks
Licensed June 1905			
Lea Sere	________[2]	1922[4]	
Rebecca Balikurungi	[2]	1915	husband dismissed
Licensed January 1909			
Sara Kageye		1922[4]	

TABLE IV
NUMBERS OF BAPTISMS AT EARLY CMS CENTRES IN TORO

	1896	1897	1898	1899	1900	1901	1902
Kabarole	38	42	105	84	303	284	224
Ngoma	4		2	28	68		22
Burungu					10		
Kibimba					2	3	
Busaiga						11	
Butanuka			10	9	4	3	19
Butiti	18	12		15	42	75	40
Kitagweta				4	8	10	15
Nyakabimba							8
Kicumu							5
Kibare					3	14	16
Kitagwenda					6		
Nyagwaki	1				4		17
Busita							10
Buweza							3
Katwe						9	9
Mboga		13	11	10		56	92
TOTALS	61	67	128	150	450	465	480

Chapter III

Bunyoro

1

INTRODUCTION

In Bunyoro, as in Buganda, the spread and acceptance of Christianity was closely connected with the political aspirations of the people, and was affected by the type of social and political institutions in existence. The situation in Bunyoro differed from that in Toro, and the type of development which will be traced in this chapter differs as a result, but the two areas also have much in common.

Bunyoro has the longest history of all the interlacustrine kingdoms, and is the most conscious of her past. Toro and other principalities broke away from a kingdom which had once been much larger, and the people of Bunyoro are mindful of the vast areas over which it is claimed that their *Mukama* ruled in the past.[1] By the nineteenth century the area had shrunk greatly, and Cwa II Kabalega, who became *Mukama* in 1870, made a bid to recover the power and lands lost by his predecessors. He succeeded in driving out those who had set up an independent principality in Toro, and in holding at bay his most dangerous rivals, the Gaṇda.[2] The rulers of a number of areas to the north, north-east, west and south were brought into a loose tributary relationship to the *Mukama,* and the area over which he ruled directly was considerably larger than the present day district of Bunyoro.[3]

The heartland of Kabalega's kingdom is shown on Map 2 surrounded by a broken line. From 1900 to 1966 the rivers Nkussi and Kafu formed the southern boundary—the reason for this will emerge in this chapter—but it can be seen that during Kabalega's reign a good half of the kingdom lay to the south of this, and included parts of modern Toro as well as areas which for many years were under Ganda rule. The heartland of the kingdom was not ruled with the same bureaucratic intensity as was Buganda. The *Mukama* ruled through chiefs, the most important of which were the *bajwarakondo* (crown-wearers). All chiefs, including those of lower rank than the *bajwarakondo,* had to have their authority formally validated by the *Mukama,* since 'all political authority was seen as stemming from the *Mukama* himself; it was held subject to his approval, signified through a ceremony of "milk-drinking" which a candidate for any kind of political office had to undergo'.[4] The *Mukama* granted rights over land and over the people living on it to his chiefs, and through the chiefs tax was levied and labour recruited. Looser ties existed between the *Mukama* and those chiefs who ruled territories outside the heartland of Bunyoro. These ties seem to have fallen into two main categories. In certain Bantu areas which had formed part of the original kingdom, but were too far from the heartland to be administered effectively from it, a kind of indirect rule was exercised through members of the Bito clan, the royal clan from which the *Mukama* himself came. These became semi-independent rulers. The founding of Toro as a separate kingdom in about 1830 seems to have been a case when a Bito ruler arrogated to himself authority which should have been granted to him by the *Mukama*, and seized a more complete independence than was tolerable. Burega, Mboga, the northern part of Bugerere, Kamuli Budiope in Busoga, and possibly Busongora as well were in this kind of relationship to the *Mukama*. To the north and east of the heartland lived non-Bantu peoples, and with some of these alliances had been made and links of a second type established. In recognition of these alliances a drum, stool and spear were given by the *Mukama* to the ruler concerned. An informant who, as a child, had been a page at the court of the *Mukama* Andereya Duhaga, stated:

> I saw all the chiefs and Babito. They used to bring cattle and goats to the *Mukama,* and there was a special spear that they came with, presented to the *Mukama,* and then took back again, and that spear stayed there to shew that that part belonged to the *Mukama*. Chiefs from Burega brought spears . . . and many came from the north, from Acoli and so on . . . When a person became *Mukama,* he gave these people a stool (*ekitebe*) and a spear to shew the place belonged to the kingdom (*bukama*). The spear was brought back to the *Mukama* to shew continued allegiance.[5]

This statement is made from the point of view of Bunyoro, and it should not be taken to mean that the peoples of Burega or Acoli were subservient to Bunyoro, only that their rulers had entered into an alliance which was mutually beneficial. 'Sphere of influence' is a better description than 'empire' for much of the territory claimed by Kabalega. This sphere of influence was to prove important for the spread of Christianity.

In order to achieve his reconquests, Kabalega relied largely on raiding bands known as *barusura.*[6] The men in these numbered from 3,000 to 5,000. A good many of them were not Nyoro but people in alliance with or subject to Bunyoro. From the areas into which Bunyoro raided captives were taken, and some of these became *barusura*; other *barusura* were simply adventurers. The name is thought to be derived from a now obsolete verb, *okurusura*, meaning to take by force. When an example of the word's usage has been asked for, several informants have said that it might also be used of a person who tore meat ravenously from the bone with the teeth, and that the *barusura* were so named because they lived by plundering other people's cattle and food supplies.[7] This they did not only when raiding outside Bunyoro, but also when staying in Bunyoro between campaigns. Their social significance will be discussed later.[8]

The beginning of Kabalega's reign saw a resurgence of Nyoro power, but in the 1890s he met with a complete reversal of his fortunes, and Bunyoro suffered humiliating defeat.[9] In common with the rest of East Africa Bunyoro suffered from severe epidemics of smallpox and rinderpest during this decade which seriously reduced the human population and the vast herds of the cattle-keeping people. Even more serious were the wars against the Ganda and the British. The British accepted the views of Sir Samuel Baker who fell foul of Kabalega in 1872 and of the Ganda who were their enemies. The latter skilfully manoeuvred the British into deciding that Kabalega was a menace to peace who must be put down at all costs.[10] This is not the place to describe in detail the years of warfare between 1893 and 1899 when Kabalega was captured and deported to the Seychelles, but some account of them must be given, since the beginning of Christianity go back to 1894 and were affected by the war.

In 1893 a British officer named Colvile led an all-out campaign which drove Kabalega out of the county of Bugangaizi, through the northern areas of his kingdom, and across the Nile. Kikukule, a Nyoro chief who paid allegiance to Kabalega, and whose headquarters were at Bukumi in Bugangaizi, was driven out with the *Mukama.* Shortly after this the whole area south of the Kafu and Nkussi rivers was ceded to the Ganda. At this date it was still agreed that Catholic expansion should take place in the south and west of Uganda, and Protestant expansion in the north and east. When Kabalega and Kikukule were driven northwards and the area ceded to the Ganda, the White Fathers saw an opportunity of opening a mission in the ceded area, and established themselves at Bukumi in

1894. The population was predominantly Nyoro, though Ganda catechists and others came with the missionaries, and Ganda chiefs were appointed. Kikukule at first remained in hiding with Kabalega, but both soon crossed the Nile again southwards, and Kikukule determined to reassert his authority against the Ganda at Bukumi. He also gave aid to Kabalega, and used the mission to his own advantage: the presence of the missionaries meant that the Ganda were held in check for the time being. Because the mission was in constant danger of attack, a fortified compound was built by Frs Achte and Houssin in the early months of 1895. The mission drums were sounded whenever Kikukule and his men approached, so he eventually withdrew to the north. The White Fathers planned to evangelize the Nyoro people, and many of their converts were won from the Nyoro living close to the mission; but because the area had been placed under Ganda rule, the real beginnings of work in Bunyoro had to await the opening of Hoima mission.[11]

Kabalega was shocked at the extent of the devastation wrought in Bunyoro by the Ganda hordes who had perforce lived off the countryside during their campaign. During 1894 his generals had been decisively beaten. Byabacwezi, an important chief and a *mujwarakondo,* had suffered two defeats, the first at Musaijjamukuru, a precipitous hill a few miles south of Hoima hitherto thought to be impregnable, and the second at Mparo, the old capital where it had been decided to make a last stand. Because of this desperate situation, Kabalega decided to ask for peace. He sent Kikukule to the White Fathers at Bukumi to ask for help in doing so, and at the same time he asked for catechists to evangelize his people. Later, in November, an emissary was sent direct to the British, but by this time Kabalega's complete defeat had been decided on. In the same month he was attacked again in north Bunyoro and driven back across the Nile into Lango. Although he occasionally made sorties into Bunyoro after this, and continued to give the British much trouble, he never again succeeded in establishing a firm foothold in Bunyoro.

However, he was by no means defeated yet, and in 1895 a group of *barusura* took advantage of a temporary truce to fetch more guns from Toro.[12] Among these was a young man named Lubaale, son of a Soga chief.[13] Early in the reign of Mwanga he had gone to Buganda and taken service with the *Kabaka* as an *askari,* a warrior armed with firearms. During the Muslim seizure of power in 1888/9 he had joined the Christians in exile in Ankole, and afterwards visited Bunyoro and stayed there, becoming one of the *barusura.* Here he earned the nickname Fataki by which he was always known.[14] In Toro he came into contact with Christianity again, for he met Mako Lweimbazi at Kasagama's capital.[15] He therefore decided to learn to read, and for a fortnight he studied the *Mateka* (first reading book). Instead of returning to Bunyoro with the others, he went to Buganda to continue learning. At Mengo he made friends with a young man named Daudi Kagiri who taught him in the evenings. Soon he had finished the *Mateka* and had started on the gospels. He then persuaded Kagiri to return with him to Bunyoro, after he had overcome Daudi's understandable reluctance to go to such a war-torn place.

2

BEGINNINGS OF EVANGELISM IN BUNYORO

During Fataki's absence much had happened in Bunyoro. Kabalega had twice been attacked in Lango, and though he himself had evaded capture, one of his sons, Kitehimbwa, a princess and the queen mother had been captured. The two children were taken to Mengo and brought up by the CMS.[16] By May 1895 the Ganda armies which had been ravaging Bunyoro had to be sent home because it was impossible to feed them any longer. Forts were built at Nyakabimba, Masindi, and Mruli, and the passage of arms and gunpowder to Kabalega had been checked. In June Kabalega again sent emissaries to try and arrange a peace, but again they failed Several Nyoro chiefs including Byabacwezi and Rwabudongo surrendered to the British and were reinstated in their chieftaincies.

In November the Rev. A. B. Fisher, who was then working in Singo, received a request from Byabacwezi at Fataki's instigation for catechists to go to Bunyoro. Fisher went to Kahora, site of an old royal capital, escorted by fifty men carrying guns whom Byabacwezi had provided as an escort.[17] Fataki later described the visit:[18]

> So in May 1896 [sic] I wrote to Mr Fisher at Bamusuta, and they gave him a guide and fifty men with guns, among them being Matayo Mpanga, seeing the country was at war. He reached Hoima in February, and when I went in the afternoon to see him he asked me about the people who were not interested in religion. He then asked me whether I needed teachers, and when I agreed that I wanted two, he asked me how I was going to feed them since

> the land was in an uproar. I assured him that they would live with me. Then we discussed whether the church should be at Rwabudongo's or Byabacwezi's, and we chose a site near Byabacwezi's because he was the *omusigire* [deputy] whom the *Mukama* had sent to strengthen Bugahya, and therefore people were likely to collect there. Finally he gave me sixty copies of the *Mateka* to teach people with.[19]

The British administration in Kampala was disturbed that Fisher had ventured into Bunyoro without their permission or protection, and Ternan had some misgivings about the safety of the two Ganda catechists whom Fisher had left there. There was, in fact, trouble in store for them. After a week or two Byabacwezi and Rwabudongo lost interest and used the pages of their *Mateka* for covering beer-pots. Fataki was imprisoned for a time, and was only freed when news came that a European was approaching, and a princess named Karujuka who was particularly interested in learning to read was threatened with being dragged off to Kabalega with her book. For the time being the catechists stood their ground.

The European was the Rev. A. H. Sugden of CMS. In September 1896 he travelled to Toro by way of Bunyoro, and at Hoima found that 'the work was progressing under native teachers, but harried by local disturbance and hunger'.[20] Sugden talked with the man who had imprisoned Fataki and secured his co-operation, but Rwabudongo and Byabacwezi were not won round, and eventually sent the catechists away. Nothing daunted, Fataki went off to Mengo again to ask for more catechists. There he was sent from one person to another on what must have seemed a hopeless quest, for everyone thought it useless to ask catechists to go to anywhere so ravaged by war and famine. The Rev. Henry Wright Duta Kitakule, to whom Fataki went first, sent him on to Archdeacon Walker. Walker passed him on to Pilkington, and Pilkington sent him to Apolo Kagwa. Kagwa was sceptical about the desire of the Nyoro for catechists, and told Fataki that they were nothing but pagans whose country the Ganda intended to come and devour. Nevertheless he told Fataki that he could wait until the next meeting of the Church Council if he liked, and see if anyone would volunteer. Surprisingly, two men expressed willingness to do so, and Fataki set off with them. They quickly aroused hostility by the tactlessness of their preaching, so that when their house was attacked by a leopard in the night and they shouted for help, no one came. One can only wonder why they had volunteered in the first place. When Fataki wrote his account of this many years later he noted: 'Then I was left in great trouble. I was left to pray alone in my house.'

At about the same time that the catechists left and returned to Buganda, the mission at Bukumi was burnt. Byabacwezi and Rwabudongo changed their minds about catechists, perhaps wishing to clear themselves of responsibility for this act, or at any rate deciding it was prudent to appear co-operative. Once more Fataki went off to Mengo at their behest, and returned with Yairo Musenziranda and Danieri Kamukukulu, both of whom spent several years in Bunyoro.[21] There was trouble in 1897 when the Sudanese burnt down a newly built church, and they retreated for a while, but were soon back at work.

In March 1898 a rumour of Kabalega's death led the British to declare him deposed, and to set up an administrative post at Hoima. However, another year was to elapse before he was finally captured, and two of his generals, Ireeta and Kikukule, were still able to harry the enemy in north Bunyoro. They were driven across the Nile in July 1898, but in September were able to return and destroy the post at Hoima whilst the British were temporarily absent, and they remained at large until the end of the year.

In February 1898 Fataki had once again gone up to Mengo, this time to complete his baptismal instruction. He was baptized on 24 July by Duta Kitakule.[22] Fataki's narrative recounting the coming of Christianity to Bunyoro breaks off at this point, ending with the words, 'That is how Christianity first came to Bunyoro . . . now the light is shining.' In spite of his Soga origins, Fataki considered himself the first Nyoro convert.

Two months later, in September, Kitehimbwa, the son of Kabalega, who had been captured three years earlier and looked after by the CMS since then, was appointed by the British to be successor to his father. The Rev. H. B. Lewin met him as he was travelling back to Bunyoro and decided to accompany him, also taking along Tomasi Semfuma, a licensed lay-evangelist, who remained with Kitehimbwa at Masindi in order to give him further Christian instruction. At the beginning of 1899 Bishop Tucker arrived in Bunyoro at Semfuma's request to baptize Kitehimbwa and a few others, and to instal Fisher as the first resident missionary.[23]

3

CHRISTIANITY TAKES HOLD

By this time the country was in a deplorable state and the people were hostile and afraid, yet Christianity made headway. Fisher noted that conditions in 1899 were worse than when he had visited four years earlier.[24] Years of warfare had reduced the area to desolation and famine, its herds of cattle had been destroyed, and the population had been quartered.[25] Forty per cent of the remainder of the people lived in the 'lost counties' under Ganda rule.[26] Great distress had been caused by the callousness of the British and Ganda armies: 'It is a sad inditement [sic] of our rule and the many young officers who pulled down everything and built up nothing except their own reputation for bravery measured by the number of wretched natives they could shoot down or drive into the Nile.'[27] Thus Fisher: and Thruston in *African Incidents* provides plenty of further evidence of such behaviour.[28] In spite of people's loyalty to Kabalega there was some fear lest he should return and revive the *barusura,* allowing them to prey on people as in the past.[29] Grain had been hidden from them in deep pits, and the people themselves had sometimes hidden in these when the *barusura* were known to be in the vicinity.[30] It was many years before the people overcame their fear and dislike of strangers.[31]

The appointment of Kitehimbwa by the British made more serious still the conflict of loyalties among the Nyoro. As long as Kabalega remained at large he was able to collect taxes, and there was a general expectation of his return. This was particularly evident at Kitehimbwa's first gathering of chiefs. Byabacwezi presented the chiefs to him, and 'the pain on their faces as if they were doing something shameful' was plain to see.[32] The capture of Kabalega a month or two later did not relieve them of their dilemma: it only deepened their fear and despair. Months later Fisher found a group of old men afraid to talk about Kabalega and still believing that he would return. A further difficulty was that Kitehimbwa did not get on with Byabacwezi. The latter was one of the regents and wielded more power than did the *Mukama.*

Byabacwezi's position and character are something of an enigma, and he epitomizes the conflict of loyalties. Thruston said he was a coward and the first to run away from the battle of Musaijjamukuru, but in view of Thruston's scornful attitude to Africans and to the whole Bunyoro campaign (unjustified, since what he described as a *chasse aux nègres* was in fact a campaign skilfully enough conducted to keep the British and the Ganda occupied on and off for seven years), his evidence must not be taken too seriously.[33] CMS opinion was divided. Lloyd shared too easily the point of view of officialdom and repeated the statement that Byabacwezi was a coward. He described him as being in terror of Kabalega and said he would rather feign illness than come into his presence. Because of this Lloyd thought him no friend of Kabalega's and held that the *Mukama* had been in the habit of giving him particularly severe orders because of his attitude. Lloyd had, of course, never seen them together.[34] This is impossible to reconcile with the evidence of Fataki and others that when Kabalega went into exile in Lango, Byabacwezi was appointed to act as his deputy.[35] Fisher, who was more sympathetic to the Nyoro than any other missionary, admired Byabacwezi greatly.[36]

Yet some explanation is needed of the fact that neither Byabacwezi's name nor that of his father appears in extant lists of those who held chiefly office in Kabalega's reign. Two such lists are known, both drawn up by Sir Tito Winyi, a son of Kabalega who became *Mukama* during the colonial period.[37] A further list of *bajwarakondo* past and present was drawn up for the 1967 *empango* celebrations, and Byabacwezi and his father were omitted from this also. These omissions must be deliberate, and there would seem to be two explanations for them. Firstly, there was a long-standing quarrel originating from the time when Kabalega had given precedence to the wishes of the *barusura* rather than the landed chiefs.[38] Out of this arose personal animosity between Rwabudongo and Byabacwezi, the former being the foremost general of the *barusura* and the latter representing the landed chiefs' interests.[39] This enmity was increased when the British appointed Rwabudongo as chief minister of Bunyoro.[40] They decided that there must be a functionary in Bunyoro analogous to the chief minister (*katikiro*) of Buganda.[41] There was no such person, but both Byabacwezi and Rwabudongo put themselves forward as entitled to the new office.[42] Because Kabalega had appointed Byabacwezi as his deputy he would probably have been more acceptable to the people, who in any case feared the *barusura,* and the choice of Byabacwezi by Kabalega in spite of past disagreements suggests that Kabalega was aware of the people's feelings. But at this juncture Byabacwezi is said to have arrogated to himself the mode of address reserved for the *Mukama* alone, and had tried to make people greet him with the royal greeting of *zonna okaali,* meaning 'there is none greater'. At this stage the breach with the royal clan became permanent.[43] This seems to account for the deliberate omission of Byabacwezi and his father from the lists of chiefs and *bajwarakondo,* as well as to explain why some people were willing to defame him to Lloyd and others. But even Lloyd admits that during the years of Kabalega's exile he played a crucial role in keeping the people together.[44]

Bishop Tucker and Fisher arrived in Bunyoro at the end of 1898 and went straight to Masindi where Kitehimbwa was awaiting baptism. The bishop wrote optimistically of the welcome given him by the young *Mukama*, by his royal sister, and by Tomasi Semfuma, together with the group of people Semfuma was instructing. Five people, including the *Mukama* and his sister, were baptized on Sunday, 25 February 1899 after being catechized by Fisher,[45] who thought Kitehimbwa good-looking and intelligent, but lazy. The royal sister struck the missionary favourably too, but the queen mother did not appear, and Fisher and the bishop were told that she refused to break with the traditional religion, and was in close touch with Kabalega and those of the chiefs who were still with him.[46]

These baptisms did not indicate a breakthrough into Nyoro society as did the baptism of the *Mukama* of Toro or, at a later date, that of the ruler of Ankole, for Kitehimbwa was not accepted by the majority of the people. He had been brought up in Buganda and when he returned to Bunyoro he was accompanied by Daudi Mbabi, a Christian who had served in the households of the queen mothers of *Kabakas* Mwanga and Mutesa, and was conversant with Ganda court etiquette. Thanks to Fisher's influence he had been appointed *Kawuta* to Kitehimbwa, in which capacity he was in charge of the *Mukama*'s cooks, and his determination to introduce Ganda court customs made him so hated that he thought of returning to Buganda. In 1900 he was made county chief of Buruli, and once away from the court he engendered less hostility, but his presence in Bunyoro added to the difficulties of Kitehimbwa's position.[47]

From Masindi Fisher and the bishop went to Byabacwezi's headquarters at Hoima. Here they met the group of people who had been receiving instruction from Danieri Kamukukuru and Yairo Musenziranda. The bishop was delighted to find a group of converts who had 'been brought to a saving knowledge of Christ as God and Saviour' almost without European teaching.[48] Fataki's wife and a man called Masuleta, who became a catechist, were baptized shortly after this visit, and in October a larger group received baptism. These included Byabacwezi, Karujuka (whose desire to learn has already been mentioned) and a large number of Byabacwezi's children.[49] A few days later Byabacwezi married Karujuka as his 'ring' wife, having sent all the others away.[50] His baptism marked the real breakthrough into Nyoro society.

Perhaps the final decision about baptism was precipitated for these people by the capture of Kabalega in South Lango on 9 April. A month later Ireeta also surrendered. He had been made a *mujwarakondo* for his loyalty to Kabalega, but because of the trouble in the country he was never able to receive his *kondo*.[51] Fisher was moved to deep admiration by his unswerving loyalty and described him as a 'tough old warrior who denied himself so much all these years out of love to his master by living anywhere on anything never giving up hope to the last'. A regency council was set up under Rwabudongo and Byabacwezi, and most of the chiefs moved to Masindi, which now became the seat of government. So many of Kabalega's children began to receive Christian instruction that Fisher nick-named the church at Masindi 'the chapel royal'. Byabacwezi, Rwabundongo and some other chiefs came regularly to church classes. At Hoima the Rev. Nuwa Nakiwafu was in charge of CMS work. He knew the language well, having spent several years in Toro. He was helped by Danieri Kamukukuru and Nasanieri Masuleta.[52] At some of the outstations there was considerable trouble, however. At Kibero on Lake Albert the catechists reported serious opposition, and at Pajao on the Nile the catechists were turned out and only reinstated on the orders of Captain Hicks.[53]

Although the fighting had ended, conditions in Bunyoro did not improve immediately. The long rains failed in 1899 and the north of the country suffered from severe famine, made worse by the loss of the cattle. Because of hunger people wandered from place to place looking for food, many moving further south where conditions were less severe, and catechists had to be withdrawn from some places. A further humiliation came in March when the (B) Uganda Agreement was signed. By the terms of this, the northern boundary of Buganda in the west was fixed at the Nkussi and Kafu rivers, and the land south of this, which had formerly been part of the heartland of Bunyoro, was placed under Ganda rule, and became a long-standing bone of contention as the 'lost counties'. The listlessness of the Nyoro at this time is reflected in their failure to get on with building new churches: 'the people know how to build nothing but their beehive huts and have no desire to learn'.[54]

In mid 1900 Fisher was moved to Toro because Ecob could not get on with the people there, and Ecob took his place in Bunyoro. Roscoe remarked, 'it leaves the work in Bunyoro in a poor way'.[55] Fisher had a greater understanding of and sympathy for the people of Bunyoro than any other CMS missionary. He succeeded in getting them to talk fairly freely to him, and he was the one European who realized that the commonly accepted picture of Kabalega as 'the human fiend' was wrong.[56] In December 1899 he wrote: 'I have never yet heard an old man speak unkindly of the old king and am now convinced that he was not as bad as painted.'[57] Few missionaries or government officials achieved this degree of understanding, and by the 1950s it was found that Nyoro considered missionaries as well as government officials to be hostile to them.[58] Government policy was understood to aim at keeping them in a humble and submissive state, and missionaries had gone along with this.[59] It was fortunate for the Anglican church that Fisher returned after a few years.

In view of this depressing state of affairs the problem arises: why did large numbers of Nyoro become Christians during the early colonial period, and why were many Nyoro chiefs keen on their clients becoming Christians? In trying to find an answer to this question we should note first the strength of the early Anglican identification of reading with Christian instruction (it had its weaknesses as well). This ensured that people did not just learn the catechism but also had to read at least one of the gospels. No matter, therefore, how bad the catechist, they were brought into contact with the source of Christianity, and many were attracted by what they found. They might not be able to live up to the demands of Christianity, as they came to understand them, and the catechist or missionary might not be able to live up to them either, but this was a human failing and not the failing of the religion. For whatever reasons of expediency people started to receive religious instruction, some of those who did so were, in the process of learning, genuinely converted. The Protestants had no monopoly of genuine conversion, and regular attendance at prayers and mass brought Catholic catechumens into the same confrontation with Christianity as gospel reading brought Protestants.[60] It is sometimes forgotten today that the gospel and epistle read at mass were translated into the vernacular from the beginning.

We must also consider the creation of a climate of opinion which was favourable to the initial acceptance of Christianity, and made people willing to attend catechism classes. The influence of Byabacwezi and Rwabudongo was very important in this. Byabacwezi was the first to come to the conclusion that further resistance to the British was useless, both for himself and for Bunyoro, and that he should make as good a deal as possible with the new regime. Part of that process lay in acquiring literacy and hence in attendance at church classes. Once he had made this decision, he directed much energy to that end, insisting that his sub-chiefs and clients became Christian also. He followed the lead of his counterpart, Apolo Kagwa, by building himself a large brick house, a further sign of his intentions. He was a more forceful leader than either of the two who ruled as *Mukama* during the remainder of his lifetime, and had he lived (he died in 1912) he might well have been remembered as the foremost protagonist of Christianity in Bunyoro rather than Andereya Duhaga, who succeeded Kitehimbwa as *Mukama*. But because of British attitudes to Kabalega and to Bunyoro, which they treated as a hostile though subjugated kingdom, his position was more ambiguous than that of other modernizing leaders in Uganda, and when co-operation with the British seemed to mean submitting to an attempted takeover by the Ganda, as it did in 1907, it was too much for him, and he rebelled. Only two senior chiefs did not take part in that uprising, Mika Fataki and James Miti, neither of them Nyoro by birth. To the missionaries, 'loyalty' to the British administration became one aspect of being a good Christian. Byabacwezi and all Nyoro whose first loyalty was to their own people and kingdom were placed in an impossible position.

Rwabudongo was more hesitant than Byabacwezi in opting for an alliance with the British and with Christianity. He was an older man for whom a change of loyalties would have been more difficult. By mid 1899 he too was 'reading' in church, however, though he was also quarrelling with Byabacwezi over precedence, and objecting to the latter's aspirations to power. He died in 1900, and after his death Byabacwezi was left as the undisputed leader after the *Mukama*.[61]

This brings us to a third point which must be considered in answering the question why many Nyoro accepted Christian teaching. Once Byabacwezi had been baptized, anyone who wanted promotion to a chieftaincy under him had to follow suit, and as other Christian chiefs were appointed, they took the same line. All appointments were in the hands of British officials, but the chiefs were well able to see that only the men of their choice came to the notice of the officials. Chiefs showed their zeal by supporting catechists and encouraging their clients to receive Christian instruction. The Rev. H. B. Ladbury noted an apathy among the readers which he put down to the fact that they were being forced to attend classes by their chiefs.[62] The chiefs were supported in this by British officials. Captain Hicks gave it out that he wished all chiefs to learn to read (and a wish would have been tantamount to an order), and 'witchcraft' was suppressed with unusual vigour in Bunyoro.[63] The administration thought the Nyoro chiefs obstinate and inefficient, and constantly dismissed them and moved them around. Yet obviously the chiefs did their best not to get themselves turned out of office: they found themselves unable to cope with the seemingly incomprehensible demands made on them. One way of trying to show willingness to co-operate with the regime was by getting their clients to go to catechism classes and learn to read. But as Ladbury noted, they could not enforce enthusiasm, so their efforts were of doubtful usefulness to the cause of Christianity.

Much more helpful was the lead given by Andereya Duhaga who became *Mukama* in succession to Kitehimbwa in 1902 when the latter was dismissed by the protectorate government. Duhaga had been Lloyd's star pupil at Masindi and he was sincerely attracted to Christianity and prepared, if necessary, to be pro-Ganda rather than compromise his position with the mission.[64] He gave the CMS missionaries every possible support, and his people every possible encouragement to become Christians, and set an example which won him the praise of the mission. Of all the traditional rulers in Uganda he seems to have been the most deeply convinced Christian, and the least concerned with possible political benefits. His conversion occurred before there was any thought of his becoming *Mukama*. After Byabacwezi's death, there was no one beside him of comparable stature as a leader in Bunyoro.

A number of the first Christians in Bunyoro, both Catholic and Protestant, had previously been *barusura* or were sons of *barusura*. Among these were Sira Dongo, a well-known evangelist to Acoli; Mika Fataki; Yafesi Isingoma, who became a catechist; Leo Kaboha, a county chief; Zakaliya Kyopaali, a mission workman; Aloni Mutunzi, whose father had carried the *Mukama*'s spear; Yonosani Wamala, a sub-chief; and Franswa Kyaherwa, an outstanding catechist.[65] With the capture of Kabalega their whole way of life was shattered, and some of them found a new purpose in life when they became Christians. The *barusura* were known as adventurers, more willing than most people to try out something new, and perhaps this was why a number of them became early adherents of Christianity, and some of them outstanding Christian leaders.

The final point we should note is perhaps the most interesting, and it is peculiar to Bunyoro. It would seem from the available evidence that one aspect of the introduction of Christianity to Bunyoro, namely the requests which were received from time to time that catechists should go to areas not yet reached by the missionaries, may have helped the Nyoro to regain a little of their lost self-respect. In a new way they were able to keep up some of Bunyoro's old political ties with areas to the north. Since the *Mukama* and most of his senior chiefs were Protestants, this concerned the Protestants more than it did the Catholics. As the Ganda often sent catechists to peoples over whom they had previously exercised some kind of suzerainty, so in Bunyoro something of the same thing happened.

The *Mukamas* of Bunyoro had claimed suzerainty over areas both to the north and to the south of the modern Bunyoro District. To the south lay Toro proper, Kyaka, Mwenge, Nyakabimba, Kitagwenda, Busongora and Bwamba, all of which were absorbed into Toro. Two other areas, Buzimba and Buhweju, were incorporated into Ankole.[66] These areas received Christianity before Bunyoro, or else became the responsibility of Toro evangelists, as did Mboga to the south west.[67] This left areas to the north, and these became the evangelistic responsibility of the church in Bunyoro. These areas were Burega just west of Lake Albert and in British hands at the beginning of the century; Bunia, which lay just within the Congo Free State; Arulu Madi, as the Nyoro called Alur country, which then formed part of the Lado Enclave leased to King Leopold of the Belgians; Ganyi, as the Nyoro called Acoli; Lango; the northern parts of Busoga (described as Kamuli Budiope); and part of eastern Teso.[68] It must be emphasized that Bunyoro had never ruled directly over Acoli, Lango or several other areas listed here, but friendly relations had been maintained with them and with their rulers, trade had been carried on, or sometimes the areas were subject to raids for tribute. If the *Mukama* of Bunyoro established friendly relations with a chief, he would present him with a special drum, stool and spear, and the chief so invested would bring the spear to Bunyoro once a year, probably at the time of the *empango,* to show that the relationship still continued. There is some evidence that this continued well into the colonial era.[69] To such of these areas as were under British rule, Nyoro went as catechists. In two cases it is known that a request for catechists was a result of these diplomatic ties, and in other cases it may be safely assumed that interest in evangelizing the area arose from the same cause. The *Mukama* and his chiefs took a great interest in these ventures. From an account given by one of the first catechists to Burega, it is clear that his presence was only tolerated because it became known that he went there by the wish of a son of Kabalega.[70]

4

EARLY DEVELOPMENTS AND DIFFICULTIES

We must now trace the early development of Christianity in Bunyoro. The year 1900 saw forty-seven baptisms in the Anglican church, mostly of Byabacwezi's followers, while a few were followers of other chiefs already committed to Christianity such as Kapiri, who was baptized later in the year, and Rwabudongo, who joined those receiving instruction.[71]

In mid 1900 the capital was moved to Hoima; Kitehimbwa and most of the chiefs took up residence there, and the Rev. A. B. Lloyd arrived to take charge of CMS work. The White Fathers opened a mission in Hoima the same year. For some time three Ganda Catholic catechists had been at work led by Placidi Mutyabi, a catechist whose devotion impressed all who knew him.[72] The Catholics suffered the usual frustrations of finding great difficulty in getting any of their converts appointed chiefs once the ruler had been baptized as an Anglican. Yet the mission records do not show quite the same degree of animosity between the two groups as in Toro and Buganda, perhaps because the Catholics quickly gained a numerical advantage.[73] In part this seems to indicate the strength of opposition to those chiefs who had decided to throw in their lot with the new regime. The fact that there were two opposing Christian factions made it possible for Christianity to gain adherents from the two opposing Nyoro factions.

Lloyd quickly introduced Runyoro as the medium of instruction in the work under his supervision, and found that the numbers attending catechism classes doubled. Ecob at Masindi maintained that Luganda was preferred in his area, probably because the Ganda there persuaded him that this was so.[74] Between October 1900 (when the first entry in the Hoima Baptism Register occurs) and the end of 1901 eighty-five people were baptized at Hoima, and only twenty-one at Masindi, eight of whom were infants.[75] Although part of the explanation lies in the removal of most of the chiefs to Hoima, the continued use of Luganda was a contributory factor.

In May 1901 Daudi Kasagama, *Mukama* of Toro, visited Bunyoro. Past custom forbade one *Mukama* to meet another face to face, so this was a major break with the past. On 12 May some of the Toro chiefs were invited to address the congregation of the Anglican church after the morning service. Petero Tigwezire, county chief of Bwamba, and Samwiri Kwitakulimuki, county chief of Kibare, did so, and Kasagama led the people in prayer.[76] The two *Bakama* discussed the question of language. The CMS missionaries were still undecided as to whether Luganda or Runyoro/Rutoro should be used in teaching once the elementary grades had been passed,[77] and the two rulers petitioned for the use of the local vernacular. They were to act together on this matter again in later years.

In Hoima things did not always go smoothly. Some of the chiefs complained to Bishop Tucker about the numbers of Ganda whom Lloyd encouraged to enter Bunyoro, and felt he was responsible for Ganda being appointed to certain chieftaincies.[78] Like many missionaries of the time, Lloyd took it for granted that Ganda influence was Christian influence, and hence he encouraged Ganda 'sub-imperialism' in a way which was to have unfortunate consequences later.[79] Already by 1902 the Rev. Nuwa Nakiwafu reported the first stirrings of trouble between Ganda and Nyoro: 'In our church at Hoima the Christians do not love each other as they should. The princes do not love the common people, and the Banyoro do not love the Baganda.'[80] Shortly after this the White Fathers began trying to replace Ganda catechists with Nyoro because the Nyoro people found the Ganda hard to please and too demanding.[81] Government policy of bringing in Ganda to teach the Nyoro how to administer continued unchanged, and James Miti, the most influential Ganda chief in Bunyoro, arrived early in 1901 and was made *Kago,* one of the most important county chiefs. His headquarters were at Nyamirima, in a fertile valley a few miles from Hoima, where he built a church, maintained a catechist, and saw to it that his people received religious instruction.[82] Mika Fataki was made county chief of the Masindi area, and both these appointments pleased the CMS missionaries.[83] The British administration were less impressed by Fataki than were the missionaries,[84] and perhaps the fact that he was not Nyoro born lessened his influence among the people, though there is no doubt about his sincerity as a Christian. The missionaries were rather less happy about Paulo Byabacwezi. They recognized in him a loyal supporter of the church, but they felt that his private life was not all that it ought to have been, and they did not think him a strong Christian, though they had great hopes of Damari Karujuka, his wife, and hoped she would have a good influence on her husband. His dilemma as a Nyoro they did not understand at all.[85]

The mission also became increasingly disillusioned with Yosiah Kitehimbwa. They felt he showed no promise as a leader, and was easily led into bad ways. They were very upset at his 'learning the vices' of the Swahili who lived nearby, and at the dancing and drumming which went on in his enclosure. Lloyd, Mika Fataki and Daudi Mbabi once spent a whole day pleading with him to mend his ways.[86] By 1902 the British administration had also come to the conclusion that he would never be fit to rule, so he was deposed and Andereya Bisereko Duhaga was appointed *Mukama* in his place.[87] The missionaries were delighted for he had already spent a time acting as a catechist, and it was felt that he had a good influence on the other members of his family. He had spent some time in Buganda in the household of the Rev. Henry Wright Duta Kitakule, and had shown himself quick to pick up new ideas.[88] He proved a quiet and sensible, if uninspired leader, and a sincere Christian.

The head catechist at Masindi for a number of years was Naşanieri Kyawola. He arrived from Buganda in September 1900, and was first sent to work at Rukondwa for two or three years before being transferred to Masindi, where he remained until at least 1909. He was more friendly with the Nyoro than were most of the Ganda, and was consequently well-liked, and he was a hard-working catechist. He used to return and visit from time to time after he had returned to Buganda.[89] At Hoima the head woman catechist from 1904 to 1912 was Juliya Kulope, also from Buganda, who is still remembered by some as a well-liked and respected teacher.[90]

Benjamini Kitugwanide first arrived in Bunyoro some time before 1899. He was the son of one of the first Ganda converts to Christianity, who had been killed in the battle of Kijungute between Christians and Muslims in 1891. From 1899 onwards he worked at Bugoma, and was chosen by the Church Council as a candidate for ordination. After his ordination in 1912 he continued to work at Bugoma, but in 1918 returned to Buganda to work in Singo.[91] Other Ganda catechists worked in the villages.

Nasanieri Kyawola's first convert at Rukondwa was Petero Bitaka.[92] He was a tenant on church land who had originally come from Mwenge or Bugangaizi to settle in Bunyoro. He was baptized just before Easter 1902 and worked as a catechist until he was made a lay-reader in 1918 or 1919. Ladbury met him at Kiryandongo in 1908, and in 1910 he went to Acoli at a time when there were no European missionaries there, and played a leading part for a while. He eventually retired to his own land, and died in 1938.[93] An early convert at Kigumba Kiryandongo was Erenesiti Ifunza, who spent his whole life in and around Masindi, working as a catechist. He was baptized in 1906 and worked until his death in 1964.[94] Most of the catechists, however, were moved from place to place in Bunyoro as they were in other parts of Uganda. Yafesi Isingoma, for instance, started as a catechist in 1902 and spent a year and a half at Kibingo, and was then moved to Nyamirima, James Miti's headquarters. From 1904 to 1905 he was at Kikungo, and was then sent to Kiziranfumbi, twenty miles south-west of Hoima. In 1909 and 1910 he was back at Nyamirima, and was posted there again from 1911 to 1912 after completing some further training. After obtaining his third letter, he went to Buraro, but here his health failed and he went back to Nyamirima and taught James Miti's children. He too was a loved and respected catechist.[95] There were not many who worked as long and devotedly as these.

Providing for the material support of the catechists was always a problem. In each place where there was a church there was a plot of land known as the church *mailo,* and the tenants living on it were supposed to supply the catechist with food. The system was not satisfactory, and Ladbury's journals are a graphic record of the troubles which occurred. Of catechists in general he wrote: 'The teacher is always quarrelling with the milo men about his food. Frequently this includes a fight and an appeal to the chief's lukiko [council]. In all my itineration up to the present I have not found a single teacher who could be said to be on good terms with the milo men.' There are many references in the Ladbury journals to unsatisfactory catechists: 'The teacher, Sirasi, is very unsatisfactory and quarrelling with the milo men.' 'The teacher here is slack and unsatisfactory, and the daily readers are few.' 'The teacher, Isiraeri, I fear, despises the people and does not think it is any good staying since only one or two will read.' 'The teacher here is Nasanaeri Kyakuhoirwe, the people are afraid to approach him.' 'Am disappointed to find so few people reading here. The teacher, a Muganda named Kabukuku is a filthy dirty fellow, and much too familiar with the women of the place.' Occasionally a happier note is struck: 'Katongoli Kangao [the chief] is a man of intelligence and tact far above the ordinary. The Christian work under his kindly and wise patronage is progressing favourably.' 'Eriya, the blind teacher, a Muganda, seems to be doing a good work. Crowds of people come to see us.'[96] One gets the impression that Ladbury was quicker to see the failures than the successes, the latter being taken for granted. Fisher, writing in 1905, assessed the situation very differently:

> In examining the standard of Christianity in the native church I can only express a feeling of gratitude and encouragement on the whole . . . One cannot withhold admiration for some of these teachers who are labouring under the most trying circumstances,

> and in some cases, real privation. For instance, at the Salt Mines at Kibiro . . . there are two Baganda teachers stationed, their food consists of cold, cooked millet brought in by canoes in exchange for salt. Others are living on one meal a day rather than withdraw from their posts.[97]

It had been the normal practice to send out catechists in pairs, and not to send out anyone who had not been confirmed as well as baptized (confirmation required an extra year of instruction), but neither of these practices was strictly adhered to in Bunyoro, and it is not surprising that catechists working entirely alone, as were several of those whom Ladbury mentions as unsatisfactory, and who had received only a bare minimum of Christian instruction, should sometimes have failed to make good.

5

INDIGENOUS MISSIONARY EXPANSION FROM BUNYORO

We have already noted that the Anglican church in Bunyoro became involved in spreading Christianity to places which had formed part of Bunyoro's sphere of influence in Kabalega's days. This movement began from Kyangwali, known then as Bugoma owing to its proximity to the Bugoma forest. In 1899 and 1900 Fisher had passed through there on his way to and from Toro, and had decided that catechists should be placed there.[98] Its population had grown considerably as people who had fled from Buyaga and Bugangaizi when these were ceded to the Ganda had taken refuge at Kyangwali Bugoma.[99] The Rev. H. W. Tegart worked there from 1902 10 1906, and was joined by the Ladburys. When Tegart went on leave in 1906 the Ladburys were transferred to Masindi, and Benjamini Kitugwanide was left in charge.[100] He was reposted to Bugoma after his ordination in 1912 and remained until his return to Buganda in 1918.[101] By this time the population had declined greatly as the refugees from the lost counties had mostly returned home. From 1900 to 1907 the chief was Daudi Bitatule, and he and his wife were helpful to the missionaries. Petero Bikunya, who followed him, was a good leader and sincere Christian who later became Bunyoro's first chief minister.[102] In 1902 Tegart made an expedition round the lake shores to investigate the possibility of placing catechists with the chiefs of Burega.[103] The hills of Burega were visible from just beyond the mission house at Bugoma, and it must have been pointed out to Tegart that the people living on the lakeshore and in the hills had once been subject to Bunyoro.

On his second visit to Burega, Tegart became fully aware that there were connections between the chiefs of Burega and Bunyoro, and he learnt that further into the hills there lived a subject population described to him as *baddu,* the Luganda term for slaves.[104] On this occasion he went right round the lake by canoe, and three catechists were left to work in Burega. Two of them, Andereya Dwakaikara and Asanasio Bafirahara, stayed with a chief named Mpigwa, whose headquarters lay due west of Butiaba.[105] Mpigwa did not really want them, and the people were hostile, but with the help of a Ganda who was staying in the place, they found somewhere to live where they were not troubled by the local people. They were given a hut which no one else dared to approach because it was the shrine of a spirit called Nyamunsule, and trespass might be rewarded with death. It was, perhaps, a less than ideal place from which to make contacts with the people. However, the catechists were approached by a few Konjo and Nyoro who said they wanted to be taught, but they insisted that the teaching must take place somewhere safe from Mpigwa. It was arranged that they should be taught at night, provided they came with enough dried reeds to make a fire by whose light they could read. It was not unusual for slaves to slip away at night to visit people who had plenty of food and who might be generous and allow them to stay and share the meal, so their absences caused no comment. They warned the catechists that Mpigwa wanted to get rid of them, and thanks to this warning the catechists were alerted against a trap which was laid for them a day or two later. Their situation was entirely changed by the arrival of a messenger from Kitehimbwa. He made it clear to Mpigwa that he came from a son of Kabalega, and that the catechists had Kitehimbwa's approval. Presents sent by Tegart to Mpigwa a month or so later eased the catechists' path still further, and their position was assured when Mpigwa was summoned by the Belgians and the catechists were able to advise him on how to approach these people so as to win their approval. In gratitude and deference to the now-proven wisdom of the catechists, Mpigwa advised his people to go and learn whatever it was that the catechists could teach them.

This is Andereya Dwakaikara's own version of the story. The manner of telling shows the interpretation the two catechists put upon their adventures. Dangers and hostility had been braved for the sake of the gospel. By the grace of God these had been overcome; the evangelists had been vindicated; the enemy had undergone a change of heart and in gratitude had recognized the value of their teaching and advised his people to accept it. Dwakaikara saw the hand of God at work in events, and this is a perfectly valid explanation. We may, however, probe into the situation further. The catechists originally arrived in Burega as emissaries of the white man, and without the presents for the chief which etiquette demanded, and they were therefore suspect. By staying in a hut which was a shrine to a local spirit they had probably outraged local sensibilities, or possibly they had been offered the hut in the hope that they would bring upon themselves the expected penalty for trespass. Mpigwa's trap was either a punishment for their sacrilege, or else an attempt to see that they got the punishment which Nyamunsule was being slow in administering. It is significant that the only people who came and asked for instruction were slaves, and natural enough that they should want to keep their activities secret from the chief who would probably have punished them as traitors had he discovered what was happening. We are left to guess at their motives in asking for instruction. The most interesting part of the story is the arrival of Kitehimbwa's messenger. Once he had vouched for the catechists, and they were recognized as emissaries of Kabalega's son, they became *persona grata,* and this is emphasized in Dwakaikara's account.[106] From this point on both they and Tegart behaved more astutely. Tegart sent the presents which he should have sent in the first place, and when the catechists saw an opportunity of gaining Mpigwa's favour, they were not slow to take advantage of it. In commending the new teaching to his people, Mpigwa was probably doing so because he saw its usefulness as a means of learning how to cope with the colonial order; the account given by Dwakaikara of the speech Mpigwa made is open to this interpretation. Dwakaikara's narrative offers no explanation of why Kitehimbwa should have sent an embassy to Mpigwa at this juncture. Whatever his purpose may have been, it was surely a sign that Kabalega's empire was not dead, and that Kitehimbwa was interested in maintaining ties with Burega. The catechists helped to strengthen these ties.

Just as the catechists had achieved this understanding with Mpigwa they had orders to withdraw from his territory because it was found to lie within the Belgian sphere.[107] For some years the territory closer to the lakeshore remained under British rule, and catechists continued to work there. Among the best known of these was Petero

Bikunya, who was in Burega from 1903 to 1905, and who afterwards succeeded Daudi Bitatule as chief at Bugoma.[108] Later a catechist whose name is simply given as Mikaeri worked here. He may well have been Mikaeri Buligwanga, a Ganda who had been appointed to a chieftaincy in Burega in 1900, and who is known to have become a catechist.[109] By the end of 1902 fifteen catechists were to be found in Burega, mostly from Bugoma, which was almost denuded of Christians in order to supply Burega. Tegart felt that it would strengthen rather than weaken the Bugoma church to have to take on this responsibility. A few catechists came from Hoima and Toro.[110] In 1905 the Belgian officer sent away catechists who entered Belgian territory, and Dodoi, son of Kavalli and chief of Bubyasi, got into trouble for allowing his people to learn with CMS catechists. Ladbury visited the following year, and Dodoi crossed into British territory in order to meet him. Some baptisms took place, but according to Ladbury, the remoteness and lawlessness of the area made work difficult, and catechists, who had often had little training, quickly lost heart in the unfamiliar and somewhat hostile environment.[111] But in 1907 Dodoi was baptized by Fisher, and others also became Christians.[112] In 1910 the western lakeshore was ceded to the Belgians, and CMS work there came to an end.[113]

The evangelism of Burega had been a challenge to the church at Bugoma and had provided an outlet for the energies of the Christians there, and a way of expressing their enthusiasm for their newly-adopted faith. After the departure of Tegart from Bugoma, things never seem to have been quite the same again. The Ladburys who took over from him were an inexperienced couple not long out from England and still unsure of themselves, and no one seems to remember anything about them today. Benjamini Kitugwanide who took over as parish priest does not arouse the enthusiasm that some of the other clergy do among those who still remember and talk about the old days. It is Tegart's drive, energy, and hard work which people recall when they show you the dilapidated little brick church which he built, and the spindly gum tree which he planted and which for sentimental reasons no one will cut down, and it is Tegart's name which is remembered in connection with the Burega mission. He seems to be held in some respect in spite of his somewhat unsympathetic character which caused difficulties elsewhere.

In Hoima the CMS mission made quite good progress. Several chiefs were enthusiastic about Christianity and reading, though by no means everyone shared their enthusiasm. In 1902 Nakiwafu noted considerable hostility among both chiefs and others.[114] A section of the populace considered that loyalty to Kabalega required them to have nothing at all to do with either the colonial administration or with Christianity. In 1907 when the news of Kabalega's baptism in the Seychelles went round Bunyoro, old people and men and women who had never been near the missions before are reported to have gone to the missions in bewilderment to try and find out what had happened, and to see if Christianity could possibly have anything in it for them.[115] Nakiwafu found that those Nyoro who became Christians were eager to teach others, and he respected their enthusiasm, though he knew they had little training, and he allowed a number of them to become catechists. There were only 135 baptized Christians in the Anglican church in Hoima in 1902, but twenty-two of them were working as catechists, and Nakiwafu praised them for their zeal.[118] He tried to oversee their work, and to give them such training as he could.[117] In the same year four catechists from Hoima were working in Bugungu, where the people possibly represented an earlier stratum of the population and were hostile at first; and two Palwo were at work in north Bunyoro among their own people.[118] The Palwo were Lwoo, and this was the first contact between the Lwoo peoples of northern Uganda and Christianity. Another and more important contact was soon to be established.

In 1903 *Rwot* (chief) Awic of the Payira clan of the Acoli, who had been imprisoned in Kampala for two years for failing to co-operate with the British, was allowed to return home. He passed through Bunyoro on his way back to Acoli, and we may be sure that Andereya Duhaga, now the *Mukama,* recommended him to follow the example of Bunyoro and accept Christian teachers. Awic would be inclined to listen to Duhaga's advice because close links existed between the Payira clan and the royal Bito clan of Bunyoro. Shortly afterwards Awic sent messengers to Duhaga saying he would like catechists to come to his headquarters, and Duhaga sent the request on to Lloyd. As a result, Lloyd set out in 1903 on an exploratory safari to Acoli. He took some catechists with him, some of whom agreed to stay and begin teaching while Lloyd went back to get the bishop's permission to establish a European-staffed mission. From 1903 until the 1920s the church in Bunyoro continued to send catechists and teachers to Acoli. They were well-received and never suspected of imperialist designs since Bunyoro, as a conquered kingdom, was in no position to have such ambitions, but there is no doubt that pre-colonial links between the two areas were important in building up good-will for the mission.[119]

Two years later the Anglican church in Bunyoro received another request, this time from Odora of south Lango, another non-Bantu area which had old links with Bunyoro. Odora came from the area in which Kabalega had taken refuge when driven out of Bunyoro. He was a flamboyant character, adventurous, eager for new experiences, a lover of dancing, wrestling, and running, and involved in a number of clan feuds which made him fear for his life. He knew, of course, of political events in Bunyoro, and of the advantage of possessing guns. As he worried over the threat to his life, he is said to have dreamed that if he wanted to save himself and the members of his household, he must go to Masindi. Deciding that this was an important dream which must be acted on, he set out for Masindi. He met traders on the way, who advised him to ask for guns, but he could not obtain the necessary permission at Masindi. In search of this, he seems to have travelled half round Uganda, meeting Cook and Fisher of the CMS in the course of his journey. In 1904 he finally obtained the guns he wanted from Andereya Duhaga (with or without permission the story does not say). The following year he returned to Bunyoro, and one day attended church with all his entourage. The sermon was specially translated for him, which pleased him greatly, and he too asked for catechists for his country. Two were found and sent, Yosua Konge and Yosua Katono, and the *Mukama* presented him with a royal drum for calling the people to church, the shell of which is still preserved at Aduku in south Lango. These catechists, and others who came later, lived in Odora's village and ate with him, and when he was baptized at Aduku in 1913 by Fisher, the *Mukama* of Bunyoro and the *Kabaka* of Buganda sent him presents. In 1917 Duhaga presented him with two new drums because the old one was worn out: these were fetched specially from Bunyoro by *Rwot* Oluol and two catechists, and they were still in use in the late 1960s. The gift of these drums to Odora recalls the drum, stool and spear which the *Mukama* presented to a chief with whom he wished to ratify an alliance. Odora was not a chief at the time when he visited Bunyoro, though he became one later under colonial rule: did the gift call to mind the old method of making alliances, and what significance did the episode have for Andereya Duhaga? The careful preservation of the drums by the church at Aduku shows that they were of special importance in the eyes of the recipients. The story of Odora's dream is well known in Lango, and like Dwakaikara's adventures in Burega, is cast in a Biblical form in which the dream is clearly thought of as being divine guidance which led Odora to findint salvation.[120]

6

CHURCH AND STATE IN BUNYORO

Fisher returned from Toro to Bunyoro in 1904 and took over the work of training catechists at Hoima, and difficulties soon arose. There was trouble in several parts of Uganda when Anglican catechists demanded better pay, and threatened to go on strike unless they got it. It was clear to all the missionaries that they had a genuine grievance, and the Rupees 1½ per month, which was the new rate of pay awarded to catechists working in their home areas, was still pitifully inadequate. The mission was far from happy, however, about the threat to stop work.[121] The Church Council in Bunyoro decided that it could not afford to pay even this small increase (its whole income in 1904 was Rupees 455, though this was doubled the following year, and continued to rise). It also decided that in future it would not send the Easter offering to the bishop to be pooled but would use it to pay an increased allowance to the Rev Nuwa Nakiwafu. Thirdly, it decided that since plenty of Nyoro were now offering to work as catechists, and were willing to receive the old and lower rate of pay, the services of the Ganda catechists would be dispensed with on the completion of their present tours of service in the district. The Bunyoro Church Council further decided that it would in future take control of all work done in Bunyoro, instead of being under the remote control of the Mengo Church Council, to which Bunyoro sent a representative, but which was, of course, Ganda dominated. Finally, a motion was passed on the question of a translation of the Old Testament into Runyoro/Rutoro, and a strongly-worded demand for a vernacular translation was made. Most CMS missionaries in Uganda felt that Luganda was well enough known to make such a translation unnecessary, but the people of Bunyoro and Toro thought otherwise. Fisher noted a 'strong feeling of racial and linguistic divisions' at the meeting, and felt it was exacerbated by the fact that the Kabarole Church Council of Toro was free of control from Mengo, whereas the Bunyoro Church Council was not.

These resolutions were not tactfully phrased, and Bunyoro's move for independence shocked the bishop and drew a strong reproof. Fisher then tried to withdraw from his previous position, in which he had sided with the people of Bunyoro, and tried to persuade the bishop that 'the Bunyoro church have absolutely no desire to break away from the Buganda church or to stand alone. They merely expressed a wish to meet their own expenses and to no further hamper the much overtaxed funds of headquarters at Mengo', noble sentiments which do not seem to represent the feelings of the Bunyoro church at all, as the bishop doubtless realized. Personal feelings also crept in, and Fisher ended a long letter to Tucker with an appeal: 'When you were here last you encouraged me to take up the training work particularly, and I must say I feel rather hurt that workers in Toro, a country similar in every way to Bunyoro, should be entrusted with the choice, training, examining and dismissing of teachers, when you point out to me that I was out of order in doing the same.' As in so many disputes, other issues were being brought in to complicate matters. Fisher then invited all the members of the Church Council to tea to try to talk them round, but this only made matters worse. They had been counting on him as an ally. Fisher wrote to the bishop again: 'There are endless difficulties in my position here, partly owing to the fear of the king and chiefs of in any way coming under the Baganda and losing their independence, and all I can say has in no way lessened it but rather increased the suspicion that we teachers are at the bottom of it.' The chiefs who formed the Church Council saw clearly that in order to gain their independence from Mengo in church affairs, it was essential to make themselves financially independent, and they insisted that Fisher tell the bishop that they wanted a separate church fund. Fisher, for his part, realized that the activity provided by teaching was an outlet the young church needed, and that a coherent policy was required on the posting of teacher-catechists so that men from one area where there were already sufficient catechists might be sent to another where they were in short supply, and he wanted to be able to send some right outside Bunyoro to Acoli and elsewhere. The Ladburys had been difficult about catechists and feared that if they accepted a catechist trained by another missionary, it would mean interference with their work. Although one can detect a note of personal pique in some of what Fisher had to say, the point of view he presented fitted well enough with the desires of the Bunyoro Church Council.[122]

Fortunately the bishop recognized the delicacy of the situation, and he granted autonomy to the Bunyoro Church Council in 1906. Its inaugural meeting was held on 30 June of that year. In future it was to meet twice annually, and was to consist of twelve representatives elected by the communicants of Hoima, Masindi and Bugoma parishes. In the months between meetings, district councils would meet at these three centres and deal with less important matters. The Council had 'purely spiritual and ecclesiastical powers, and is exclusively engaged with the conduct of Christian work, the discipline of its members, of church organisation and finance. In regard to the latter the council has absolute power to control the expenditure of all native funds.'[123] The wording suggests an attempt to dissociate the council from politics.

The bishop wisely did not allow Fisher's request for a lower standard of training for catechists in Bunyoro, but he did order that there should be only one place in Bunyoro where teachers could be trained, and that was to be Hoima. Fisher was put in charge of the training. The catechists had to take the same examinations and reach the same standards as catechists anywhere else in Uganda. Twice a year they were all called in to a conference. In spite of this administrative tidying up, the Ladbury diaries reveal that not all unsatisfactory catechists were eliminated, and in 1912 Fisher carried out what he described as 'a great weeding out of teachers'.[124]

The ecclesiastical crisis passed, therefore, with a victory for Bunyoro, but two years later what was essentially the same trouble flared up again in the rising against the Ganda chiefs which became known as *Nyangire.* The name refers to the refusal of the *lukiko* (chiefs' assembly) to reinstate Ganda chiefs who had been intimidated into retreating to Hoima.[125] The root cause lay in the desire of the people of Bunyoro for independence from Buganda. In 1901 and 1902 a number of Ganda had been brought in by the administration as chiefs since they were literate and had experience of working under the Protectorate government, and knew what would be required of them. Eight of James Miti's followers were given chieftaincies, and eleven other Ganda were appointed. Although Miti was the only Ganda to be given a county chieftaincy, the others were given key positions immediately below the county chiefs, and 'the new *Mukama*, surrounded by an atmosphere of intrigue, leaned upon Miti's relatively disinterested counsels.'[126] The chiefs in Bunyoro were not salaried at this time, or else received only a pittance, but they were allowed tribute rights, and these were sometimes abused.[127] This caused dissatisfaction, but *Nyangire* was a protest by Nyoro chiefs against the continued presence and power of people who had been their enemies and were still suspected of having designs on the country, rather than a peasant uprising against extortionate overlords. They had endured equal extortions from the *barusura*: such was a peasant's lot. The people of Toro had entertained fears of the Ganda chiefs and had managed to get rid of many, at least for the time being.[128] Perhaps the Nyoro could do the same.

A letter written by Fisher had, unknown to him, greatly

strengthened these fears. In December he had written to Maddox in Toro on the question of translating the Old Testament, and a large part of this letter must be quoted in full:

> One might urge against the translation of the Old Testament into the Runyoro language for use in the Kingdom of Bunyoro the following:
> 1. Fully one third of the original population and one half of the Kingdom of Bunyoro, now belongs to Uganda, and are, by force of circumstances, forced to learn Luganda.
> 2. Nowhere, except in the extreme north is the Kingdom of Bunyoro more than one long day's march from Uganda.
> 3. Two of the six sazas and five of the six myukas in the Kingdom of Bunyoro are Baganda, and together with a very large number of minor chiefs do all they can to encourage Luganda.
> 4. A very large proportion of the entire trade of Bunyoro is in the hands of the Baganda, hence the Luganda language is very generally known throughout Bunyoro as compared with the knowledge of that tongue in Toro.
> 5. In attending the Hoima church services the Baganda Christians stick to their own books and cause great confusion in the responses and psalms.
> I have not been able to see the king or chiefs on the matter as they have been away now for some time, but I do not think that they are at all keen on the translation of the Old Testament, nor that they would be prepared to buy the books now that they are mostly supplied with Luganda books.[129]

This letter had been read aloud by Maddox to the Toro Church Council, which, like the Council in Bunyoro, had among its members the *Mukama* and several county chiefs. Every sentence of it was politically explosive, and its contents had been faithfully reported to the *Mukama* and chiefs in Bunyoro, though Fisher was unaware of this. He was aware, however, that the flames of the trouble in Bunyoro had been fanned from Toro. Towards the end of 1906 emissaries had arrived from Toro with letters begging the people of Bunyoro to insist on having a translation of the whole Bible in their own language, and this had inflamed anti-Ganda feeling.[130]

Feelings against the catechists did not run as high as feelings against the chiefs, since the catechists did not wield formal power, but they came in for a share of the trouble. At Masindi, Nasanieri Kyawola had all his *matoke* (plantain) and maize stolen, and at Hoima a Ganda woman going to a confirmation class was attacked and beaten up, though her companion who was Nyoro was not touched. For a time scarcely anyone went to church classes, and work on building the new church at Hoima ceased. Some of the CMS missionaries came to believe that the movement was anti-European, anti-progressive, and anti-Christian, and the involvement of men such as Daudi Bitatule and Paulo Byabacwezi was incomprehensible to them, for being law-abiding seemed to the missionaries part of being a Christian. Paulo Byabacwezi's personal ambitions played a part in *Nyangire*. He was one of the ring-leaders of the uprising, and the people spoke openly of having a new *Mukama* and of Byabacwezi being the first minister.[131] Until 1917 no first minister was appointed, however, and James Miti tended to be considered the most senior chief. Andereya Duhaga made him a *mujwarakondo* because of his friendship with him, and Byabacwezi was jealous.[132]

The Ganda chiefs and agents seemed to the people of Bunyoro to constitute a dangerous and alien element. To the administration and to the missionaries they seemed to be a legitimate and indigenous authority: were they not Africans? Were they not a co-operative and Christian group of more advanced people called in to help when the Nyoro were judged still incapable of ruling themselves? Even Fisher, more sympathetic than most Europeans to the people of Bunyoro, thought *Nyangire* showed nothing but rebellion and ingratitude. Because of his influence with the people he was called in to help when the Commissioner's orders were publicly read out. He tried to plead with the CMS adherents to give in to the demands made; but his pleas were useless, and fifty-three Nyoro chiefs were imprisoned and sent off to Kampala for refusing to obey the Commissioner. Fisher's action helped to give the Nyoro the impression that the missions were in league with the government to humiliate them. A few days later, when the ring-leaders were out of the way, Fisher was able to persuade Duhaga to call a special meeting of the *lukiko* and get all those who were by this time willing to submit to the Commissioner's demands to go and make their peace with him, and after much debate this was done. The rebellion thus came to an end, the Ganda were reinstated under police protection, Byabacwezi was fined £500 and had to give up some of his estates to the *Mukama* (which was particularly humiliating in view of his desire to be a king-maker), and Leo Kaboha and two others were deprived of their estates and sent out of the country. Atogether forty new chiefs had to be appointed.[133]

The *Nyangire* rising affected the Catholic mission less than the CMS but the listlessness of the people was apparent to the White

Fathers. Their attitude to the rising and to Byabacwezi was different from that of the Protestant missionaries. They were less aware than the Protestants of impending trouble, and were amused when troops were sent to protect their mission and themselves, 'nous qui savent le pays si calme'.[134] Leo Kaboha, the one Catholic who held a county chieftaincy, was deeply implicated in *Nyangire,* and perhaps because of this Wilson, the Commissioner, wrote the White Fathers a letter which they construed as virtually an accusation of having helped to foment the trouble. They referred the matter to Mgr Streicher, who wrote back asking for clarification of Wilson's remarks. As a result, Isemonger, the Collector, was sent on what appears to have been a mission of appeasement. The White Fathers had some sympathy for Byabacwezi and realized how deeply humiliated he had been when taken as a prisoner to Kampala, and wished he could see his way to becoming a Catholic. They were also distressed at Kaboha's demotion and removal from Bunyoro, and noted that almost all the new chiefs appointed were Protestants.[135] It was an odd turn of fate that the Protestants should have benefited from an uprising for which they were far more responsible than the Catholics.

The Protestant church did not suffer too serious a setback as a result of *Nyangire.* The *Mukama* had remained 'loyal' to the Protectorate government, for which he was rewarded, and his position *vis-à-vis* the powerful Byabacwezi became more secure as he received the strong support of the British and of the church. His sincerity as a Christian and his loyalty to the church probably helped him to survive this crisis.

In 1908 he decided to revive the *empango* celebrations, as did Daudi Kasagama. Because Kabalega was still alive he had not undergone the full accession rituals. The only eye-witness account of the *empango* of 1908[136] suggests that even less of the traditional ritual was carried out in Bunyoro than had been the case in Toro earlier in the year. Duhaga, like Kasagama, needed to choose a significant occasion, and the day he chose was 17 September, the day when the new church in Hoima was to be dedicated. After the church service everyone flocked to the *Mukama*'s palace and there Fisher placed the crown upon his head. For this ceremony the *Mukama* and his chiefs were assembled on the verandah of the palace where they could be seen by many: in the traditional rituals the crowning was not public and took place at night. At the moment of crowning there was a great outburst of music and cheering from the crowd. Speeches followed, and after this a tea-party was given by the sub-commissioner for the *Mukama* and his chiefs. The celebrations ended with a torchlight procession to the beating of drums. The Rev. Apolo Kivebulaya was present on this occasion, probably representing the Anglican church in Toro, and the Rev. Henry Wright Duta Kitakule was another guest: he was the Senior Native Clergyman at Mengo. He had a personal interest in the proceedings as well as being present in an official capacity, as he had used his influence to help get Duhaga appointed *Mukama* in 1902.[137]

What did this occasion signify to the people of Bunyoro? Probably its primary significance must be sought in relation to the *Nyangire* rising of the previous year. This had been firmly quashed by the Protectorate government, and they had been helped in this by the missionary Fisher. This rising had questioned Duhaga's position as *Mukama* as well as refusing the Ganda chiefs. Duhaga had finally committed himself against it when he called together the remnants of the *Lukiko* after the fifty-three dissident chiefs had been marched off to Kampala, and he had persuaded the *lukiko* to submit to the Protectorate government, thus bringing the rising to an end. His chief rival, Byabacwezi, had been severely punished for the part he had played in *Nyangire*, and the fine exacted from him had been paid over to the *Mukama*. Duhaga's revival of the *empango* was in part a gesture affirming the new strength of his position, and a demand that all should recognize it. But it was also in part a gesture made by the people of Bunyoro to the Ganda. *Nyangire* may have been suppressed, but there was already evidence that the Anglican church had recognized the validity of some of the claims of Bunyoro. The first Nyoro ordination candidates had been chosen so that the church in Bunyoro should not have to rely indefinitely on clergy from Buganda. The government had had to reinstate the Ganda chiefs who had been refused in order to maintain its position, but the many vacancies caused by the deposition of the chiefs who had rebelled were not filled by Ganda; from this time on only Nyoro were appointed to chieftaincies, so it could be said that the Nyoro had won their main point after all. After the divisions of the previous year, the holding of the *empango* was also something of a unifying ritual occasion. It brought together all the different parties involved in the events of *Nyangire:* the *Mukama*; the loyal chiefs; James Miti, of whom Byabacwezi was jealous; the British administration; and the missionaries; and it did so on an occasion when the *Mukama* was the focus of attention and honour. And apparently it was a very successful occasion when great cordiality reigned.

We have also to ask what the Anglican missionaries, on the one hand, and the people of Bunyoro on the other, learnt from these crises in church and state. There is no evidence that either had enough insight into what had been at stake for any real stock-taking to take place. The CMS missionaries had used the traditional institutions of the kingdom to further the cause of Christianity, and it was the more natural for them to do so because they came from the background of the established Church of England whose head was the monarch. In the Bantu kingdoms of Uganda the Anglican church achieved an official semi-established status which is well illustrated by the role which the missionaries played in the *empango* in Toro and Bunyoro, and they were convinced that they were witnessing the birth of Christian kingdoms. The people of Bunyoro, for their part, had hoped that the Anglican church might help them to regain something of the kingdom's lost glory. They had used the mission to enhance the traditional institutions of the kingdom, only to find that just when they thought they were achieving something, the missionaries drew back. Yet they were willing enough to participate in an *empango* in which the *Mukama* demonstrated his readiness to play the role assigned to him under the Protectorate government. Throughout the Bantu kingdoms one senses a disenchantment with Anglican Christianity once the first adventurous meeting was over; a discovery that it was not, after all, relevant to the people's ultimate concern of upholding the glory of the traditional institutions. But this discovery did not become articulate, nor was a deeper understanding reached of the truth that the Kingdom of God is not of this world, except perhaps in the case of a few individuals. The false trail was only slowly abandoned, and faith placed on a surer base.

After the crises of 1906 to 1907, the Anglican church in Bunyoro settled down to more routine development. Schools were founded, and became a focus of great interest; teachers were trained; their training became more organized and formal; and the first steps were taken towards the formation of an indigenous clergy. As in Buganda, Toro, and elsewhere, there came a time when things seemed to regress. In 1910 Fisher noted a falling off in the number of baptisms, and few people came to communion. Two years later he had to 'weed out' the catechists. 'There are other things for people to do now,' he wrote, 'not only going to baptism classes.'[138] Perhaps the true measure of the mission's success was that after *Nyangire* people did not leave the church in spite of their disappointment, recognizing that they and the missionaries were at fault rather than the religion if things went wrong, even if the religion was only half comprehended.

The Catholics had suffered a setback in 1907, but by 1908 things were looking up again. They still had only one station, at Hoima, but there were also large catechumenates at Bugoma under Jowanna Kaparaga, and at Masindi under Placidi Mutyabi.[139] Each had two assistants. There were some seventy other catechists at work in Bunyoro, though they were not easy to recruit because the mission could pay them so little. The year 1910 saw the establishment of a mission at Kilo Mines in Burega, the area west of Lake Albert to which Anglican catechists from Bugoma had gone in 1902. In 1911 a Catholic mission was opened at Masindi which was then the *Mukama's* capital. By this time Andereya Duhaga was on more friendly terms with the White Fathers,[140] but Byabacwezi, whom they had once hoped might turn to Catholicism, was their most bitter opponent.[141] In 1912 the White Fathers were concerned about fairly numerous defections to the Anglicans,[142] and there was intermittent friction between the two groups, but relations never became as embittered as elsewhere in the Bantu kingdoms, and the death of Byabacwezi in 1912 eased the tension.

The history of Bunyoro since 1900 is dominated by the humiliation which followed the defeat of Kabalega, and the annexation by Buganda of the 'lost counties'. Some Nyoro found a personal fulfilment in dedicated Christian service, but the frustrations of defeat hung over the area until the referendum held in 1964 restored the lost counties to Bunyoro. But only three years later the kingdoms were dismantled under Uganda's second independence constitution. Something of the listlessness of the people affected some of the missionaries who worked there, as far as one can judge by their writings. Yet the publication in the 1930s of the *Bunyoro Church Magazine* reflects a vigorous concern with education, and shows Andereya Duhaga giving a strong lead. It has to be admitted, however, that the acceptance of Christianity did not lift the people as a whole above the defeatism and suspicion which retarded development in Bunyoro, nor above the frustration which characterized much of her life in the colonial period.

Chapter IV
Ankole

1

INTRODUCTION

The last of the Western Kingdoms to receive Christianity was Ankole (the more correct 'Nkore' is often used by historians of the pre-colonial period). If Buganda was the most intensively administered of the interlacustrine kingdoms, Ankole was the least so. It was more sparsely populated than any other part of Uganda that we have so far considered: the eastern counties of Kashari, Nyabushozi, Nshara, and Isingiro are predominantly cattle-grazing country. To the west and forming an arc around this area there lies more fertile country, more wooded and with steeper hillsides, which is predominantly agricultural. The open country in the east was of necessity sparsely populated; the forests and steep hills of the west meant that the people there were also scattered. Map 4 shows two main areas where the agricultural and pastoral peoples were mixed.

These two groups of people seemed to the first Europeans to enter Ankole to be ethnically as well as socially distinct, though later studies have shown that there has always been the possibility of movement from one group to another.[1] The pastoralist Hima people comprised about five per cent of the population and were the traditional rulers. They were thought by many Europeans to be of Hamitic stock. They lived a semi-nomadic life with their vast herds of long-horned cattle, and milk and cattle-blood formed a large part of their diet. Most of the rest of the population was made up of agriculturalist Iru who did various tasks for the Hima including the making of millet beer, and a *modus vivendi* had been established between the two groups. The distinguishing mark of the Hima was their possession of wealth in the form of cattle. Tension between Hima and Iru seems to have increased during the period of colonial rule, and was no doubt exacerbated by the European misunderstanding of the relationships between the two groups.[2]

The pre-colonial kingdom of Nkore was only a small part of the modern district of that name, and its ruler was styled the *Mugabe*. He was always a member of the Hinda clan. Like the rulers of

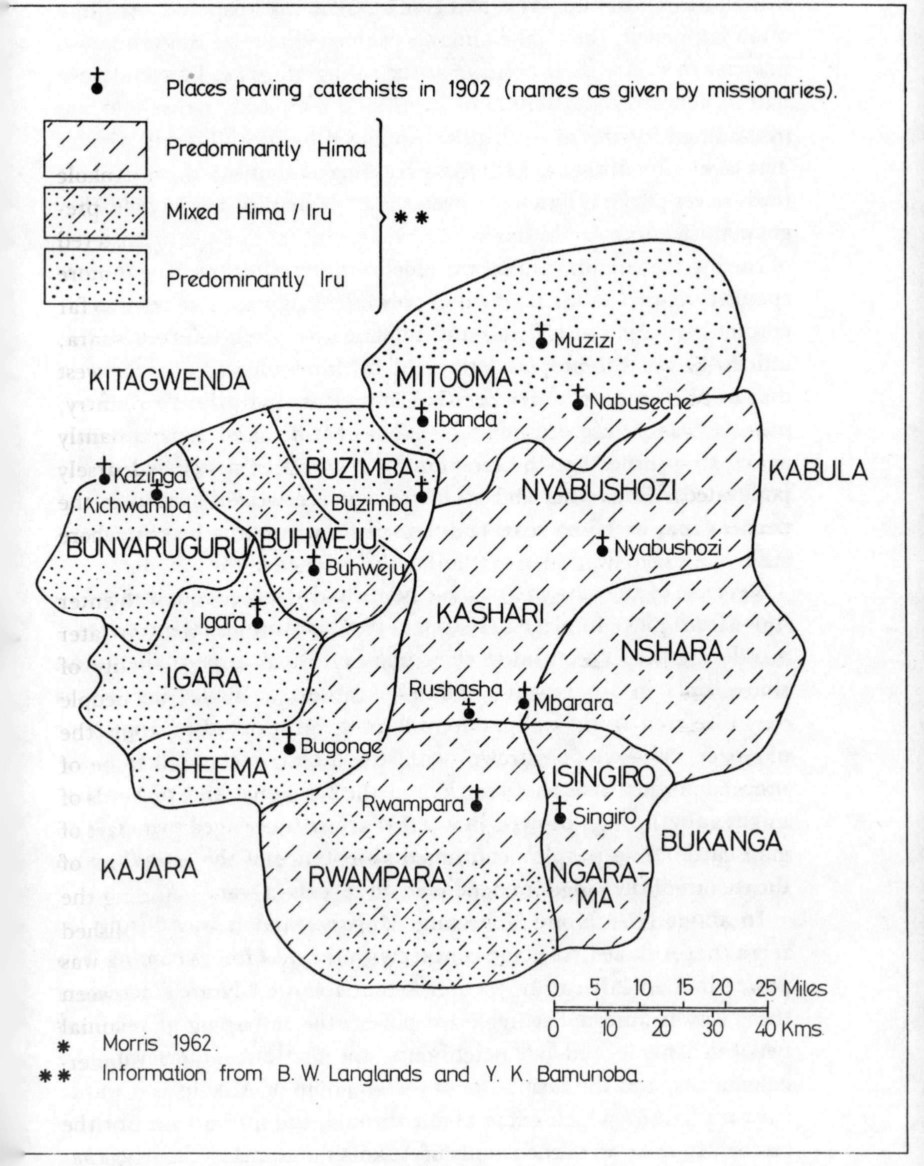
SPREAD OF THE ANGLICAN CHURCH IN ANKOLE
COUNTIES AS AGREED IN 1901 *
Places having catechists in 1902 (names as given by missionaries).
Predominantly Hima
Mixed Hima / Iru
Predominantly Iru
**
KITAGWENDA
MITOOMA
Muzizi
Nabuseche
Ibanda
BUZIMBA
Buzimba
NYABUSHOZI
KABULA
Kazinga
Kichwamba
BUNYARUGURU
BUHWEJU
Buhweju
Nyabushozi
Igara
KASHARI
NSHARA
IGARA
Rushasha
Mbarara
Bugonge
SHEEMA
ISINGIRO
Rwampara
Singiro
BUKANGA
KAJARA
RWAMPARA
NGARA-MA
0 5 10 15 20 25 Miles
0 10 20 30 40 Kms.
* Morris 1962.
** Information from B. W. Langlands and Y. K. Bamunoba.

Map 4

Bunyoro, Buganda, Rwanda and other kingdom states, he traced his ancestry back through many generations, and the people of Ankole share with those of Bunyoro and Rwanda the legends of the mysterious Cwezi kings who preceded the present dynasties. Kingship in Ankole was focussed not only on the *Mugabe,* but also on the royal drum, Bagyendanwa. When the succession was disputed, as quite often happened, the rival claimants each tried to seize Bagyendanwa in order to secure their position as the ruling *Mugabe.* Bagyendanwa had its consort and attendant drums, and a separate household was maintained for the royal drums, supported by special herds. On his accession the *Mugabe* had to strike Bagyendanwa; thereafter he must never strike it again, or even see it. If he did, it was held that grave misfortune would follow.

During the colonial period the chief minister after the *Mugabe* was entitled *enganzi,* a word which denotes the brightest star next to the moon. The colonial officials and missionaries often referred to this official as the *katikiro,* and thought his function was analogous to that of his Ganda counterpart. It is not clear that prior to 1900 the *enganzi* was so important as he later became, and it is certainly wrong to assume that the kingdom of Nkore was structured in the same way as Buganda.[3] Other chieftaincies were filled by relatives of the *Mugabe,* by Hima from the clans of his wives, and by some from other clans who lived in areas vital to the defence of the kingdom.

Because of the vast size of their herds and the consequent need to move from place to place in search of fresh pasture, the Hima lived a wandering life. To outsiders their houses seemed impermanent and flimsy huts in what were essentially cattle-kraals, yet inside was exquisite reed work, well-made milk pots, an ordered arrangement of space, and floors strewn with the finest grass. Their main preoccupations were their cattle and the influence and power they might gain through prowess in war.[4] Warfare was waged primarily to gain cattle. The people's continued acceptance of the *Mugabe* and the wealth of the kingdom depended on success in war.[5]

In about 1870 Ntare V became *Mugabe,* and it was during his reign that Ankole first made contact with the new forces coming into power in East Africa. In the years that followed Ntare's accession there was an internal struggle for power, the reshaping of relations between Ankole and her neighbours, the first encounters with the colonialists, and the formation of the kingdom of Ankole as it was to exist until 1967 which came about through the interaction of these factors. In the eyes of the people of Ankole the coming of Christianity was closely associated with the imposition of colonial rule, and to a lesser extent with relations between Ankole and Toro. The arrival of Catholic missionaries soon after the CMS was yet another complication. The establishment of Christianity cannot be studied in isolation: it must be viewed in the whole context of events.

Ntare V is remembered as a great warrior *Mugabe* in whose reign the influence of Ankole was considerably extended, especially in the west. The original heartland of the kingdom lay in the counties of Kashari, Nyabushozi, and Isingiro. From this area the rulers had slowly extended their domain, and in the reign of Ntare V the states of Buhweju, Buzimba, and Igara came to acknowledge him as suzerain. The more distant Kitagwenda, Busongora, and Bwera to the west and north gave him presents to avert invasion. At the same time Ankole had to reckon with the growing power of Buganda in the east, and she suffered incursions from Rwanda in the south.

The first Christians to reach Ankole were fugitives from the persecutions of *Kabaka* Mwanga who took refuge on the borders of Ankole in 1885-6. They were allowed to stay in Bukanga, near the border with Koki. Most of them returned to Buganda when the persecutions ceased, but a few remained permanently.[6] In 1888 when Mwanga was deposed and the Muslims turned against the Christians, it was again in Ankole that the latter took refuge. Kiboga, Ntare's mother, tried to dissuade her son from allowing them to settle, for she remembered what Ankole had suffered from Buganda in the past.[7] But the Ganda had rightly divined that Ntare would welcome the assistance of a large band of warriors in his troubles with Mpororo and Rwanda, and the refugees were given land in the empty border country of Kabula.[8] In 1889 H. M. Stanley passed through Ankole, and the *Mugabe* refused to meet him. Perhaps he had heard from the Ganda of the troubles that had beset them since Europeans had entered their country.[9]

When Mwanga was reinstated in 1889, most of the Ganda returned to their own country, but again a few refugees stayed on in Ankole. Mbaguta, a young man rising to power at court, was allowed to form them into a warband. In 1890 Mbaguta led them on a successful raid into Mpororo, returning with 200 head of cattle. Four years later he led them into Rwanda, and they captured a further 700 cattle. Success in raiding was a sure way to gain favour and promotion, and because of these and other successes, Mbaguta was rewarded with rulership over some areas of Ankole.[10] A year before the successful raid into Rwanda he had been sent by the *Mugabe* to treat with Cunningham, who came to Ankole partly because German and Belgian encroachments were feared, and partly because Ntare was said to be harbouring Ganda trouble-makers. The choice of Mbaguta as emissary is another indication of his rising importance.

By 1895 various troubles beset Ankole. A retaliatory raid from Rwanda penetrated far into the country. Rinderpest had struck the herds, and remained endemic for some years. Thousands of cattle died. In 1896 the *Mugabe* died in a smallpox epidemic, and strife followed as the succession was disputed.[11]

The succession was extremely involved as Ntare had left no indubitable heir. A boy of sixteen named Kahaya was eventually accepted as *Mugabe.* His supporters appealed to the Ganda for help, and the British were also marginally involved as a result. Mbaguta claimed to have played an important part in securing Kahaya's accession[12] but this seems doubtful. Mbaguta's chief rival was Igumira,[13] in whose homestead Kahaya had been reared, and Mbaguta's claims seem to have been made long after the event.

Mbaguta's early contact with the Ganda was important to his eventual success. It opened his eyes to the need for adjustment to the new order which was coming, and placed him in an advantageous position. If the example of Mwanga's fate deterred the *Mugabe* from trafficking with Europeans, the example of Apolo Kagwa had just the opposite effect on Mbaguta. For if Mwanga's power had diminished as a result of the upheaval caused by the arrival of Europeans, the power of Kagwa, Mbaguta's counterpart in Buganda, had been greatly enhanced. Yet a year or so after the events described here Mbaguta was suspected of helping Mwanga's rebel leader, Gaburieli Mujasi. If the suspicion was correct, and it may well have been false, it would suggest that Mbaguta was not yet sure of how to play his cards.

2

OPPOSITION OVERCOME

Ever since 1888, when Christians had found refuge in Ankole, messengers had gone backwards and forwards between Buganda and Ankole, and Apolo Kagwa had kept in touch with the *Mugabe* Ntare.[14] But it was not until 1894 that any attempt was made to send catechists to Ankole, and nothing came of the first attempt.[15] No further attempt was made until 1897. In July 1897 a conference was held for catechists working in the nearby principality of Koki, and three European missionaries, Pilkington (the translator of the

Luganda Bible), the Rev. R. H. Leakey, and the Rev. H. Clayton urged the need to evangelize Ankole.[16] The administration did not consider the area safe for missionaries yet, but a catechist had been sent just before the conference to find out how Kahaya would react.[17] On the Sunday following the conference the missionaries in Koki heard the news that Mwanga and other Ganda leaders had rebelled, and nothing more is found in the missionaries' letters or journals about this embassy.

A further attempt was made in 1898. Apolo Kagwa sent two catechists to Kahaya's court, and the *Mugabe* received them kindly, but a conservative group led by Igumira opposed them. There was also difficulty over food. As strangers, known to eat foods never touched by the Hima, they could not be given milk, lest they should bring about the death of the cattle. Kahaya gave them sheep, but *matoke,* the staple food of the Ganda, was unobtainable, and no substitute could be found. After a few weeks the opposition of Igumira as well as the embarrassment they were causing because of food taboos was too much for the catechists, Nuwa and Timoteo, and they had to return to Buganda. They reported their failure to the bishop and to the Mengo Church Council, though there is no record to show that the bishop understood the difficulty over food.[18] Apolo Kagwa was disappointed at their failure, and thought that Kahaya should have made greater efforts to find food. Maybe this was being used as an excuse. He therefore urged the *Mugabe* to send for catechists because of the good they would do in Ankole, and Mbaguta was persuaded that Kagwa was right.[19] He was astute enough to see that he would do well to take the advice of Kagwa who had so profitably thrown in his lot with Christianity. But his position was far from secure, and he could not protect the catechists as he might have wished.

In May 1899 Clayton paid a visit to Ankole, leaving Koki on the eighteenth.[20] With him were three 'boys', five porters, two Hima herdsmen to look after the cows they took with them for milk, a Koki chief called Zabuloni Musalosalo who travelled with two of his servants, and finally the two catechists whom Clayton wished to leave in Ankole, Isaka Nyakayaga and Stefano Kabumunsa.[21] Isaka was a Hima who had been taken to Koki as a child, and Stefano was a native of Koki.[22] The journey to the *Mugabe's* capital at Rushasha some miles west of Mbarara took them six days altogether. For the first two days they passed through an area inhabited by Muslim Ganda, and after that they were among the Hima. At the government fort at Mbarara the Collector, R. J. D. MacAllister, told them that a Roman Catholic catechist had recently visited, but had failed to find any support. The party then went on to see the *Mugabe* who gave the travellers a bullock and a sheep, and allowed them a formal interview with him the following day when they discussed the question of catechists coming to his kingdom. On 25 May Clayton wrote:

> We have had our interview with the king and tried to tell him about our religion, but he says the Bahima don't want to read. They have their cows to look after and they move about from place to place looking after them and wish for nothing more. Nor does he wish his people to be taught. The king is very much under the influence of an old chief named Igumira who was, I believe, his guardian, and who is a determined old heathen and opposed to any change.[23]

But it was Mbaguta who won the next round, against the wishes of the majority. He provided accommodation for Clayton and his party, and told them that he would have been glad to learn to read, but that he feared the power of Igumira and the other chiefs. 'He says that if he were to start reading, the others would secretly get rid of him, lest in time he should drive out the king, as they say the katikiro of Buganda drove out Mwanga.'[24] Nevertheless on 29 May Clayton was able to record that Kahaya had changed his mind and had agreed to a catechist instructing his people, though he refused any suggestion that he should learn himself. But the two catechists fared no better than the previous ones had done, and remained only about a week before making their way back to Mengo and reporting their failure to the Church Council.[25]

But the opposition was beginning to crack. Zakariya Kizito Kisingiri, now senior chief and a deacon of the Anglican church, himself went on an embassy to Ankole. He called in at the mission in Koki on his way home and told Clayton that the *Mugabe* was now willing for a catechist, and that he would give land for a house and a garden as well so that the catechist could grow his own food. Kisingiri suggested that Clayton himself should go and inaugurate the mission, and then leave it in charge of Ganda catechists until a European missionary could be permanently appointed.[26] Kisingiri had been instrumental in getting Kasagama appointed as *Mukama* of Toro, and his influence was clearly of great importance in Ankole also. The episode convinced Bishop Tucker that the time had come when he should visit Ankole to see the situation there for himself. He set out in November 1899 accompanied by Dr Albert Cook, who had arrived two years previously to take charge of medical work in Uganda for CMS. They travelled through Koki to confer with Clayton, and learnt that two more catechists, Andereya Kamya and Firipo Bamulanzechi, were willing to go to Ankole in spite of past setbacks.[27] A young Hima, who had once been a slave in Koki, went with them as a guide.[28]

The meeting between the bishop and his party and the *Mugabe* took place on 2 December 1899.[29] With the *Mugabe* were many of his princes and chiefs: with the bishop and Dr Cook were the two catechists who had volunteered to work in Ankole. The interview had to be conducted through interpreters, and there was a good deal of arguing and quarrelling between these as to what was being said.[30] In the message which he had sent through Zakariya Kizito Kisingiri, Kahaya had asked for European missionaries, and he was disappointed and a little put out when offered Ganda catechists, though Kisingiri had apparently guessed that he would agree to catechists provided that Europeans followed.[31] Kahaya knew that there were Europeans at the courts of his neighbours, the *Mukama* of Toro and the *Kamswaga* of Koki. The latter was only a no-longer-independent principality, tiny in comparison with Ankole, and to have a European at court was something of a status symbol. Moreover there were genuine difficulties about accepting Ganda catechists. So far they had not been satisfied with the hospitality they had been offered, and it is a serious matter in African custom for guests to leave because no suitable food is available. Kisingiri had persuaded Kahaya to think of the catechists in these terms rather than as undesirable intruders who could be conveniently discouraged from staying by the use of local food taboos. Neither Tucker nor Cook understood the food issue. They taunted Kahaya saying that a king who boasted that he possessed 20,000 head of cattle must be able to do a little thing like finding food, and both thought they had scored a debating point. An outburst of excited and indignant conversation among the Hima was misunderstood by the bishop and his party as being directed against the meanness of the *Mugabe* instead of against their own suggestion. No one told them that what they were asking was well nigh impossible because of the Hima belief that if milk was given to strangers who ate forbidden foods, the cows would cease to give milk, or would even die. Finally Firipo and Andereya offered to bring their own food from Koki, and on this suggestion the discussion was temporarily adjourned to give Kahaya and his chiefs time to think things over. The following day permission was given for the catechists to stay in Ankole. The bishop and Dr Cook left for Toro, not entirely satisfied, but feeling that they had done all they could, and the two catechists returned to Koki to fetch food, and arrived back at Rushasha about a week later to begin work.[32] And this time they were able to stay permanently, and were supported in their work by both the *Mugabe* and Mbaguta.

It is noticeable that Ankole's resistance to the presence of catechists arose from several different causes. Firstly there was the desire to preserve the traditional way of life, and the recognition that any intrusion would upset its delicate balance. This is seen in Ntare's refusal to meet Europeans and in Kahaya's statement that the Hima wanted only to be left in peace with their cattle. Early contacts with Ganda Christians who had turned out their *Kabaka* and then reinstated him with severely limited powers served as a warning of what might happen if new ways were accepted. When opinion began to shift a little, and the idea of Christian catechists became just tolerable, the difficulty of providing food for them arose, and although this was exploited by the opposition, the difficulty was real enough, and underestimated by the bishop.[33] Resistance to the catechists was strengthened by the fact that it was Mbaguta who was their chief protagonist. He was considered to be an upstart Mpororo, and the Hima were jealous of his rising power. By this time, British colonial administration was beginning to impinge on Ankole, and the arrival of Christianity at the same time meant that the two became confused in people's minds. The missionaries of the time were glad to shelter under the colonial umbrella: the disadvantages of doing so are more apparent today.

The elements in the situation which made the eventual acceptance of Christianity possible were sometimes simply the obverse of those factors mentioned above. Firstly, there were the reversals which had recently befallen the Nyankole in their feuds with their neighbours, and through the epidemics which had struck both them and their cattle. These had to some extent undermined the faith of the people in their traditional religion, which was largely directed towards the achievement of prosperity.[34] To begin with the resulting insecurity may have heightened their fear of anything which seemed to threaten their traditional way of life; later it seems to have made it easier for the people to drop certain practices. Then, whereas contacts with the Ganda made the *Mugabe* and many of his chiefs fearful of new ideas, Mbaguta learnt a different lesson from the same events. The part he came to play was crucial because he was supported by the British and used to implement their policies. His personal ambitions must be borne in mind. Next, the exile in Ankole left the Ganda Christians with a sense of responsibility towards those who had given them refuge. Apolo Kagwa and Zakariya Kizito Kisingiri both played an important part in persuading Kahaya to accept catechists. Finally, the imposition of colonial rule occurred at a turning-point in Mbaguta's career, and in the slowly changing climate of opinion in Ankole. Kahaya's youthfulness—he was only about sixteen years old at his accession—left him in a weak position when confronted with the conflicting aims of Igumira, Mbaguta and the colonialists, and the combination of the last two was beyond his control. It is possible that he did not carry out the full accession rituals when he came to power.[36] He was, like Mwanga, faced with a more complex and difficult position than a new *Mugabe* was normally called upon to handle, and, again as in Buganda, his powers were diminished to the advantage of a chief.

3

THE FIRST TWO MISSIONARIES: FIRIPO BAMULANZECHI AND ANDEREYA KAMYA

For a year before the arrival of Europeans, Firipo and Andereya worked in Ankole, and gradually won the confidence of a number of the people. Kahaya gave them permission to build a small reed church in front of the royal enclosure (*rurembo*),[37] and his people started to attend classes.[38] They had little idea of what they were there for, and it is said that they shouted a good deal, carried on with their conversations, and would not obey the catechists. The people were now more accustomed to the presence of Ganda—a number were employed by the administration—and were therefore more willing to come to learn. Firipo and Andereya taught in Luganda, and if people wanted to learn to read, they had to learn Luganda also. This had a permanent effect upon the language of some people. The catechists sold reading-sheets, and the people brought chickens, eggs, milk, and occasionally money in payment. Mbaguta was the driving force, though he could not do anything without referring it to Kahaya. In April 1900 Clayton received a letter from the two catechists, telling him that Kahaya had made a start in learning to read, and that he had become very keen to continue in spite of opposition from some important chiefs. He repeated his request for a European missionary. The letter contained confirmation that Mbaguta was the driving force behind Kahaya.[39]

Clayton visited Ankole again in September 1900, but when he arrived Kahaya was away ill at his uncle's homestead an hour's journey away from Mbarara, and most of the chiefs were with him. The *rurembo* had been moved close to Mbarara, and the catechists were building themselves a house about 300 yards from the fence surrounding it.[40] Clayton met Mbaguta and found that he was attending classes with about twenty other Hima.[41]

Late in November Clayton received a letter from the bishop enclosing a message from Saulo, the Ganda county chief of Kabula, adjacent to Ankole. The letter from Saulo contained yet another plea for Europeans. A Catholic chief had visited Ankole and persuaded some of the Hima to join him, but Kahaya apparently wanted to be a Protestant. The *Mugabe* could have had no idea of the difference between Catholics and Protestants in doctrine or practice. The explanation of the urgency apparent in this appeal seems to lie in Mbaguta's quarrel with Igumira and the Hima chiefs. If Catholics came to Ankole, they would be likely to turn for support to those chiefs who opposed Mbaguta, and therefore opposed the Anglicans. Neither Kahaya nor the administration wanted a repetition of the strife which had taken place in Buganda and Toro. At this juncture Kahaya seems to have decided that it would be wiser to cast in his lot with the occupying power than with Igumira and the Hima who opposed Mbaguta. Clayton was not free to respond to Kahaya's invitation immediately because he was awaiting the arrival of the Rev. (later Bishop) J. J. Willis who was on his way up from the coast, but he sent off a messenger to say that the arrival of European missionaries would not be delayed much longer.

Right at the end of 1900 the Rev. Aloni Muyinda, a Hima who had spent most of his life in Buganda, visited Ankole. He was surprised to find a little church outside the *rurembo*, for he did not know that catechists had begun work there, and on enquiry he was directed to their house. He arrived in time to witness a momentous event, the burning by Mbaguta of his fetishes, in the *Mugabe*'s courtyard. Many people followed Mbaguta's example until he himself stopped them, saying they were only doing this to please him, not out of conviction.[42]

Clayton and Willis arrived in January 1901. They did not find that much progress had been made in the mechanics of reading, and Willis noted in his journal:

> The native teachers have been away for a few days, Clayton and I have been doing the teaching in church. They have been learning to read here off and on for about a year, and yet they don't know A

> from O, nor any of the vowels (much less the consonants) by sight. They seem to have been learning in a queer way, if learning it can be called. The teacher says 'a' and they say a . . . but what a letter is and means they haven't the slightest notion. The result is they know a certain number of things by heart, parrot-like . . .[43]

So Clayton and Willis tried to devise a new method of teaching, and were no more successful than Andereya and Firipo, probably less so, since neither of them knew the language, and though Clayton knew some Luganda, Willis knew nothing at all. One admires the persistence of the catechumens. No one had as yet expressed a desire for baptism. Had anything been accomplished? The fact is that in spite of the lack of progress in reading, the point of which the Nyankole probably did not understand, Firipo and Andereya had accomplished a good deal. They had succeeded in staying in the country, which no one else had done, and during their stay the *Mugabe* had become increasingly open to their teaching. It is clear that a certain amount of their teaching had been absorbed. Mbaguta had realized that acceptance of the new meant turning away from certain aspects of the old, and had therefore burnt his fetishes. Also, as Willis noted, the people had learnt certain things by heart. The *Mugabe* had learnt the creed, for instance, and this meant quite as much as learning how to read syllables. Finally a small church had been built, and people had begun to come to it on Sundays as well as to weekday classes. Professor Oliver speaks of 'Andereya and Firipo who converted the king and prime minister of Ankole',[44] and although when the missionaries arrived neither had as yet asked to be baptized, the initial conversion, the beginning of the turning from one way of life to another, had certainly taken place.

4

ROYAL AND CHIEFLY CONVERTS

During the period 1901 to 1904 the work of the CMS mission in Ankole was dependent on European missionaries, and on catechists from Koki, Buganda and Toro. In 1904 the first Christians in Ankole were ready to go as catechists and missionaries to their own people, and the spread of Christianity there entered a new phase. The first two years, 1901 and 1902, saw the consolidation of work at Mbarara and the decision of the *Mugabe,* the *enganzi* Mbaguta, and a number of leading chiefs to accept Christian baptism. These years also saw centres of Christian teaching established at the headquarters of a number of chiefs throughout the kingdom. Not all of these were destined to grow into permanent church centres, but a number are still parish centres today. There was also a clarification of the position of the church and the catechists vis-à-vis the civil administration and the chiefs, as well as the beginnings of the White Fathers mission.

From the moment that Clayton and Willis arrived it was clear that they would be able to count on the whole-hearted support of Mbaguta, and as things turned out, the *Mugabe* always proved willing to ratify the steps he took. To begin with the CMS was dependent on the goodwill of Kahaya and Mbaguta not only for land on which to build, but also for a supply of food. Willis wondered why Mbarara should ever have been chosen for the capital, since it was in an area wholly given over to pastoralism, and it was at least a day's journey, if not more, in any direction before cultivation was reached.[45] Fortunately for the CMS missionaries, Mbaguta had begun to undertake some cultivation by the time they arrived, and food had to be grown for the Ganda police.[46] As yet no *matoke* bananas were available, but sweet potatoes, beans, and other vegetables could be found, and Mbaguta arranged for the mission to receive a plentiful supply. One day he sent a sheep to the mission, which was received with gratitude, and he followed this up with a further gift of thirty the next day.[47] Even more were soon to be forthcoming. But this was less generous than the missionaries thought, for there was a surplus of sheep in the country.[48]

On Sundays people crowded into the tiny church, emulating the example of Kahaya and Mbaguta. Willis described the church as like a little barn, into which you crept through a low doorway some four feet square. There were no seats inside, and the pulpit was a little raised platform, surrounded by a reed fence plastered with mud. The walls were of reddish mud; the thatched roof was supported by trunks of trees; and the floor was spread with fine grass, as were the homes of the Hima. At most it held about a hundred people. By June the congregation had grown far too large for this tiny building, and a second service was held in the enclosure of either Kahaya or Mbaguta. An afternoon service was held in the open air so that more people could attend. By the end of June a site just below that chosen by Kahaya for the new brick palace he wanted to build had been marked out for a larger church. Earlier in the year the *Mugabe* had visited Mengo at a time when great enthusiasm was being shown over the rebuilding of Namirembe Cathedral, and he determined that his people should build their church with equal enthusiasm. It was used for the first time on 22 December, although it was not quite finished. The congregation grew in size steadily, but it was about a year before women began to come in appreciable numbers. It was a breach of custom for Hima women to venture out at all, and when they came to church, they were completely veiled. They sat in the centre of the church with even their faces wrapped in bark-cloth, their unveiled servants sitting round them as a sort of screen. They were able to come because the *Mugabe* expressed his willingness for them to do so.[49]

Among the women being instructed in Mbaguta's household was his niece, Kacibala, and another relative, Kyenkuhaire. The former remembers how, in April 1902, she and a party of others went to meet a group of people who were accompanying Mr Fisher from Toro. Among these was the elderly widow, Hana Kageye. Her husband had been a senior chief in Toro, and she was, by virtue of her husband's position and her own force of character, a person of consequence at the *Mukama's* court. In the days when Toro had been at the mercy of Bunyoro, she and others had fled to Ankole as refugees, and as a result she knew something of the language and customs of the people.[50] She had now volunteered to come back and work as a catechist. She worked among the high-class Hima women near Mbarara who were secluded and veiled, and hence unapproachable by Clayton, Willis and the catechists. She taught them to read and gave them instruction in the Christian faith, and is also remembered for teaching them sewing, knitting, and mat-making, and she caused much astonishment by being the first person in Ankole to wear spectacles.[51] To the consternation of the mission staff at Mbarara she arrived with a retinue of chiefly proportions, and the problem of feeding them all was so great that some had to be sent back to Toro. Even so, Hana Kageye had a large household.[52]

The first of her pupils to be baptized, and indeed the first Ankole converts to receive baptism, were Kacibala and Kyenkuhaire. They and four Ganda were baptized by Willis at a crowded service on the afternoon of 8 June 1902. Kyenkuhaire took the name of Keziah, and Kacibala, Malyamu. Both were later confirmed and made Christian marriages. As they were both unmarried girls at the time of their baptism, the problem of seclusion did not arise, for it was only married Hima women who had to cover their faces in public.[53] Almost immediately after her baptism, Malyamu Kacibala started to help in the work of teaching the women, and when European women missionaries came to Mbarara, she went round with them visiting the Hima women in their homesteads. Thursday was the day set aside for visiting the Hima women, and on Fridays the Christian women met to pray and discuss the previous day's work.[54] Later Malyamu received some training as a teacher in Toro, and over sixty years later she was still remembered there for her energetic support of the church.[55]

In 1901 and 1902 when the European missionaries were not away on safari it was usual for one of them to preach at the morning service in Mbarara church, and for one of the catechists to preach in thy afternoon. From time to time a visitor from Toro or Buganda would be among the latter. On 13 January 1901 Saulo Lumama, county chief of Kabula, was the preacher. 'He told the people how the Europeans had come, not to get rich . . . but because Christ constrained them.' In the afternoon his companion 'took the line of showing how people in Buganda, Toro, Koki, Busoga, etc., had once, as in Ankole now, been believers in witchcraft etc., but how marvellously the gospel had changed the people there, and how it would do the same in Ankole.' Later in the year, in July, the chief minister of Toro, Nasanieri Mugurusi, was the preacher. His language was more readily understood by the people than Luganda, and his rank ensured an attentive hearing for what he had to say.[56]

At first all teaching and preaching was in Luganda, but a visit from Maddox, the missionary in Toro with special responsibility for translation, made the Ankole missionaries realize that Runyoro/Rutoro would be much more satisfactory. But there was considerable opposition to the proposed change, both from the Ganda catechists and from some of the people of Ankole themselves. Luganda had acquired a prestige value, and therefore they wanted the opportunity to learn it. However, by the beginning of 1902 Willis reported that even those catechists who had at first favoured Luganda had reluctantly agreed that it was unsatisfactory, whereas Runyoro/Rutoro was universally understood.[57] When a person was initiated into an *emandwa* (spirit) cult, he had had to learn a secret vocabulary, of no particular usefulness except that it was a distinguishing mark of members of the cult. This may have had something to do with the passivity with which instruction in a foreign tongue had been accepted at first.[58]

In August 1902 both Kahaya and Mbaguta asked to be registered as wanting baptism. Mbaguta was the one to take the initiative. He sent a note down to the missionaries saying that both he and the *Mugabe* had agreed to send away all but one wife, and to give up beer-drinking. Their decision was announced to the people, and was confirmed by Kahaya and Mbaguta in their own words.[59] Catholic catechists had arrived the previous month, and this was perhaps significant. Permission had for some time been refused to the Catholics, who had wanted to start a mission at Mbarara, and there was strong opposition from Hima who were adherents of the CMS. A panic was started about the likelihood of war if Catholics were allowed into Ankole, and Mayindo, a chief who had declared himself Catholic, was deposed because of alleged political dealings with the Catholics.[60] The White Fathers arrived in October 1902 and found their catechists had collected some 430 catechumens, an astonishing achievement in so short a time, and perhaps indicative of the extent of opposition to Mbaguta's growing ascendancy over Igumira and to the acceptance of new ways which this indicated.[61] When Mbaguta and the *Mugabe* were baptized in December the White Fathers suspected that the baptisms had been hurried through before Catholic influence became too strong.[62]

As the missionaries expected, once the *Mugabe* and Mbaguta had definitely committed themselves, others followed their lead. On 1 September the news reached Willis, who was away on safari, that twenty people had been registered as wanting to be baptized, and others followed shortly. In November Willis examined all of these, and twenty-three were allowed to go forward for baptism. The service was delayed until Clayton should have arrived back from leave in England, and could take it. Of the twenty-three, eight were men, nine were women (three of these were among those who had accompanied Hana Kageye from Toro), and six were boys, including two Ganda. Clayton arrived on 22 November, and the baptisms took place on 7 December. The Rev T. B. Johnson from Toro was also present.[63]

The occasion was memorable for the breaking of two traditional customs. Firstly, the women, encouraged by Hana Kageye, decided to unveil. They appeared at the baptism service dressed in white cloth instead of in the traditional bark-cloth.[64] Then at the close of the service the missionaries were called to witness the breaking of another custom by an action whose significance they did not understand until it was explained to them. They were invited to watch the *Mugabe* beat the royal drum, and they at first supposed he was doing so to express joy. When they arrived in the grass-strewn court of the *rurembo,* where the four chief drums were standing, spread with bark-cloth, Mbaguta explained the old belief that if the *Mugabe* were to beat the drums after the accession ceremonies were over, disaster would follow. Now that Kahaya had been baptized, he wanted to show his people that he was free from old taboos.[65] Many of those who witnessed the scene were horrified and looked for calamity to come upon their country.[66] Criticism of Mbaguta and Kahaya mounted for breaking custom and for allowing the Ganda too much influence, until it reached a peak where it eventually became politically dangerous. Kahaya vacillated in his attitudes, and Mbaguta survived because he was in favour with the British.[67]

5

CHRISTIANITY SPREADS AND MEETS RENEWED OPPOSITION

At the same time as the CMS were consolidating their work in Mbarara, catechists were being posted to other parts of the country, and small groups of catechumens were forming. The places to which Anglican catechists went are shown on Map 4, and it will be seen that all counties except Nshara had catechists. An account of a few of these places will serve to illustrate the developments which took place. Everywhere the importance of the chiefs will be apparent.

Within a few months of the arrival of the CMS, catechists were sent to Ibanda, and this has remained an Anglican church centre until today. Although right on the border with Toro and sparsely populated, Ibanda was important because the chieftainess who ruled the area was a key person in the politico-religious system.[68] She was descended from a woman remembered simply as *Murogo* (diviner), who had served the *Mugabe* who had reigned about six generations before Kahaya.[69] The chief functions of *Murogo* and her successors was to provide the *Mugabe* with intelligence concerning the neigbouring peoples, and to give advice about cattle-raids, and ensure their success by magical means. She stood in a special relationship to the *Mugabe* and ranked as one of his wives, holding her chieftainship directly from him. Her traditional place of sacrifice was the great, smooth-sided, flat-topped hill which dominates Ibanda, and five miles away to the east was the pool of Kijongo, where each new *Mugabe* had to undergo certain rites in which *Murogo*'s successors played an important part.[70]

At the turn of the century the chieftainess at Ibanda was Kishokye. In December 1899 she heard that Europeans had arrived at her place, and she went out to meet them. She found Bishop Tucker and Dr Cook resting under the shade of some large trees. They told her of their hope that the people of Ankole would accept Christian teachers, and she replied very hesitantly that she would wait and see what happened at the *rurembo,* and that if the *Mugabe* accepted teaching, so would she. Later the news reached her that Kahaya had begun to learn, and she quickly decided to follow his example, since she could no longer rely on her old occupation as a means of holding influence over him.[71] In December 1901 she therefore told messengers sent by the missionaries that she was willing to accept catechists. The first to be sent were two youngsters from the missionaries' household who, in the absence of proper catechists, agreed to begin the work at Ibanda. Kishokye did not really want to learn at all, and covertly put obstacles in the way of her people doing so, but since the *Mugabe* had given the lead, what else could she do but accept the catechists and bide her time? The arrival of two such youngsters did little to impress Kishokye, and although she arranged for them to be fed, she did nothing about arranging for a church to be built, and they taught under a tree. When Clayton and Willis visited Ibanda in April her reluctance was apparent. She conveyed to them that she feared to lose her position if she did not follow the new fashion of reading.[72]

By this time the youngsters had been replaced by catechists called Yona and Yusufu. Even so, when Willis passed through Ibanda at the end of June, no progress had been made, and Kishokye had beaten two of her girls who had wanted to learn. She tried to pacify Willis with vague promises such as she had made before, but she was told that unless she built a church and encouraged people to read, the catechists would be withdrawn.[73] Kishokye did not want this to happen. News of it would reach Kahaya and she feared the withdrawal of his favour and the loss of any chance of regaining her old authority. When Willis passed through Ibanda a week after making this threat, a church was almost completed. Willis was pleased and the danger averted. In September Willis visited again and found a larger and more responsive congregation than previously.[74] Shortly after this Kishokye died.[75] Before her death her attitude had so changed that she was thinking of giving up her instruments of divination and becoming a Christian.[76] She was succeeded in the chieftaincy by her younger sister, Kibubura, who started to learn to read at about this time. In May 1903 Clayton found her among a group of thirty-six catechumens at Ibanda. During his Ascension Day sermon she was ready with comments and with answers to questions he asked during the course of his preaching.[77] In September she and ten others were waiting to be examined for baptism when the missionary arrived. She had handed over her instruments of divination to the catechist some months before, and he now gave them to Clayton. Kibubura was one of seven people baptized the next morning, 15 September, and she took the name Juliya.[78] The conversion to Christianity was easier for Kibubura than for her elder sister. She was a much younger woman; and she had never, like Kishokye, achieved power through divination.[79] She was confirmed in her chieftaincy by the Protectorate government and became the only woman to hold a sub-county chieftainship under the British in Uganda. She became a Christian leader of her people, and she made the upkeep of the church at Ibanda her personal responsibility until her death in 1961.

The next place to which catechists were sent was Kazinga in the extreme west. The chief of the low-lying land between Lakes George and Edward and the escarpment of the hills of western Ankole was Kaihura, '. . . a fine specimen of the old regime, though now quite an old man and feeble . . . heavy with bracelets, anklets and charms, but with a dignified manner and quite a distinguished looking face.'[80] He asked for catechists to please Kahaya and they went in April 1901. A good start in reading was made by some of the boys. Kaihura himself took no interest at all in their work, and in less than a month one of the catechists made his way back to Mbarara to report that the chief had stopped building the church, and was refusing to give the catechists food. A complaint to Kahaya by the missionaries was quickly effective. One of Kaihura's sons was sent to Kazinga with messages to his father, and for the time being no further difficulties were put in the way of the catechists.[81]

Kazinga quickly became the most promising Christian outpost in Ankole. The boys were quick and intelligent, and the catechists were among the few who showed freshness and originality in their teaching. It was reported to the Catechists' Conference in January 1902 that thirty people in the whole of Ankole were able to read a gospel, and fourteen of these came from Kazinga. Kaihura had ordered all the boys there to learn. In February, however, he reversed this order and dismissed the catechists. This was the consequence of a meeting held in Mbarara at which government officials announced that, contrary to previous expectations, *mailo* land would not be granted to the missions. They tried to explain that the missions were entirely separate from the kingdom government: the government could not order the people to accept the missions, and chiefs could not be forced to provide land, build churches, and supply food for catechists. These things had to be done voluntarily. The *Mugabe* and

Mbaguta had, however, been ordering chiefs to do precisely those things which the Protectorate officials said were voluntary, and Mbaguta was unpopular. The people, therefore, could not understand what the government officials were driving at, and many of them concluded that Willis had got into trouble with the administration (and, indeed, something must have provoked the administration into making this statement, probably both the mission's use of the chiefs, and the chiefs' high-handedness). An immediate reaction was that Kaihura sent the catechists away from Kazinga, saying that he thought this was what was intended. Whatever the Protectorate officials may have intended, Mbaguta intended the chiefs to accept and maintain catechists, and he had the means to make things unpleasant for them if they demurred. In May Kaihura arrived at Mbarara very repentant and asked for the catechists to return. Like many other chiefs, he was torn between his own and his people's inclinations, his relationships with the traditional authorities, and the need to ingratiate himself with the Protectorate officials. He allowed the catechists to remain at Kazinga, and the boys to learn to read. But he forbade the women to be instructed, and the adults stood with him in refusing to learn.[82]

In May 1902 Willis visited Kazinga and was delighted with the boys and with their clear answers to his questions, and did not feel that he should delay before baptizing four of them. Two of the four had come into contact with Christianity before they began to receive instruction at Kazinga. This was often the case when a first group of people decided to ask for baptism.[83]

In August 1902 there was further trouble at Kazinga. New catechists acted so high-handedly that the church was burnt down in protest. The catechists were promptly sacked and replaced by two 'picked' men, and when Willis went to deal with the situation, he took with him the head-catechist, Sedulaka Kamagu.[84] Just after this Kaihura, the old chief, died.[85] His successor was Kasigano, who was baptized with the name Daudi on 14 July 1903.[86] It was hoped that under a Christian chief Kazinga would make good progress. By the end of 1904 a total of twenty-seven people had been baptized and at least one Christian marriage had taken place, but after 1904 no further baptisms are recorded. There were a number of reasons for this. Firstly, there was trouble between Kasigano and the British administration, because Kasigano became involved with the Belgians in disputes about the frontier. After one of the *Mugabe*'s soldiers had been killed, he took refuge in Belgian territory. In 1906 he was sacked.[87] After this, life at Kazinga was further disrupted when fighting broke out between two of Kaihura's sons, Lazaro Bwasuba and Paulo Kajangwa. During the unrest, Matayo, the Ganda catechist, returned to Buganda and was not replaced.[88] Finally, with the outbreak of sleeping sickness in about 1910, the whole population was moved to the higher parts of Bunyaruguru.[89]

Catechists were placed at three centres in eastern Ankole in 1901: at the headquarters of Mayindo, county chief of Nyabushozi; with Bucunku at Nabuseche; and at Muzizi, which lay to the north of Nabuseche. A brief account of these three centres will illustrate some of the difficulties in the early days of the CMS in Ankole.

The first of these chiefs to ask for catechists was Mayindo at Nyabushozi. He was one of the very few Iru chiefs, and many of his people were Ganda settlers who had entered Ankole fairly recently. Two young Ganda catechists, Satulo and Isaka, were sent to his place, and at first all seemed to be going well. But in August Mayindo was deported because of 'political dealings' with the Roman Catholics, and he was replaced by Matsiko. The people did not really know the difference between Catholics and Anglicans, and decided it was safest to keep clear of Christianity altogether, though a visit from Willis did something to restore their confidence. In 1902 it was Matsiko's turn to be sacked—the administration found him inefficient—and Mayindo was reinstated.[90] He was now definitely committed to the Catholics, and his people followed his lead.[91]

Bucunku was chief at Mitooma. He had once made blood-brotherhood with Stanley.[92] His sub-chief at Nabuseche was Rwakaikaga. In 1901 Bucunku came to Ibanda to meet Willis and ask for catechists. None were immediately available, but when five arrived from Mengo at the end of July, two were sent to Nabuseche, and were warmly welcomed. By September a little grass church had been built, and sixty or seventy people came to service when Willis arrived on a visit. Later in the year, towards the end of the long dry season, there was a severe shortage of food, and Jemusi, one of the catechists, wrote to Mbarara to complain of their sufferings:

> Here things are in a bad way; hunger is going to kill us; for many days now we have been fasting; the food in the gardens is finished; there is not even bulo [the coarse red millet]; sometimes we eat muhogo [a native vegetable]; sometimes a very little matoke. Nowadays hunger has made the Bahima refuse to read . . . Well, as soon as I have finished my time in November, I shall return home again.[93]

Food was promptly sent to them when this letter reached Mbarara, but Jemusi left and returned to Buganda. This left the other catechist, Samwili, alone, and because Nabuseche seemed so much more promising than Nyabushozi, Isaka was sent from Nyabushozi to join Samwili. These two together were most unsatisfactory. They were both Ganda, and they despised anyone not of their tribe. More than one missionary in Uganda had cause to complain of the Ganda in this respect, but fortunately few cases were as bad as that of Isaka and Samwili. In February 1902 they wrote to Willis to complain that no one would come to learn any more. The reason was not far to seek. They had, on their own showing, done virtually everything possible to antagonize the Hima. They had stolen their goats on 'paltry pretexts', constantly complained about the people, and made preposterous demands on them. Both teachers were promptly dismissed. When Willis visited the following April, he discovered that things were even worse than he had supposed, but that the people were too frightened to take any steps against the catechists lest they should get into trouble with the Europeans. So afraid were they that when the catechists had threatened to leave, they had offered them presents to stay.[94]

Two months later a group of catechists had arrived from Toro, and the best of these, Eriya Lujumba and Yosiya Kamuhiigi, were sent to reopen work at Nabuseche. In the six months that they remained there, they gained the confidence of the people, and taught so well that six were able to read a gospel and several wished to have their names registered as baptismal candidates.[95] Willis considered these two men much better than the average catechist at that time. They both came from the chiefly class: Yosiya Kamuhiigi had been a sub-county chief, but had given up this position in order to become a catechist. In 1901 he worked for his 'first letter' under Fisher at Kabarole, and as soon as he qualified he went to Ankole. He was an outstanding man, and one of the first Toro to be ordained. These two men, and the catechists at Kazinga are a commentary on what could be achieved when really good men were available. It seems from Willis' accounts that the average catechist was of comparatively poor quality at that time.[96]

But, as everywhere, Anglican work in Ankole was bedevilled by a lack of continuity engendered by the system of posting a catechist for only six months or a year, and then recalling him and posting him elsewhere (if he continued to work as a catechist at all, that is). When Lujumba and Kamuhiigi left, no one took their place for six months, and enthusiasm waned in spite of Rwakakaiga's efforts to keep the catechumens together. For about a year no missionary visited. New catechists who got on quite well with the people had been at work for some months when Clayton visited in 1903, but only one boy was willing to commit himself about baptism, and only four people remained who had reached the stage of reading a gospel.[97] Gaburieri Rwakakaiga was baptized in Mbarara in March 1903, and Apolo Bucunku two months later, and when Bucunku died the next year, Rwakakaiga was appointed county chief in his place. In May 1905 he was one of those accused of the murder of the sub-commissioner, Galt, and although he was acquitted by the Appeal Court, he was deported.[98] This had repercussions on progress at Nabuseche, and although a few of those baptized at Mbarara during the next few years gave the names of Bucunku or Rwakakaiga as their chief, no baptisms were recorded at Nabuseche itself, and the work there died out.

We must here digress a little. The murder of Galt has been one of the unsolved riddles of recent Ugandan history. Particularly puzzling is that no motive has been found for it, though there is a measure of agreement among Nyankole informants that it was in some way that they cannot explain designed to harm Mbaguta.[99] In an article devoted to the subject, H. F. Morris writes: It is unlikely that the mystery of the murder will ever be solved. Those who know the secret are taking it with them to their graves.'[100] He was, however, unduly pessimistic, for the Mbarara Mission Diary, now available in the White Fathers' Archives in Rome, contains information which has not previously been seen, and which opens up new possibilities.

From October 1903 onwards the Diary records growing tension between Igumira and Mbaguta, and growing animosity to the latter among the Hima and Hinda chiefs and princes. They blamed Mbaguta for the intrusion of the colonial administration, the Ganda, and the missions, all of which threatened their way of life. More than one plot was hatched against Mbaguta.[101] The crisis came in May 1905. Igumira's headquarters lay between Ibanda and Mbarara, and the *Mugabe* and most of the leading chiefs and princes were assembled there, and were arming themselves with spears.[102] Mbaguta was with Knowles, a Collector in the service of the Protectorate.[103] They went to see Igumira and then returned to Mbarara.[104] Meanwhile Galt, then Acting Sub-commissioner, had been instructed to hand over to Knowles and report to Entebbe. He informed Knowles that he would come to Mbarara, stopping over at Ibanda.[105] The chiefs seem to have been misinformed about the movements of Knowles and Galt, though they will have known that Knowles and Mbaguta were together. They planned to kill Knowles and the hated Mbaguta, but the plan misfired, and Galt was killed instead.[106] The plot was hatched by Igumira and the chiefs, together with Kahaya, but they themselves did not carry out the murder. This was done by a peasant called Rutaraka who, after he had murdered Galt, apparently shouted out: 'Look! I have killed a big pig!'[107] He himself was murdered shortly afterwards (though at first the chiefs said he had committed suicide), and one may conjecture that he was killed for bungling his assignment. It was correctly concluded by the British officials that there were others behind Rutaruka, and much time and energy was spent in trying to follow up anyone who might have had a grudge against Galt.[108] Rwakakaiga and Nyakayaga were eventually suspected, but acquitted by the Appeal Court, as has been noted, because of the garbled and unsatisfactory nature of the evidence.[109] In December 1905 Knowles announced the findings of the Entebbe trial to a meeting of the *lukiko* (assembly of chiefs), and Kahaya and Mbaguta were confirmed in their positions. The Mbarara Diary records Kahaya's immense relief, and that later there were all night revellings at the headquarters of Ruhara, a chief in Rwampara.[110] It is not surprising that Ankole in general, and Ibanda in particular, were disturbed and unresponsive to the missions after an upheaval of this sort, and as the chiefs waited tensely for the results of the trials and enquiries that were held.

At the third place, Muzizi, the work was no more permanent. There was a small colony of Ganda here. In April 1902 Willis found the people indifferent, and few attended classes. In October of that year no catechist was available for Muzizi, so when Catholic catechists arrived from Villa Maria in Buganda, the people started to learn with them.[111] In 1903 an Anglican catechist was again posted to Muzizi, and the chief was a boy who had been baptized by the CMS in Mbarara, but he lived at the capital, and his uncle, who was a Catholic, ran the chieftaincy for him. Catholic pressure and the shortage of Anglican catechists brought work to an end here.[112]

Catechists were also sent to the counties of Igara, Shema, Rwampara, Buhweju, Isingiro, and Buzimba, and although they met with much the same kind of difficulties as have been described, Anglican work in western and central Ankole has for the most part survived.

The most promising area of Catholic work outside Mbarara was Bunyaruguru, a mountainous region in the west of Ankole. Whereas the Anglicans had first started at Kazinga, down in the Rift Valley, the Catholics opened their first outstation in the more densely populated highland area among the vigorous Nyampaka people.

There were several Catholic sub-chiefs in this area, but they were Ganda who exploited the people, and they were a hindrance rather than a help. For a time a Ganda political agent, Yohana Ssebalijja, worked in Bunyaruguru. He too was a Catholic, and the White Fathers had a fairly high opinion of his helpfulness, but the real key to success in this area was the catechist, Yohana Kitagana, who served, led, and taught the people. Apart from Apolo Kivebulaya, his is deservedly the best-known name among Ugandan African missionaries. He succeeded in remaining on good terms with the Protestant county chief, Kasigano, took a firm stand against the extortions of his fellow-Ganda Catholic chiefs, and helped to bring the genuine grievances of the people to the notice of the administration, and to get redress for them. He also successfully challenged the power of the traditional religion in a manner which won the respect of the people, and he was remarkable for the way in which he cared for the sick. He acted with sensitivity, and when the first Christian marriages took place in Bunyaruguru, an attempt was made to include everything possible of local custom, the decision being taken after discussion between the missionaries, Yohana the catechist, and the two young couples concerned. The zeal of the catechumens from Bunyaruguru was often remarked on by the White Fathers, and in 1909 their second mission in Ankole was opened in Bunyaruguru at Rugazi. Kitagana then went with Ssebalijja to Kigezi and was responsible for starting work there, where he was greatly loved and respected.[113]

Although there was rivalry between Catholics and Protestants in Ankole, it never reached the proportions that it had done in Toro. Once the White Fathers had been given permission to open a mission in Ankole, there were difficulties over the acquisition of land, but at no time was the mission dependent on the chiefs to the same degree as in Toro because land could be obtained through registration. Although the agreement of the chief was required, the missions were less at his mercy than they had been before land could be obtained in this way. There was a period in 1903 and 1904 when opposition to British rule, centred on Igumira, reached considerable proportions, but when he was finally removed from the country the possibility that Catholicism might become a rival party disappeared. Factionalism in Ankole is more complex than in Toro because of the Hima/Iru division of society. Although practically all Christian Hima are Anglican, the Iru are divided between Catholic and Anglican allegiance, and nowhere else in Uganda did religious cleavage follow so exactly the lines of social and political cleavage as in Buganda and

Toro. The Catholics did not try to compete for the Hima in Ankole: they concentrated on the Iru.

6

PROBLEMS OF CHURCH GROWTH

At the end of 1903 Bishop Tucker visited Ankole and confirmed fifty-seven people, including a few Ganda. After a brief training under Clayton, some of the people from Ankole were appointed as catechists. Canon Buningwire, himself baptized in 1903, remembered eighteen men baptized between 1902 and 1905 who served as catechists. All but two were Hima, and seven had to give up teaching within a few years when they were made chiefs. A further six left teaching to return to their traditional way of life with their cattle. Two died, and Canon Buningwire himself was the only member of the group to remain in the service of the church (one of the Iru died within a year or two, and the other returned to cultivating). The careers of these men are shown in Table V and they highlight some of the difficulties in building up the church in Ankole.

The first was the difficulty experienced by the Hima on becoming Christians, and especially on becoming catechists. The main preoccupations of the Hima were their cattle, and the achievement of chiefly power. Although the CMS concentrated most of its attention on the Hima to begin with, few Hima have been able to separate themselves sufficiently from their traditional way of life to follow a vocation in the church, nor has the church considered reforming its structures so as to allow the Hima the possibility of following such a vocation without abandoning their pastoralism (other occupations in the 'modern sector' are, of course, equally incompatible with pastoralism). In consequence there were, in 1970, only three Hima Anglican clergy: Canon Buningwire; the bishop of Ankole, Bishop Shalita; and the Rev. (now Bishop) Yustasi Ruhindi, then Principal of the Anglican Theological College. A further difficulty in Ankole, as in almost every area of Uganda, was the demand made by the government on the small numbers of educated men—literate men were needed as chiefs and clerks, as well as catechists, and government could pay more than the pitifully low wages offered by the church. It was to the best leaders that chieftaincies were offered. The missionaries usually overestimated the influence of Christian chiefs on their clients, and the Anglicans leaned on the civil administration more than the Catholics did.

Some of the catechists who worked in Ankole deserve mention. For several years catechists from Toro helped in Ankole, and the contribution of Hana Kageye and Yosiya Kamuhiigi has already been mentioned. A third catechist from Toro was Gabulieri Kiza who is still remembered in Ankole, as are the other two. He first arrived in 1902 with Hana Kageye. He had been a church elder and was of the chiefly class. He had a commanding personality, later becoming over-authoritarian.[114] The catechists from Toro had an advantage over those from Buganda in that their language was virtually the same as that in Ankole. Rebecca Alibatafudde was a widow from Buganda who had done her 'second letter' at Namirembe. Like Kageye, she spent much time with the Hima women, and is remembered for her kindness and generosity. She was a very active Christian, and whenever she visited she preached to the women, telling them that God could see them wherever they were.[115] Esita Mbaitamu was among the Christian women who regularly went visiting their pagan neighbours on Thursdays. When Miss Baker, who was normally in charge of this visiting, was on leave in 1906, Esita took over.[116] In 1914 she took charge of the women's baptism class when there was no catechist available.[117] One of the first Iru women to achieve influence and be remembered as an active church worker was Melinda Mukenshakho.[118] The important part played by Juliya Kibubura and Malyamu Kacibala has already been mentioned.

The catechists from Buganda were a mixed bunch. Most of them were very young and stayed only six months or a year, and a few caused trouble, as at Kazinga and Nabuseche. Nevertheless the church in Ankole owed much to them. By far the most remarkable was Johana Kitagana, the Catholic catechist responsible for the evangelization of Bunyaruguru. The Ganda catechists often experienced hardship, and in the early days, when the chiefs wanted to get rid of them, the method usually employed was to try and starve them out by refusing to supply food. In 1906 it was reported that all but four of the Anglican catechists were from Ankole itself,[119] but we find Ganda and Toro working in Ankole for some years after this. Several Ganda who originally came as catechists were offered sub-county chieftaincies and accepted them. Among these were Isaka Nyakayaga, who became a chief in Mitoma under Gaburieri Rwakakaiga and was arrested with him on suspicion of being involved in the murder of the sub-commissioner. Although he too was acquitted, he was deported from Ankole. Mikaeri Mangasi probably first came to Mbarara in 1902 from Buganda. He was a lay-reader from Nakanyonyi near Mengo, and, being an active and cheerful man, got on well as a catechist at Mbarara. However, women and beer eventually proved his undoing, and in about 1918 he was dismissed. Nuwa Mbaguta thought him a capable man and in 1920 appointed him sub-county chief at Birere in Rwampara. He lost all interest in Christianity and eventually retired to Masaka.[120] Zakariya Mujendada arrived from Koki in 1902 and his name frequently appears among those who preached at Mbarara that year. Later he became sub-county chief at Bumbeiri in Igara. He was a large, cheerful and talkative man, and he too reverted to polygamy and was disciplined by the church.[121] In contrast to these was Shadrak Kamagu, who arrived in 1901. He refused a chieftaincy in order to continue to work as a catechist.[122] Another person from Buganda who is remembered with respect is Yoweri Daki who was the first catechist at Kitojo in 1906. He was a good teacher and preacher, and fond of children. In 1911 he went to Buganda to read for his 'second letter', but he returned to Kitojo for a further period.[123] In 1913 a small school was opened at Kyagaju and Obadiah Kamya came as catechist. Lazaro Kamugungunu, who later became first minister and had always been a staunch supporter of the Anglican church, was then chief in this area. He persuaded the parents to send their children to school. Kamya was a young, unmarried man who had not reached a very high standard of education, but he could read and write and do some arithmetic, and he had a very good moral influence. When he left in 1915 the school had to be closed down because no one could be found to take his place, but he had made his mark. Many who had been his pupils found employment with government; others became catechists, and several were ordained.[124]

Canon Buningwire has been the most outstanding of the catechists from Ankole trained in this early period. He was also the first man from Ankole to be ordained. He tells of the difficult days he had in Ibanda in the early years of the century. After Rwakakaiga had been deported because of his possible involvement in Galt's murder, a Muslim from Buganda, Abdul Aziz Bulwadda, was appointed to take his place as county chief of Mitoma. This man was prejudiced against the Christians and looked after the catechists very badly, which is hardly surprising in view of his religious persuasions. Daudi Ntate, a lay-reader from Buganda, had resigned because of this, and Stefano Kahondore who followed him found things extremely difficult and was moved to Bugonge in Shema in 1906 to work with an experienced catechist from Buganda. Buningwire went to replace him. By this time there were about fifteen baptized Christians at Ibanda, and Juliya Kibubura was the sub-county chief. Buningwire, who had known Kishokye, now became Kibubura's personal friend, and acted as her clerk. When people came to pay hut-tax, he took the opportunity of preaching to them. Because of his efficiency as a clerk, Abdul Aziz became kindly disposed to him. Buningwire realized that there was one matter on which he and Abdul Aziz could co-operate, and that was the suppression of witchcraft. Aziz was anxious to help, for he greatly feared witchcraft, and as a result of their working together on this, Abdul also gave his support to the building of a church. The partnership did not last very long, however, as in 1907 Buningwire was sent to Kabarole in Toro to read for his 'first letter', and a year later, in 1908, Abdul Aziz was deposed for cruelty and for oppressing the people.[125]

Nasanieri Riang'ombe became a 'third letter' catechist before being appointed to a chieftaincy. He was the first evangelist to go to Kyagaju, about twenty miles west of Mbarara. He was baptized in 1905 and went to Kyagaju soon afterwards when still a young, unmarried man. He had cows at his home in Kakoma, but at Kyagaju he had to cultivate, and he had his small-holding just across the path from where the church stands today. It is still possible to see a mound by this path where he had his first small church. Tujunje the chief, although not a Christian, wanted his children to have a chance to learn, and had therefore asked for a catechist. About sixty people came to church classes, both Hima and Iru. Riang'ombe was moved elsewhere at the end of a year, but the work he had started grew and prospered.[126] Paulo Ntundubaire was a quiet man, a Hima, who first went to work at Kahihi in 1904 with Yoweri Buningwire. Later he worked at Rubinga, also in Kashari county, and then he went to Nsike in Buhweju. He was eventually appointed sub-county chief in Igara county. Stefano Kahondore taught for a number of years, first at Ibanda and then at Bugonge in Shema, and later in Kashari and Nyabushozi. At length he returned to his cattle and went with them to Kabula just across the boundary into Buganda.[127] These three are remembered as having made a significant contribution to the early growth of the Anglican church in Ankole.

It was not easy to find men willing to work as catechists. Table VI gives numbers, where these are available, of men in training as catechists at Mbarara, but the picture it gives is incomplete on two counts. Firstly, many young men went as catechists without any training, and secondly we know that some went to Toro. For training as 'second' and 'third letter' catechists, men from Ankole went to Buganda. Table VI does not, therefore, give a complete account even of trained catechists in Column 5, but it does show fluctuations in numbers which reflect general trends. In 1908 the number of catechists in training had dropped markedly, and so had the numbers of those baptized. The missionaries complained that the church was in a bad state, and that few people attended church services or showed any desire to evangelize. They also stated that 'the baptized women at Mbarara are very unsatisfactory'.[128] The CMS *Annual Report* makes no attempt to account for this state of affairs.

There had been a number of difficulties over the years which together may have produced the situation of 1908. 1904 was the year of the boundary disputes in western Ankole, when a number of people decided they were no longer under British rule, and that they must therefore give up their profession of Christianity. 1905 saw the murder of Galt, and as a result of this the missionaries were not encouraged to travel without a police escort for about a year. In such circumstances they found it better to call the people in to Mbarara for baptism rather than go out to the villages. Igara was affected by the trouble already recounted at Kazinga, and in 1907 they refused to have catechists because they were angry at having to pay hut tax. Christianity was confused in their minds with colonial rule, and they could not distinguish between catechists and the new type of chief being appointed. The missionaries also reported difficulties in making contact with the Iru, who said they were too busy cultivating to come to catechism classes. It was soon realized that special efforts would have to be made to reach the Iru, who, after all, formed the bulk of the population.[129] The policy of converting the chiefs first was not too effective in Ankole where the Iru felt under no obligation to follow the lead of the Hima. By the time the Anglican mission turned seriously to the Iru they had to compete with the Catholics. Willis had by 1908 left Ankole for western Kenya; previously his safaris had been effective in keeping in touch with widely scattered congregations. There were no unmarried male missionaries at the CMS station in Ankole, and married men were more station-bound than unmarried ones. There was a measure of unrest in Ankole in 1907 and 1908 of the same sort as that in Toro and Bunyoro when there was resentment against the Ganda. Probably the enthusiasm which had marked the first acceptance of Christianity had worn off, and this, coupled with the various causes of unrest listed here, accounted for the low state of the church which the missionaries commented on.

The recovery which began in 1909 is easier to explain, however. There was a concerted effort to increase the numbers of catechists. Eighteen men volunteered for training, a class was held for them in Mbarara, and the total number of catechists employed by the CMS rose from thirty-seven to fifty-four. One catechist refused a chieftaincy in order to continue with his work—an example which would have had its effect. The missionaries talked over the decline in numbers of catechumens and school children with some of the leading women, and among those who were consulted were Esita Mbaitamu, wife of the *Mugabe*, and the wife of Nuwa Mbaguta. They were invited to the mission house 'to pray that an improvement might take place, and from that time the numbers of pupils increased.'[130] These ladies were influential enough to see to it that their own prayers were answered. In 1909 the first Ugandan clergyman, the Rev. Aloni Muyinda, arrived in Ankole. He was Hima by birth, but as a child he had been taken off to Buganda and had there been converted to Christianity. He had worked in Kyagwe with the missionary Baskerville for some years, and now both he and the people of Ankole felt that he was returning home. By this time the church was well-established at Kyagaju, and at Kitojo, some twenty miles west of Mbarara. This was where Yoweri Daki and Nasanieri had done good work, and it was one of the first areas in which there had been a response from Iru as well as Hima. The area is fertile, and was and is a centre of population. Among other well-known figures who worked in the Kabwohe area were Aberi Balya, the first East African bishop of the Anglican church, and Lazaro Kamugungunu, later to be Prime Minister of Ankole. Kamugungunu remained as chief until 1918 and did much to help the growth of the church. In 1913 the Rev. Silasi Aliwonya was put in charge of a pastorate there—the centre was then at Kitoju—and the results in numbers baptized became apparent at once. Forty-six people were baptized at Kitoju the year he arrived, and in the following year the number rose to 347.[131]

In 1910 there were still complaints that although Ganda chiefs were encouraging their people to come to church classes, the Hima chiefs were doing little, and that the women showed no desire for instruction; but for the first time we hear of large numbers of Iru coming to learn. One or two new county chiefs were appointed at about this time, and these were active in promoting Christianity. In 1908 George Sefasi Togo was made county chief of Igara, and this area became more settled and easier for catechists to work in. In 1911 Yonosani Mpira was appointed to Nyabushozi and Yeremiya Kabarime to Mitooma—the latter appointment ended several years of unrest in that area. Nuwa Mbaguta was county chief of Shema and Kashari as well as being first minister. In 1910 we read of 'efficient service' being given by the Christians of Ankole, and by the Christian women especially (the tide has turned); and the doubling of the number of people being baptized reflects the increasing responsiveness of the Iru.[132] By 1913 the baptism figures had doubled again and the number of catechists in training at Mbarara had trebled. These figures continued to rise steadily throughout the next few years.

TABLE V
CAREERS OF SOME CATECHISTS IN ANKOLE

Name	1	2	3	4	5	6	7
Stefano Kahondore	1902	/		/			
Paulo Ntundubaire	1902	/	/				
Yakobo Nyindo	1902	/		/			
Nasanieri Komakocwa	1902	/	/				
Yoweri Buningwire	1903	/				/	
Andereya Kuhondeire	1903	/	/				
Musa Kagondozi	1903	/		/			
Yeremiya Kimenjere	1903	/	/				
Matayo Rwakatiagisi	1903	\			/		
Yona Kabwigunda	1903	/					/
Esau Kyatuka	1903	/	/				
Stefano Rukurucira	1904	/		/			
Musa Rwabutere	1905	/		/			
Nasanieri Rwakeizanda	1905	/	/				
Paulo Ntagarama	1905	/		/			
Erisa Mucucu	1905	/					/

1 Year of baptism
2 Hima / or Iru \
3 Became chief
4 Went back to his cattle
5 Went back to cultivate
6 Remained in church work
7 Died within a few years of baptism

Name	1	2	3	4	5	6	7
Nasanieri Riang'ombe*	1905	/	/				
Petero Bitama	1905	\					/
TOTALS			7	7	1	1	3

* Became a 'third letter' catechist before becoming a chief.

TABLE VI
NUMBERS OF CATECHISTS WORKING IN ANKOLE 1904–14

Anglican catechists

Year	Men	Women	Total	Number in training	Number baptized	Catholic Catechists
1904	37	8	45		127	
1905	39	19	58	16	103	28
1906	40	12	52	9	110	
1907	43	3	46	0	147	42
1908	31	6	37	0	105	49
1909	47	7	54	0	126	69
1910	108	4	112		130	84
1911	89	6	95	9	259	
1912						97
1913	124	4	128	27	587	
1914	172	2	174		809	
1916*						104

Figures taken from CMS *Annual Reports, Ankole Baptism Register,* and White Fathers: *Rapports Annuels*.

No information is available as to how many catechists were from Toro, how many from Ankole and how many from Buganda.

*this year is added to show the general trend of Catholic catechist numbers as no figures are available for the two preceding years.

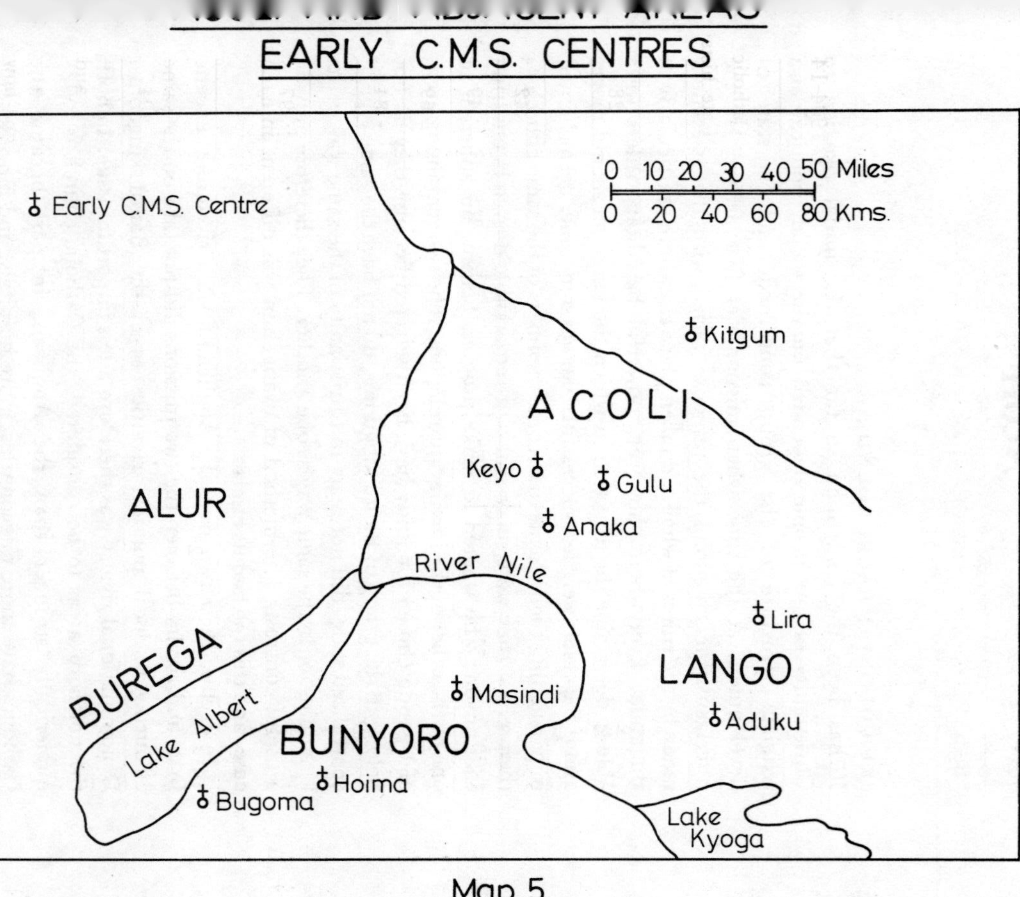
EARLY C.M.S. CENTRES
Early C.M.S. Centre
0 10 20 30 40 50 Miles
0 20 40 60 80 Kms.
Kitgum
A C O L I
Keyo
Gulu
Anaka
ALUR
River Nile
Lira
LANGO
Aduku
BUREGA
Lake Albert
Masindi
BUNYORO
Hoima
Bugoma
Lake Kyoga

Map 5

Chapter V
Acoli

1

PRE-COLONIAL BACKGROUND

It has been the contention so far that the initial reaction to Christianity of any people depended on the social, political and religious structure of the group concerned, and its state of development at the time when missionaries first arrived. In the interlacustrine kingdoms the response varied with the assessment made by the rulers of what had taken place elsewhere, particularly in Buganda. Everywhere, however, powerful hereditary rulers were able to determine the direction in which the kingdom should move, and if the chiefs were less successful than has sometimes been claimed in persuading their clients to become members of the same church as themselves, they were successful to a remarkable degree in ensuring that anyone who wanted to make progress became an adherent of one or the other of the immigrant religions. The two remaining areas of Uganda chosen for study have been selected because they do not belong to the group of Bantu kingdoms, do not have the same type of centralized state, did not react to Christianity in the same way as the kingdoms, or in the same way as one another. They therefore provide a useful contrast. The method of evangelism was different in each case, and this too had its effect.

In each of these two areas the Anglican CMS arrived on the scene first, and rivalry between the two missions did not take on the same colouring of local political rivalries as in the Bantu kingdoms. Denominational rivalry was therefore a less important issue. In both the northern areas to be considered, the Catholic church is today numerically stronger than the Anglican, in part because the Catholics have more missionaries, more hospitals, and more schools than the Anglicans, and have put a greater effort into the mission in the north. For the CMS, the north and east were important largely in relation to Buganda and to the kingdoms in general. In Acoli, the first of the non-Bantu areas to be considered, the Verona Fathers reached a goal towards which they had been working for half a century, and the Acoli mission mattered more to them than to the

CMS for this important psychological reason. The Mill Hill Mission in Teso, the second area to be considered, had not arrived in Uganda until 1895, and was for that reason less emotionally involved with Buganda. Their work was confined to the eastern part of Uganda and to western Kenya, so they came into less contact with the mystique of kingship and were less fascinated by it than were either the CMS or the White Fathers. The first contact with Christianity in the north and east was with Protestant Christianity, however, and it is this encounter which will be examined here.

The Acoli are members of the large Lwoo group of peoples who extend from latitude 10° N in Sudan, through Uganda to western Kenya and north western Tanzania. Most of the Lwoo are still pastoralists, and, except for the Luo of Kenya, have proved rather unresponsive to Christianity. A study of only one member of the Lwoo will not shed much light on the question of why the Lwoo generally have proved unresponsive, but it may shed a little. The Teso, the other non-Bantu dealt with, are members of a group of peoples inhabiting eastern Uganda and north western Kenya. They too are mostly pastoralists, and have also been somewhat unresponsive to the missions. The Lwoo used to be referred to as Nilotes and the Teso as Nilo-Hamites, but this terminology is no longer considered satisfactory. It is mentioned here only for the sake of reference. Both the missions and the colonial government came to Acoli and Teso later than to the Bantu kingdoms of Uganda, both areas remain underdeveloped still in comparison with the rest of the country, and this underdevelopment is partly due to mission politics. Comparatively little study of their history and institutions has been carried out, though this is in process of being rectified.

Acoli was the first non-Bantu area entered by the CMS in Uganda, and the people, their language and their social institutions immediately struck the missionaries as being very different from anything they had so far experienced in Uganda. The Rev. A. L. Kitching, who arrived in Acoli from Toro in 1904, noted that the 'elaborate feudal system, so prominent a feature of life in Buganda', was lacking in Acoli, and he wrote admiringly of the independence of the people, and their physique and intelligence impressed him.[1] The Rev. A. B. Lloyd, another pioneer missionary in Acoli, noticed immediately that their language belonged to a different language-group from the Bantu languages, though he mistakenly thought it akin to Arabic.[2]

Yet, whilst appreciating that there were great differences between the Acoli and the Bantu peoples, the missionaries took it for granted that the same approach and methods of work should be used, and the relative failure of these was not noticed or acted upon for some time. The first approaches of the mission were made to the chiefs, and it was assumed that *Rwot* (chief) Awic, who had invited them, was paramount chief. In this they were misled by the writings of Sir Samuel Baker who had been persuaded that Rwotcamo (*Rwot* Labvoor) of the Payira clan held a paramountcy over all the other *Rwodi,* and in *Ismailia* called him 'King of the Shuli'.[3] The first approach to the CMS had come from *Rwot* Awic of Payira, Rwotcamo's son and successor, and this strengthened the missionaries in their misapprehension.[4] As we shall see, the approach to the chiefs was largely unsuccessful.

Elsewhere in Uganda the missionaries had been virtually the first foreigners profoundly to influence the lives of the people. Where the colonial administration was established before the missions, missionaries followed at once. Only in Buganda itself had they been effectively preceded, and there by Arab Muslims, but these had been checked in their activities by the *Kabaka* and kept under control. When the missionaries had gone from Buganda into a new Bantu area they had done so at the request of the king, and, as teachers who would enable the people to follow the lead of the Ganda into new ways, they were welcomed. Initial resistance was broken down by African catechists who paved the way for them. Both the catechists and the missionaries were seen to some extent as representatives of the leading chiefs of Buganda. In Acoli also the missionaries were invited by a chief, *Rwot* Awic, but, as we have noted, he had no paramountcy, nor would his people feel bound to follow his lead in matters of religion. Then also, the Acoli had had their lives disrupted by foreigners since the 1850s when traders coming from Khartoum had entered the country in search of ivory and slaves. The missionaries were by no means the first influential foreigners; and there had been successive European governors who had been unable to control the depredations of the Khartoum traders or of their own people unless they themselves were personally present—Baker, Gordon and Emin Pasha had all visited Acoli.

That the traders had been able to enter Acoli was partly due to the Acoli themselves. The Acoli had migrated to their present home from a cradle-land in the Sudan lying to the south of the junction of the Bahr el Ghazal and the Bahr el Jebel.[5] Different clans had arrived at different times, each under its own *Rwot*. There was no overall authority, and the clans were in frequent conflict with one another, groups of clans forming temporary alliances for the purpose of warring against their neighbours. From time to time smaller groups might place themselves under the protective authority of some powerful *Rwot,* or, equally, might break away, setting up someone of their own choosing as *Rwot.* In the 1850s when the traders from the north first entered the country they were able to take advantage of this friction, and they first came into Acoli at the request of Lobai, *Rwot* of Atiak, who about 1855 sent to Gondokoro asking for help against the Jo-Chwa.[6] Crazzolara, commenting on this, says that the traders' 'establishment and stay in Acoliland was entirely based on the rivalries of the various chieftainships and their discords.'[7] For whilst we are told that this precedent was deplored by the Acoli, especially when it was realized that the Arabs were transporting out of the country their share of the captives taken in the fighting, other groups of Acoli fell into the same temptation of asking the Arabs for help and for guns when further quarrels arose.

The havoc wrought by the traders in their hunt for ivory and slaves was first noticed by Europeans when Speke and Grant passed through the country in 1862. About a year later the Bakers passed through Acoli for the first time, and noticed the devastation wrought in Chua. Their writings roused European public opinion against the atrocities of the slave-traders, and Ismail Pasha prepared to annex the headwaters of the Nile, giving out that his main reason for doing so was the suppression of the slave-trade, and he appointed Sir Samuel Baker to carry out the annexation, which was proclaimed at Gondokoro in 1871. Baker, and later Gordon and Emin Pasha who succeeded him as governors of Equatoria, did what they could to suppress the traders, but this was negligible as the annexation of Equatoria was regarded by Egypt in a double light. Baker spent a year at Patiko in 1872–3 and made friends with a number of leading *Rwodi,* and Acoli was temporarily more peaceful and prosperous. Emin Pasha was at first hampered in administering the area by Gordon's order that he was not to proceed south of Dufile. Later, during the Mahdist rising, he was cut off from Khartoum and became increasingly powerless to control his troops (Gordon had little contact with this part of his domain, passing through it only once on his way to Bunyoro). Many of the troops left behind by Emin when he was 'rescued' by Stanley made their way to Kavalli's village near Lake Albert, where they were found by Lugard in 1891; others remained in Acoli under a leader named Fadl-el-Mula, where they exacerbated the clan strife, and continued to prey upon the people.[8]

But in spite of these misfortunes, the religion of the Acoli did not suffer the same undermining as the traditional religion of the

Nyankole, nor had their morale suffered in the same way as that of the Nyoro or Toro people. Okot p'Bitek, himself an Acoli, explains that 'When all the medicines and blessings, when the prayers and supplications and rituals have failed, when the sufferings of the individual persist, the Acoli resignedly cry Wilobo! or Woko! or Run-Piny! which for lack of a better word I tentatively interpret as Fate'. He later remarks that *Wilobo* and *Woko* are representations of all the problems, risks and sufferings of a person's lifetime, whilst *Run-Piny* personifies those of a day, and against all of them man is impotent. Whilst the Acoli do all they can to avert disaster, 'When the game of ritually acting out their keen desires has produced no material changes in the situation . . . the Acoli become thoroughly sceptical and irreligious, and prefer to face the facts of life coolly and realistically'. Okot considers that traditionally the Acoli had no belief in a Supreme Creator and were not seriously concerned with what would happen to them after death.[9] Something of a battle has raged over whether or not the Acoli believed in a Supreme God before the introduction of Christianity. Some scholars claim that all Africans did so: they refuse, therefore, to accept that some peoples may have possessed no concept which could meaningfully be equated with the Christian/Muslim concept of a Supreme God. Those who hold this view seem to do so partly out of a desire to defend African religion against charges of 'primitivism'. In their zeal to do so, however, they have settled for a rather narrow definition of religion—equating religion with monotheism or pre-monotheism. Traces of this may be found in Okot's use of the word 'irreligious' quoted above. Taken in conjunction with other evidence, Okot's evaluation of traditional Acoli attitudes appears more accurate than an insistence that the Acoli believe in a Supreme God.[10] Acoli religious attitudes are different from those of the Bantu peoples of Uganda, and their scepticism enables them to meet and accept disaster without the entire structure of their traditional religion being undermined.

Nor had the morale of the Acoli suffered as had that of the Nyoro and Toro in spite of the havoc wrought by the slave-traders. In part this may have been due to a difference in social structure. Since there was no overall authority, what affected one group of Acoli or one part of Acoli country did not necessarily affect another, and since there had been much clan fighting, trouble for one clan might be to the advantage of another. In the Bantu kingdoms what affected a part affected the whole to a larger extent, and humiliation for the traditional ruler brought a measure of humiliation on the whole group. So whilst the lack of cohesion gave the traders their initial chance, it also acted as a shock-absorber for the damage they eventually caused.

12

THE FIRST CONTACTS END IN FAILURE

It was *Rwot* Awic who was responsible for inviting the first missionaries into Acoli. His father, as we have noted, was the powerful Rwotcamo whom Baker described as 'King of the Shuli'. Both Baker and Emin knew Rwotcamo and treated him with respect. Awic had also met these men; in 1872 he almost certainly accompanied his father on a visit to Baker, and in 1880 he met Emin. At this time his father had been on friendly and co-operative terms with both of them. But towards the end of his life Rwotcamo was so deeply insulted by one of Emin's commanders that his attitude towards the foreign administration changed completely. By the time he was killed in a clan fight in 1887, he had become deeply suspicious of the administration and not on good terms with the Europeans. Awic, his successor, adopted the same attitude. He lost favour with the British in 1898 because he gave refuge to Kabalega, and in 1907 Delmé-Radcliffe took him to Kampala as a prisoner because of his resistance to British rule.[11]

During his first period of imprisonment in 1901-3 Awic must have become aware of the great changes coming to Buganda, and have heard of the advent of Christianity, or 'reading'. After two years he returned home by way of Hoima and Masindi where it was doubtless hoped that Andereya Duhaga would have a good influence on him. Duhaga met him and successfully persuaded him that it would be to his advantage to invite Christian teachers into his country. Although Awic probably regarded Duhaga as a usurper, since Kabalega was still alive, clan connections between the Payira and the Bito were strong enough for Duhaga to exert considerable influence.[12] Not long after Awic arrived back in Acoli he sent a delegation asking for catechists. The leader of the delegation was an intelligent young man called Ojigi who was sub-chief at Alokolum, the land of a clan group living not far from Gulu.[13] Four other men went with him. Naturally it was to Andereya Duhaga the *Mukama* that they went with their request. He sent them on to the Rev. A. B. Lloyd with a letter in which he restated their request in his own words, rephrasing it so that it would find favour at the mission. Lloyd said the contents of the letter were somewhat as follows:

> Sir, — these men have come from far away, from the great country called Ganyi to the north of Bunyoro across the Nile. They are sent by their king Awich, and they come to see you. They are a warlike people, but their message is one of peace; they want to be taught about God. They say they have heard how we, in our country, have received teachers and helpers, and why should they not have the same help? See these men, then, my friend, and decide what you will do.[14]

An Acoli, writing in 1945, remembered the event rather differently:

> When Awic came back from Kampala it was good because he knew that the white men were good. Afterwards when he knew of the good ways of the white men, and the white people of reading who were at Hoima, he said to the white people that they should come and teach his people wisdom because their way of doing things was good.[15]

All Awic was asking for was for reading to be taught, since that had certain advantages under the colonial regime. Lloyd later laboured under an equally serious illusion about Ojigi, whose request he described thus:

> I too have longed for teachers to be sent to my country . . . we heard long ago that the Banyoro and the Baganda had learned to worship the white man's God . . . Do you think that we should mind the destruction of our old and worn out customs of religion, if you provide us with good food that shall strengthen our souls?[16]

The last sentence of this request in particular would seem to be beyond even the most imaginative interpreter's rephrasing of Ojigi's remarks, and due only to Lloyd's own hopeful interpretation of the situation.[17] Events were to show that the destruction of their customs of religion was something that the Acoli did not want at all, and it was most unfortunate that the CMS missionaries entered Acoli under such a serious misapprehension.

At any rate, when Lloyd received Awic's delegation, he heard in it a divine call, for the evangelizing of Acoli had already been on his mind. Contact with Bito and with Lwoo people who lived in the north of Bunyoro had already made him aware of the links between Acoli and Bunyoro, and he tells us that as he himself had not been free to go to Acoli, he had sent the Rev. Nuwa Nakiwafu to see if he could gain entrance, but Nakiwafu had had to turn back before he even reached the Nile, because of sickness and other difficulties.[18] So Lloyd now decided that he himself would set out on an exploratory journey, and he took with him as an interpreter a young teacher of Alur birth, who was named Sira Dongo.[19] The Alur are very closely related to the Acoli and their languages are mutually intelligible. Sira Dongo later played an important part in the planting of Christianity in Acoli and Lango.

Dongo's story is an interesting one. He was born about 1880 to Katere, wife of Anywalo To,[20] and was the third of five children, and the only boy amongst them. The family lived at Erusi[21] on what is now the border between Zaire and the West Nile District of Uganda, and Katere died of smallpox whilst Dongo was still a child. The district in which they lived was raided from time to time by Kabalega's soldiers, and in one such raid Dongo and two of his sisters, Katuku and Anyumba, were captured. They were taken to Bunyoro by a man called Bakarunga, who noticed that Dongo was intelligent and hard-working, so made him his gun-bearer, and took Katuku as a wife.[22] In 1899 when Kabalega was captured in South Lango, Bakarunga was with them, but escaped capture and returned to Bunyoro.[23] Bakarunga owed a debt to a Ganda for ten guns he had bought, and paid the debt by handing over Dongo. The Ganda concerned was named Enoka Mutalebwa, who, as a Christian, should not, of course, have owned a slave, but probably did not think of Dongo in those terms anyway: it was common among the Ganda for parents to send their child to be brought up in someone else's household, and a better-off household would probably include several such youngsters, as well as some boys or girls taken prisoner in warfare, and attached to the household of their captor. If they did well, they might eventually achieve quite a good position in society. Dongo went with Mutalebwa to church, carrying his master's bag of books, and began to attend catechism classes. He also learnt Luganda. He returned to Bunyoro in 1901 when Jemusi Miti, a Ganda, was sent to take up a senior chieftaincy in Bunyoro, and Mutalebwa—and therefore Dongo also—accompanied him. Not long after this he began to work in the household of a missionary, Mr Farthing, and again attended catechism classes.

In 1902 he decided to return to Alur country to make contact with his family. He received a great welcome from Anywalo To and from his clan, and the people got together a bride-price (and presumably a bride), in order to encourage him to marry and settle down among them. He refused their offer, saying that he wanted to marry a

Christian girl. They then offered him the position of a sub-chief. (*Won Paco*) hoping thus to bind him to his clan again, but he refused this also. His long absence from home and his contacts with the new order of things must have greatly weakened his clan ties, and to remain in Alur country would have meant giving up all further chances of education and of getting on. So he returned to Hoima and was baptized there on 3 May 1903, taking the name Sira (Silas), and immediately afterwards he was accepted as a teacher and sent on his first teaching assignment.[24] Later in 1903 we find him wanting to marry an Alur girl, and he brought her to baptism classes. She was baptized the following year, taking the name Lucira, and they were married on 11 May 1905.[25] To find the reason for the delay in marriage, we must go back to the occasion in 1903 when the five Acoli came to Lloyd in Hoima asking for teachers, and Sira Dongo went on safari with Lloyd to Acoli.

This first journey to Acoli was made during the rains: the rivers were swollen, the swamps were full and difficult to cross, and undergrowth was dense in the forested areas. After a difficult crossing of the Nile and a bad storm, the porters wanted to go home when faced with yet another river so swollen that the trees they felled in an effort to bridge it fell short and were washed away. Sira Dongo swam the river and persuaded a crowd of Acoli to help them.[26] The first village they came to north of this river was Ojigi's,[27] where Lloyd remained for about a week, 'each day being fully occupied with talking to the people, giving out medicine to the sick, and occasional lantern shows at night . . .'[28] From Ojigi's the party followed a rather indirect route to the home of Obwona Acoli (called by Lloyd Bon Acholi's), previously *ladom* (interpreter) for the Sudanese garrisons which had been in the area: Lloyd took him for a chief.[29] His village was at Keyo, about seven miles west of Gulu. From there the group travelled north to Atiak where they met *Rwot* Olia, and then they went on to Nimule on the Nile, today right on the Sudan/Uganda border. Here Lloyd met *Rwot* Awic, but only briefly: Awic was in trouble with the administration and Lloyd was annoyed to find that he had been taken into custody, and that he could not have further conversation with him. From Nimule they journeyed quickly southward to cross back over the Nile at Pajao near the Murchison Falls. As a result of this journey Lloyd concluded that Acoliland was calm enough for missionaries to enter, and that some chiefs at least would welcome catechists. Bishop Tucker agreed to the sending of missionaries, but wanted to see the situation for himself and help select the site for the mission. So a safari was arranged, and in 1904

Dr and Mrs Cook and the bishop set out from Mengo and were joined eight days later by Lloyd at Hoima. They had the permission of the Commissioner to undertake the journey, but were told they must travel at their own risk.[30]

The safari was long remembered in Acoli because of Dr Cook's activities. He treated some 3,575 patients for syphilis, bronchial troubles, eye and skin diseases, but he saw little malaria.[31] In spite of their eagerness for medicine, the people wondered if the white pills, which they called lizards' eggs, could do any good, since they had been administered without the correct accompanying rituals:

> The medicine was very strange to them. Usually, whenever they went to the witchdoctor, he would take a hoe and go into the bush, and then the medicine was brought, and he asked for a hen. The hen was to bless the medicine, and the sick man had to bring a hen with him, or something in the way of a gift. And after blessing the medicine, then it was given to him. But now there was no one who asked for that thing, and so all the people wondered.[32]

Bishop Tucker did not feel that Ojigi's village was central enough for a mission station, so they went to Obwona Acoli's, which appeared to be an ideal site. Cook wrote delightedly of it, and of the friendliness of the people.[33] The first missionaries to come here called the place Patiko after the clan which lived around Keyo. Patiko where Baker had his fort lies some fifteen miles to the north-west.

In December Tucker wrote to Baylis, the CMS Lay Secretary, appealing urgently for men to assist in opening up the mission in northern Uganda, which he suggested should be called 'The Mission on the Upper Nile'. He envisaged a chain of three more mission stations stretching northwards from Keyo up into the Sudan, and he took it for granted that the work which CMS was about to open in the Sudan would be based on the Uganda Mission. He felt this would be advantageous for two reasons: firstly because of the experience gained by the Uganda Mission in opening up new areas, and secondly because of the help Ganda evangelists would be able to give.[34] It came as a great blow to Bishop Tucker to learn that the Sudan Mission would be an entirely separate entity, and have no connection with the Uganda Mission.[35] As a matter of fact the church in Uganda did, over a period of many years, send a number of catechists to help in work in the Sudan. In the early years they were Ganda, but later Acoli were recruited for this work. It is unlikely that Ganda would have adapted themselves successfully to work there, but the decision that the Sudan should have an independent mission had serious repercussions on the evangelizing of Acoli. Keyo lost its strategic importance in the eyes of Uganda missionaries, and instead of being a vital link in a chain, it became a far-flung outpost, with unfortunate results.

Sira Dongo accompanied this safari also, again acting as an interpreter, and when Tucker and the Cooks returned, leaving Lloyd in Acoli to start immediately with opening up the new station, Sira stayed with him to help in teaching and translating. There was also another young Alur called Adimola who helped with interpreting. He came from Nebbi[36] in West Nile, and had joined the *barusura,* Kabalega's warrior force, and settled in northern Bunyoro where he married. He subsequently got into trouble with his wife's clan and took refuge with the mission from his matrimonial difficulties, having told them a sorry tale about being a slave whose life was endangered. He subsequently became a sub-chief in Acoli, and his descendants were completely integrated into Acoli society.[37] He was not yet baptized when Lloyd took him to Acoli. Another catechist who helped at this early stage of the Acoli mission was Yohanna Murusura. He was a Nyoro of good birth, and he went to work at the headquarters of Owiny of Pugwenyi who apparently did not really want him at all, and created difficulties. Other catechists stayed with Olia of Atiak and Ojigi of Alokolum, and also met with difficulties.[38] Some claimed to have been imprisoned.[39] The people made up insulting jokes about them and called them 'banana Europeans' because of the *matoke* (cooked banana) which they ate. The Acoli also made up songs which were doubtless both apt and catchy, for the Acoli are gifted at making up such songs about those they despise.[40] The links between the Payira clan and the Bito of Bunyoro did not mean that everyone in Acoli welcomed Nyoro catechists, and both Olia and Ojigi belonged to semi-subjugated clans. Some of the Nyoro catechists became discouraged and went home, but Murusura persisted. He returned briefly to Bunyoro to get married, but then brought his wife to Acoli with him,[41] and later worked in Lango where he is remembered as an outstanding teacher.[42]

Two European missionaries were sent to help Lloyd in the founding of the mission at Keyo, the Rev. A. E. Pleydell and the Rev. A. L. Kitching, the latter to take special responsibility for language work. A good beginning was made with translations in 1904. Sira Dongo worked from the Luganda Bible, putting it into Alur, and this was then put into Acoli. By the beginning of November a reading-sheet, a hymn, parts of the Prayer Book and half of St

Mark's Gospel had been translated. The first complete Acoli gospel was published by the British and Foreign Bible Society in 1905.[43] Whilst making this translation, Kitching found himself in difficulties because there seemed to be no Acoli word for 'God'. At first the missionaries spoke in Runyoro, and Dongo and Adimola in Alur. Probably those who translated from Runyoro simply repeated the Runyoro name for God, *Ruhanga.* In 1904 Kitching stated that he could find no Acoli word for 'God', 'create', or 'Creator', and that the Runyoro word *Ruhanga* signifying 'God' had had to be 'adapted' (sic).[44] The adaptation was an unfortunate one—the Runyoro *Ruhanga/Luhanga* (l and r are almost interchangeable) was perpetuated in Acoli as *Lubanga.*[45] But in Acoli *Lubanga* signified the *jok* (spirit) responsible for giving a person tuberculosis of the spine.[46] Today *Lubanga* seems to be firmly entrenched in its new meaning of Creator God, and the reactions of those who first heard the missionaries' preaching can only be guessed at.

Catechism classes and services were held at Keyo, and between forty and eighty people attended them, mostly men, but also a few small boys. Kitching noticed that Awic and a few of the others seemed really keen to learn to read, but showed no interest in the content of the Christian teaching given, and no desire to leave their old customs or their drinking, which gives us a clue as to how the gospel was presented.[47] However, on Christmas Eve, 1904, the first three men were admitted as catechumens. One was Ali, son of Gimoro, a prominent Acoli in the time of Baker. The other two were Nyoro who had come to Acoli as children and grown up there. These three were the result of Yohana Murusura's teaching at Pugwenyi.[48] Ali was baptized in November 1906, taking the name Muca (Moses), and with him was baptized Lakobo Ameda.[49] Muca Ali's baptism caused an uproar. He had two wives and had been required to send away one. The people thought him mad for he sent away his second wife, keeping his first wife who was barren, whereas the second had borne him a son. They made up songs about him saying what a fool he was to keep only a woman who could be no use to him at all.[50] The *CMS Annual Report* records: 'Mr Kitching baptized two of the catechumens in December,[51] but it was evident that the polygamy customary among the Gang would prove an obstacle in the way of admission of some of the tribe into the visible church.'[52]

The year 1905-6 was an encouraging one. The missionaries intervened in a clan feud, and were apparently successful in bringing about a peaceful settlement, and the people expressed gratitude. The colonial administration's headquarters were moved to Keyo and many chiefs and their retainers came also, and the number showing an interest in the teaching of the mission increased.[53] But an apparently small development was ultimately of more significance. The missionaries approached the chiefs, and a number agreed as a result to send their sons to live with Pleydell and receive an education. By the end of the year there were ten, and others followed later. The chiefs were made responsible for building houses for these boys to live in and for supplying them with food, and the boys did some work for Pleydell as houseboys.[54] The agreement was that each chief should send two of his sons, but in fact most sent only one of his own sons, and to make up the number sent one of the boys who lived in the household: this was less dangerous than risking two of his own sons in an unproven venture. *Rwot* Awic sent Aliker who was his own son, and Obwoya, one of his young retainers. *Rwot* Lagony of Koic did the same thing: Kibwola was his own son, but the second boy, Oyugi, was not. Others who sent their sons were *Rwot* Akelo of Patiko who sent Lagara, *Rwot* Ogwal of Puranga who sent Owiny and Oboga, and Okelomwaka who sent Olal and Otuke. Okelomwaka was not a *Rwot,* though he was a man of importance who had served Kabalega as an emissary to the Sudan, and had there learned some Arabic. He had also visited Mombasa when he had travelled with Major Delmé-Radcliffe to the coast. Both his sons became *Rwodi.* Ayong',clan-elder of Pugwenyi, sent Olok; Obwona Acoli sent Dony (later killed in a clan feud) and Odur; Aboga, the clan-elder of Patiko, sent Oryem and Odongpiny; and *Rwot* Latigo of Paico sent Odur. All these, except the two sons of Ogwal of Puranga, were baptized between 1906 and 1908. Two other Acoli boys were also baptized in these years, Culoman Okelokoko (who had been brought up in the household of Owiny of Pugwenyi) and Elia Lukwi. Two of Adimola's 'boys' were baptized in 1906, and a few infants, and no one else at all.[55] The importance of the chiefs' sons sent to Keyo to be educated is clear.

It is also clear that from the very beginning mission work in Acoli followed a different pattern from that in the Bantu kingdoms. The lack of interest of the chiefs forced the missionaries to turn to their sons. The older generation in Acoli had little interest, either at this early stage or later, in Christianity, and a new beginning had to be made with the younger generation. It is true that even in the Bantu kingdoms of Uganda the hereditary rulers were in every case new men, but some of the older chiefs, Byabacwezi, for example, were converted to Christianity, and there were strong links with the past. An attempt was made to graft Christianity on to the old structure.

Nothing of the sort happened in Acoli, and the missionaries were disappointed. They looked for a Constantine, and, failing to find one, did not explore the strengths of their position, but regarded it as a second best, and the non-Bantu areas as inferior to the kingdom states with their semi-established Anglican church. For this reason as well as the loss of strategic importance, Acoli eventually became a backwater.

A third setback to the Acoli mission had yet to occur. Despite the initial friendly welcome from the Acoli, the missionaries were never fully accepted. In May 1905 the work suffered when Pleydell accidentally shot a woman. Not surprisingly the station was for a time deserted, but the people slowly came back.[56] About a year later it emerged that both Kitching and Pleydell had temporarily been persuaded into acting for the Collector, 'giving out wages, hearing cases, and threatening the rioters'. This brought a severe reprimand from Roscoe, the Mission Secretary, who pointed out that such action was contrary to mission regulations.[57] It certainly did not help the mission in the eyes of the Acoli, and witnesses to a confusion in the minds of the missionaries concerned about the nature of their mission. There are not as many documented instances of this sort of collaboration with government as one might expect from the accusations brought against the missions by people today, and the missions' not infrequent remonstrations with government are seldom heard about. Their attitude, however, was quickly noticed by Africans, even though it perhaps did not often translate itself into overt action. In the following year the government station was moved to Wadelai on the Nile, and the Acoli hinted to the missionaries that now the government was no longer at hand to support them they too would be forced to move. The incident had not been lost on the Acoli.[58] The possibility of such a move was very much on the missionaries' minds, and was several times discussed by the mission committee in Mengo.[59] Other troubles beset the mission at Keyo: the hill was more than once struck by lightning; the missionaries were unwell; Obwona Acoli who had supported them had died; the people had begun to move away from the neighbourhood of Keyo; and at the end of 1907 Bishop Tucker decided to withdraw the missionaries.[60] The fact that Keyo was no longer to be considered as a link in a chain of missions reaching into the Sudan may have influenced his decision. It was perhaps the most serious mistake he made in mission strategy.

The reason for the unpopularity of the mission and for the people's movement away from Keyo has still not been fully explained, however. The accidental shooting and the alignment of the mission with the administration were only a part of the cause. Bishop Russell who worked in Northern Uganda uncovered a more serious reason for fear and hostility on the part of the people; one which the missionaries of the time did not realize. What actually precipitated matters seems to have been a storm that blew up over some cinematograph pictures and phonograph records of Acoli dancing and singing which the missionaries had made. They expected these to be a great success, but they were received in a silence which the missionaries interpreted as indifference, but which was really fear. An Acoli explained the occasion as follows:

> When the people heard the voice of dead people singing and saw their shadows in the picture walking, talking and blowing whistles and horns, they were very afraid. They thought that the white man was *capturing the shadows* of the people to take them to their own country; which would mean that these people died. From that time the people began to run away from the white man.[61]

The expression translated 'capturing the shadows'—*mako tipo*—is the name for a variety of malevolent witchcraft.[62] When one man shouted out, 'This is better than our own *ajwagi* (diviners); it is better than the shrines where we remember our ancestors' they were furious and some sort of fight ensued. Here was the real trouble—fear that the Europeans had a power superior to that of their own *ajwagi*, and with malevolent intentions. When lightning struck Keyo Hill and illness struck the missionaries, the Acoli must have seen in this the confirmation of their fears that the foreigners were evil.

But how to deal with such a situation? Clearly the white men had great power and open opposition would be useless. They fell back on a ruse the Patiko clan had used before when they could bear the extortions of the Egyptian garrisons no more[63]—they made the excuse that the land was no longer fertile, and one by one they moved away, and the missionaries accepted this reason as genuine. When the administration was moved from Keyo nearer to the Nile to control possible Belgian infiltration, the chiefs had a further reason to leave Keyo. The missionaries were given a wide berth, and eventually found the situation intolerable. In Teso people were said to be crying out for missionaries, so it was decided they should leave.[64]

There is no doubt that most of the Acoli were glad to see them go. The people refused to provide porters to help with the move, and these had to be sent from Bunyoro. When the missionaries had left, the deserted buildings were looted.[65] So far the mission would appear to have been largely a failure. Only a handful of converts had been won, mostly boys, and the missionaries left without making any provision for these.

3

THE INTERIM: 1908-1912

In January 1908 it was on these converts that the wrath of the Acoli fell. The reaction was such as one might expect from badly frightened people:

> At the time when the white men left, people hated the readers very bitterly. One day at two o'clock in the afternoon they were in the house of Oor reading when the people of Kerio's house came and attacked them, beat them very severely, and destroyed all their books. Among the people who were reading were Latigo [the writer] who had a bangle round his neck. When they beat him, they wrenched the bangle off his neck and stabbed him with it in the chest so that he nearly died. The reason why the readers were beaten was that they still wanted to go on reading although the white man had gone.[66]

One chief was so angry with his son for continuing to read that he shot and killed him. Muca Ali was nearly killed at this time. The trouble arose because he had no *abila* (shrine where the spirits of ancestors were remembered) in his homestead, and because he insisted on going to the church every Sunday. His clansmen tried to stop him and attempted to force him to build an *abila*. They came together and attacked him and nearly beat him to death 'because he was building another kind of *abila* which they did not understand'. After this he had to separate his home from the houses of his clansfolk and he spent much of his time alone.[67] From what one can discover about the next year or two, it seems that Muca Ali stood almost alone and kept the faith alive and the few Christians together. 'He fought hard to keep the fires of religion burning.'[68]

When the missionaries left, all the catechists left too except, possibly, a Nyoro called Yokana Nyuta who seems to have remained in the household of Ali Abete, son of Obwona Acoli.[69] Ali Abete had moved to Laminang'ol, a few miles to the north of Keyo, after

Obwona's death, and when the missionaries would not themselves move to this new homestead, a catechist was sent there and a small church built. Nyuta did a little teaching at Laminang'ol, but he did not succeed in mastering the Acoli language, and an ability to speak the language recommends a man to the Acoli as nothing else will. Nor did he get on very well with the people because he was neither very sociable nor very active.[70] He seems to have been too diffident to be a good mixer. One can only admire his perseverance, for he seems to have come to Acoli in 1904 and remained until the end of 1912.[71]

In January 1909 Sira Dongo was sent back to Acoli from Masindi with Obadia Jaganda. Jaganda was an Alur and he had first come with the missionaries in 1904 as a porter.[72] These two would both have a great advantage over Yokana Nyuta in that they would be able to make themselves understood to the people in Alur, if not in Acoli. The first thing Dongo did on arrival was to start building a small house for himself and a small church at Bung'atira, slightly to the east of Gulu. The people were afraid that this meant the return of the white men, and put up considerable opposition. One man came threatening to beat Dongo, but Dongo's quiet refusal to be provoked shamed the man into going away.[73] After the departure of the British administration to the edge of Acoli country, clan feuds had broken out again, and despite Dongo's efforts at peace-making, there was a fight between the people of Purang'a and the people of Patiko in September 1909 in which about seventy-five people were killed, including Nuwa Dony, son of Obwona Acoli, and one of the first Christians.[74] In these difficult circumstances it is not surprising that Dongo did not find many catechumens to teach, but he did find and prepare for baptism four boys, three of whom, Yosiya Okelomwaka, Jedekiya Igito and Edwadi Kija, were to become reliable and active church leaders for many years.[75] They were not baptized until September 1910 when Dongo had already been back in Masindi for some months. The four candidates had to walk a round journey of 200 miles for baptism.

Meanwhile back in Masindi where he had been recalled, Dongo did not find things easy. He had been recalled in February 1910 to be head-teacher, but the Rev. H. W. Tegart who had recently been transferred to Masindi could not get on with him.[76] Tegart took over the headship of the school, and Dongo, hurt and disappointed, went off to Kitgum as a trader, and was offered a job as a government clerk at a wage of sixty shillings a month, which he accepted for a time, until his wife persuaded him to return to work for the church.[77] Tegart's lack of sympathy for Dongo may have extended to his pupils. Against the names of the baptism candidates from Acoli whom Dongo had trained, Tegart wrote, 'Weak in ideas of sin. Also weak in gospels. They did not know how sin was remitted.'[78] There is no other comment of this kind anywhere else in the Register. When Tegart visited Acoli in 1911 he is remembered as having been very angry with Muca Ali for not having begun to teach his small son, Andereya Aluku, to read.[79]

When Sira Dongo was recalled to Masindi in 1910, he was replaced by two catechists from Bunyoro, Petero Bitaka and Yonosani Balikwata.[80] These went to the home of Muca Ali, who introduced them to the country and helped them to learn the language, as he did for many of the catechists from Bunyoro.[81] Petero Bitaka was the senior of the two new catechists—it was some months before Balikwata's name appears in the Service Book as having taken part in leading a church service, and it is Bitaka whom people remember. They held services regularly every Sunday, both morning and afternoon, in the little church that Dongo had built, and the congregation numbered from six to twenty-eight, and was usually fewer than fifteen. They did not find any new candidates to prepare for baptism, though they must have completed the teaching of the four whom Dongo had found. Occasionally one of the Acoli converts preached at a Sunday service: in September Muca Oryem's name appears several times (Bitaka seems to be away at this point, and he had probably accompanied the catechumens to Masindi), and towards the end of the year we also find the names of Jakayo Odur and Muca Ali. In the following April Edwada Kija and Jedekiya Igito, two of those who had just been baptized at Masindi, appear as preachers, and for both of them this was the beginning of many years of service to the church.

Balikwata and Bitaka remained in Acoli for a year, and then returned to Bunyoro. In January 1911 Sira Dongo paid a visit, and a record congregation of forty people came to hear him preach on 15 January. Yokana Nyuta now came to take the place of Balikwata and Bitaka, and worked alone until May. Few people attended the services, and one can only admire his tenacity for he never missed taking a service. Then in May 1911 things improved considerably with the arrival of a senior catechist called Abimereke Lukyalekere. This man was an outstanding catechist who is still remembered with love and gratitude. For the past few years he had been in the Seychelles with the exiled Kabalega who had specially requested that he should go and teach him there.[82] The numbers of those attending church services now rose, and varied between seventeen and sixty.

On one occasion 105 came—the Service Book offers no clue as to the reason for this. Abimereke also began to prepare another group for baptism, four of whom were baptized by the Rev. H. A. Brewer in Masindi in January 1912, whilst another two were ready for baptism in October of the same year when Brewer visited Gulu.[83] Abimereke continued to work as a catechist for many years and was later ordained. One reason for his success was that he learnt the language really well. He was taught by Lacito Okech, and taught Okech Runyoro in return. He came to Acoli with his wife, Eseri, but they had no children, and Eseri was difficult to get to know.[84] Abimereke's personality as well as his ability made him beloved of the people. He is remembered as being always humble and kind, and one who never quarrelled with people or got angry. He commanded the respect of his pupils, and his class would always be ready and silent on his arrival. He would invite his pupils into his house to eat with him, and unlike some other catechists, he would serve them since they were his guests, instead of expecting them to wait on him. One man said of him, 'In his speech, you could see Jesus there.' He also had a passion for cleanliness, and pupils who kept themselves and their clothes clean won his approval and the privilege of carrying his books for him.[85]

The year 1912 saw an increase of CMS interest in Acoli, as well as a greater interest among the Acoli in the instruction being given. The reason for the improvement in the situation is not far to seek. The first Catholic missionaries of the Verona Fathers Mission arrived in northern Uganda at the very end of 1909, and early in 1910 they opened their first mission at Omach on the Nile.[86] Northern Uganda had been their goal for half a century. They had established work in Sudan and had gradually made their way southwards to Acoli. In the late 19th century their progress had been impeded by a horrifying rate of sickness and death, and then by the Mahdist rising. At Omach they probably did not seem to constitute much of a threat to the abandoned work in Acoli, but when in February 1911 they moved to Gulu where the British administration had recently been established, things looked rather different. First Abimereke Lukyalekere, a senior catechist, was sent; later European CMS missionaries visited for the first time since they had left Keyo, and then in February 1913 the CMS returned to Acoli, eventually settling at Gulu on a site between that of the Verona Fathers Mission and the government site, and the Fishers were appointed to this mission. They do not seem to have met with any opposition.[87] The reopening of the mission by the CMS was encouraged by the colonial government, and the Verona Fathers quickly felt themselves discriminated against.[88]

What factors led to the increased African interest in and tolerance of, the mission? A number of different elements in the situation need to be borne in mind. The Lamogi rebellion which took place in 1912 demonstrated the uselessness of further resistance to European rule, and the moving of the seat of administration back to Gulu was a reassertion of British power.[89]. The presence of a rival Christian mission would certainly stimulate interest. It is frequently asserted that if there had been no rivalry between the different Christian churches, the Christian gospel could have been spread more effectively: it is never possible to say one way or another what *might* have happened *if* . . . but there is evidence that competition sometimes spurred the different missions to make greater efforts than they would have done otherwise, and the reopening of the CMS mission at Gulu would seem to be a case in point. A third factor which may possibly have added to the attractions of the CMS mission for a time is that the Verona Fathers were known as Khartoumers for some years after their arrival in northern Uganda. This was probably because they came along the Nile route and their mission headquarters were at Khartoum. Is it possible that the wearing of white soutanes reminded the Acoli of the dress of the Arabs? Eventually the government forbade the people to go on using this damaging nickname.[90] Undoubtedly also the perseverance of the catechists who had continued the work in Acoli in the absence of European missionaries, and the lead given by men like Muca Ali had an effect and helped to win the trust of the Acoli.

Sira Dongo returned with the Fishers, and there were soon quite a number of catechists from Bunyoro including Yokana Murusura who had returned, and Yucito Magezi, who did particularly good work. Regular teaching was started, and by the end of the year a number of chiefs had asked for catechists to work in their areas. Kitgum had been opened as a centre of Christian activity, and some Acoli Christians had gone to Lango as catechists.[91] Fisher supervised the building of a new church just below the present Gulu High School. The catechists' houses were grouped round the church, and the missionaries' houses were on the bluff of a hill about half a mile away.[92] On 18 May 1913 the first service was held in the new church, and on 3 July four hundred people attended its official opening. Later in the year Bishop Willis came to Acoli and confirmed six people, Muca Ali being one of them.[93]

4

1913: THE MISSION RE-OPENED.

The reopening of the mission in 1913 began a new decade in the life of the Anglican church in Acoli, and this was to be different in character from the first. It was a decade of steady, though not spectacular, growth. Although it falls largely outside the scope of this study, something must be said about it because one of the most marked features of the church which was developing during these years was the extent of its rootedness in the pattern of things already established. Firstly a weakness seems to have remained, resulting from the fact that the conflict between the new Christian faith and the traditional practices of the Acoli had never been brought to a head or a conclusion, except in the lives of a few people, the most notable being Muca Ali. In the moment of crisis the missionaries had withdrawn; when they came back the storm had blown itself out. Apart from the removal of a diviner who lived next door to the church compound and who was carrying on his practices in a manner which embarrassed the Christians, there is no record of further conflict between the new and the old, and in view of the initial trouble, this is remarkable.[94] Because of the arrogance with which the European culture was thrust on Africans during the colonial era, and the often tactless confusion of the Christian gospel with hygiene and western technology, there is today an over-emphasis on the need for Christianity to be linked with the past, and an attempt, which is sometimes misguided, to show that traditional African religious beliefs are compatible with Christianity. Early converts to Christianity saw the incompatibility more clearly than those who are two or more generations removed from traditional practices unmodified by contact with outside influences. Muca Ali saw the incompatibility and so did his clansmen. There is evidence from a number of different areas that Christianity took root better where this conflict was clear, and involved converts making a decided and costly stand as innovators than in areas where the issue was never dealt with.[95] A study of the conversion of Europe shows the constant tension between the need to assert the uniqueness of Christianity and the need to integrate existing social structures into the new framework. It has been well said that the penalty for refusing to look at history is that history has to be relived. In Acoli the issue of the relation between the old and the new was simply shelved, to the great bewilderment of Acoli people today.[96]

Secondly the church in Acoli continued to depend to a marked extent on the leadership of those who had been baptized prior to 1913, and did not produce a new generation of leaders to succeed them. The total number of Acoli baptized before 1913 was thirty-six. Thirteen of these became chiefs, the majority being *Rwodi*, senior chiefs. Two of the chiefs were also members of the church council, and three others started to work as catechists but had to give this up when they became chiefs. These chiefs played an important part in giving a lead to others and by helping in the establishment of church centres, but they did not have the sort of influence over their people as chiefs in other areas of Uganda. A further four men, Muca Ali, Bartolomayo Kalokwera, Culoman Okelokoko and Yosiya Okelomwaka, became the foremost leaders of the church—none of these had been son of a chief. Another man, Muca Kibwola, was among the first catechists to go to Lango, but he died after a year or two.[97] Jakayo Odur taught in Lango for many years.[98] Against the names of a further five in the Baptism Register is a note to say that they have died, and these notes seem to have been written within a few years of the mission's return to Acoli. The remainder do not appear, from such records as remain, to have played a very important part in either local or church life. After 1913 a few other Acoli came to the fore, notably Nikodemo Latigo who had been stabbed in the chest with his bangle, but the onus of leadership lay on Muca Ali and Sira Dongo.

A third strongly marked characteristic of the Acoli church was its continued dependence on catechists from Bunyoro. This was due, at least in part, to the chronic shortage of missionaries: there were seldom more than two, and sometimes only one right up to the mid 1920s.[99] This shortage was largely due to World War I. Because there were so few missionaries it was impossible for them to form a self-sufficient European community apart from the local community, and as a result they were very close to the Acoli people. Each of these missionaries—H. T. Wright, P. H. Lees, E. C. Davies, and Canon T. L. Lawrence—was loved and respected, and people talk of the good old days when these people were still among them. It is greatly to the credit of the church in Bunyoro that it continued for a number of years to supply catechists in Acoli, but the fact that the Acoli Church learnt to lean so heavily on imported help is less satisfactory. For instance, when Acoli catechists were first sent to Kitgum, each Acoli was sent as an interpreter and assistant to a catechist from Bunyoro, and sometimes he hardly acted on his own initiative at all.[100] The catechists from Bunyoro preached regularly in Gulu church, ran many out-schools, were members of the Church Council, and occupied positions of leadership. Catechists from Bunyoro were acceptable in Acoli as catechists from Buganda were not acceptable in the areas to which they went. No one could think that the Nyoro had imperialist aims, since they more than most of the peoples of Uganda were a conquered people. But the Acoli therefore had less urge to become catechists themselves, and this resulted in a serious weakness in the church.

Perhaps because Sira Dongo was such a good leader he too came to be relied upon too much. On him fell much of the burden of travelling and supervision of catechists, especially after he was ordained in 1917. He was given a bicycle, and later acquired a small car to help him travel round his huge parish.[101] He was renowned for his hospitality and generosity, and his house was always full of visitors. He was never short of food for all these visitors because he was hardworking and so was his wife, and because people would try to repay his kindness to them by helping him to cultivate.[102] Many people speak of his practical sympathy and his helpfulness to those who were in trouble. His sense of fun and humour also recommended him to the Acoli people.[103] He too had a passion for cleanliness, and encouraged the people to clean up the places from which they drew their drinking water, and to build bathing places in their homesteads.[104] Muca Ali was Dongo's friend and co-worker, but died suddenly on safari in 1929 just before he was to have been ordained.[105]

There was a dearth of catechists able to instruct people for confirmation, and between 1913 and 1922 only four confirmation services were held. In 1916 only sixteen people made their Easter Communion in Gulu, and owing to the lack of clergy, this may have been the only Easter Communion held in the whole of Acoli that year.[106] It is difficult to obtain numbers of those who were confirmed, but it is clear that a church was coming into being composed almost entirely of people who had not achieved the status of full membership. One gets the impression that confirmation was an optional extra for the few. Many catechists were not confirmed, and in their isolated places of work they would, in any case, have had little opportunity of receiving the sacrament.

The outbreak of war in 1914 was a serious setback to the work of the missions in Acoli as everywhere else. War was followed by economic depression and a failure of nerve regarding the missionary vocation, so that the numbers of missionaries remained small. The Verona Fathers Mission was able to staff its missions better than the

CMS and also had more stations, but both missions were disappointed with their achievements, and other causes must be found for this than a lack of missionaries. Among these may be the use of an inappropriate term for the name of God, but more important would seem to be the nature of Acoli traditional religious beliefs, and the inability of Christians to find an adequate presentation of Christianity in these circumstances. The Acoli quickly saw that reading and writing could be obtained without the learner becoming a Christian, or at any rate without his committing himself beyond the initial stage of baptism—hence the lack of people going on to prepare themselves for confirmation in the Anglican Church. The negative moralistic approach of the first preaching can have made little sense to the Acoli, and they do not seem to have felt the need of the salvationist teaching of Christianity in the way that some other peoples with different attitudes did.

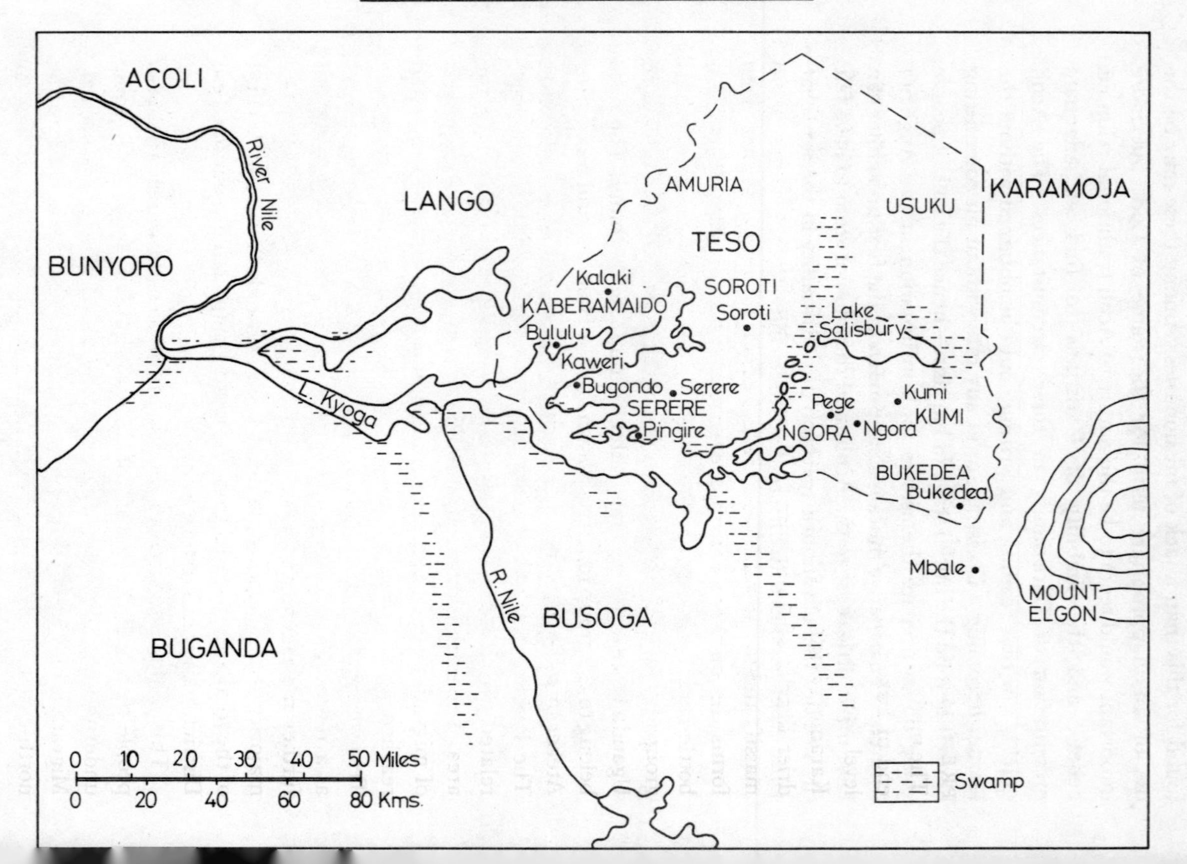
TESO AND ADJACENT AREAS
ACOLI
River Nile
LANGO
AMURIA
USUKU
KARAMOJA
TESO
BUNYORO
Kalaki
SOROTI
KABERAMAIDO
Soroti
Lake Salisbury
Bululu
Kaweri
Bugondo
Serere
SERERE
Pingire
Pege
Kumi
KUMI
NGORA
Ngora
L. Kyoga
BUKEDEA
Bukedea
Mbale
MOUNT ELGON
R. Nile
BUSOGA
BUGANDA
0 10 20 30 40 50 Miles
0 20 40 60 80 Kms.
Swamp

Chapter VI
Teso

1

PRE-COLONIAL BACKGROUND

The modern Teso District lies around Lake Salisbury and the eastern end of Lake Kyoga. The whole area lies under 4,000 feet above sea-level, and except along its northern and eastern border with Karamoja is fairly evenly populated. To the north-east lies the much drier district of Karamoja; to the south-east lies the Mount Elgon massif, and to the south-west the Lake Kyoga drainage system. Teso forms the northern end of a migration corridor where there is a bottle-neck between natural obstacles, and a mass of small ethnic groups is clustered just to the south of Teso. In this area of eastern Uganda three different major ethnic groupings are found. The Teso belong to the group formerly known as Nilo-Hamites, and now called Ateker by some scholars.[1] The Karimojong also belong to this group. The Padhola just to the south are Nilotic, Lwoo-speaking people, related to the Acoli. There are also Bantu-speaking groups in the area. The establishment of colonial rule brought to an end a process of migration which had been going on for centuries, and which had reached a point where the migration corridor was blocked by the Teso who settled in its northern end. Conflict had begun to break out as a result. The British caused the whole position to congeal, and further movement and jostling for living space was checked. The majority of the Teso people today live in Uganda, but about a third of the total are separated from the main group, and live outside Teso District, mostly in Western Kenya.[2]

This is not the place to discuss the process by which the Teso people reached the areas which they inhabit today, but some understanding of their background and social structure is needed. Migration into Teso District from the drier, less fertile lands to the north-east had taken place over a long period, possibly as long as three centuries, and there is still much that is uncertain about the chronology of the settlement of the different areas.[3] In about 1830 a major influx of people into Teso District occurred when the state of Woropom to the east was overrun by the Karimojong, and the people fled westward and took refuge among the Teso to whom they were quickly assimilated. Parts of Amuria and Serere counties were still receiving new Teso immigrants as late as the first half of the twentieth century, whilst during the nineteenth century some Teso moved still further west into Busoga and across the Nile into north Bugerere. In these areas the Teso were assimilated to the Bantu, adopting their language, but retaining some Teso clan names.[4] The absorption of the Woropom, it is suggested, turned the Karimojong and Gisu into enemies of the Teso as population pressure built up and caused friction in disputed border territory.

Migration and settlement altered the pattern of living of the Teso as they turned from being primarily wandering pastoralists to becoming settled agriculturalists. The change seems to have occurred in part because people had lost their cattle through drought and famine, and in part because the more fertile lands into which they were attracted were better suited to the practice of agriculture. The Teso adopted the means of livelihood of the people who inhabited the land into which they moved, and with whom they mingled and gradually merged. During the nineteenth century they began to acquire iron hoes through trade with Bunyoro, and this led to greater efficiency in agriculture. The Woropom also came with a knowledge of blacksmithing. Even in Teso District the people were not immune from drought and famine, and some degree of famine is recorded every ten years or so. In the years 1894 to 1896 a very severe famine occurred, sometimes named after Okadaro, an *emuron* (foreteller) who fell from power after he had repeatedly tried to bring rain through the rainmaking ceremonies, and failed. The desperation of the people inflamed the growing hostility between the Teso on the one hand and the Karimojong and Gisu who were their neighbours on the other. Finally civil war broke out which probably originated in fighting over the possession of water-holes, but also had the seizure of cattle as a motive. Although the Teso had become agriculturalists, their wealth still consisted in the possession of cattle. As we shall see later, this war provided an easy opportunity for the Ganda who were acting as agents of the British in bringing Teso under colonial rule.

The process of migration together with the settling of the people to agriculture weakened the social organization of the Teso. This was originally based on a highly complex system of age-sets by which authority was vested in the more senior members of the clans who had slowly worked their way up to this grade, and who were closely bound together as a group. The system was very like that still found among the Karimojong. But at the beginning of this century this system, around which the whole social organization of the people cohered, was brought to an end in a matter of a few years when Kakungulu, the Ganda general who for a time administered Teso for the British, banned the holding of the initiation ceremonies in the southern part of Teso. It seems unlikely that he could have done this unless the hold of the age-sets over the people had already been weakened.[5]

The most important institution among the Teso after the age-sets was the clan. Webster thinks that the members of each clan originally lived together and that clans were territorial units.[6] During the migration period the clans were broken up and the territorial unit came to be made up of members of many clans. No over-all authority developed either for the clan or for the settlement, but a wider military authority was in process of forumulation at the time of the Ganda conquest and became the basis of the later administrative structure. The extraordinary difficulty experienced by colonial officials and others in finding the traditional authorities in Teso is understandable when it is realized that these were in the midst of change at the time when alien rule was being imposed.[7]

It is difficult to know how strong the Teso were militarily at the time of the Ganda conquest. They were glad enough to secure the help of the Ganda against the Langi, and they were also in some fear of Karimojong raids, then as now.[8] They had no source of iron, and, as we have seen, obtained iron hoes from the people of Bunyoro, or occasionally made them from old hoe heads reworked.[9] They did not put up a strong resistance to the Ganda, but could have put up a stronger defence had they not been divided by advice from some of the leading foretellers who prophesied the coming of 'butterflies' (taken to be a reference to the fluttering cloths of the Ganda) and advised against resistance.[10] In spite of the fighting recorded of the last part of the nineteenth century, the Teso are basically a peaceful people. When they realized there was little they could do about occupation by foreigners, they accepted the situation and set about making the best of it. They were less inclined to resistance than many of the peoples of East Africa. Older informants consistently maintain that on balance they benefited from contact with the Ganda. Younger men, perhaps more aware of current rivalries and politics, read their history somewhat differently. The Teso also show great adaptability which may be illustrated in a number of ways. Firstly, as they themselves will point out, the closely related Kumam have taken on much of the Lwoo language; a group of Teso in Budiope in Busoga have become largely assimilated to the Soga people; others have been absorbed into Padhola and Luo clans.[11] A further example is the way in which they have adapted to settled agriculture, and more recently to cotton cultivation. Again, as will be noted later, having accepted the inevitable in the shape of outside intervention, first by the Ganda and then by the British, they accepted the new situation with less resentment than other Ugandan peoples. The Teso appear to live mainly in the present and to attach little importance to historical memories; few people can remember the names of more than three generations of their ancestors; and since there was no centralized authority, there is no traditional historical myth to dominate the present.

2

MISSION INTEREST IN TESO IS AROUSED

The CMS first came to take an interest in Teso through the activities of the Ganda general, Semei Kakungulu, a Protestant convert. After the capture of Kabalega and Mwanga early in 1899, he turned his full attention to the area beyond the Nile where these two had been hiding. All this country, from Acoli to Mt Elgon, the missionaries at first referred to as Bukedi, and the inhabitants as Bakedi.[12] The Rev. W. A. Crabtree in 1901 was the first person to use the term Teso.[13] Several missionaries visited the area in the next two years, and great interest was shown in encouraging the evangelism which they heard was being done through Kakungulu's men who were also establishing forts throughout the region. Yet for one reason and another, European missionaries did not enter the area until 1908, and Teso country was then still virtually unknown. When they did enter, they found that the evangelism supposed to have been done by Kakungulu's men was practically without results, and the Teso people, who were said to be crying out for catechists, were in fact very reluctant to receive Christian instruction in the first few years. How did it come about that the missionaries had gained such an erroneous picture?

We will first examine the missionaries' accounts of how their interest in Bukedi was aroused.[14] According to the *Church Missionary Intelligencer* Bukedi first came into the news at the end of 1899:

> During his itinerations in North Kyagwe last year, the Rev. G. R. Blackledge . . . met the Bakedi, a wild, naked people inhabiting the Nile Valley. They welcomed him, and some 500 assembled and discussed the subject of a white teacher, and came to the conclusion that as the Gospel had been such a blessing to the Waganda, and had so changed their lives, they themselves were willing to be taught, and would welcome a white teacher.[15]

This account reminds one of Lloyd's report of how the Acoli first asked for missionaries—in some way the conversation, which must have been carried on through interpreters, has been adapted to what the missionary would want to hear. In January of 1900 the Rev. T. R. Buckley paid a three weeks' visit to Bukedi, and Roscoe, acting temporarily as mission secretary in Archdeacon Walker's absence through illness, refers briefly to the impressions Buckley gained:

> The most interesting topic just now is the opening of the Bakedi country. I learn both from Mr Buckley who has visited the country and also from the chief in command of the whole country (Semei Kakungulu) there are two places where work is now going forward. There are about sixty people under instruction, and they want teachers to go there, there are two already, but these are men who have had no special training. We hope to be able to send out two or three more at once and thus prepare the country for a European.[16]

The *CMS Gleaner* published an account of this visit in the form of an interview between Buckley and the editor. It is entitled 'Among the wild Bakedi' and the title is something of a clue to its style. It contains little of any value, being largely concerned with impressing the reader with how outlandish were the dress and personal adornments of the Bakedi. It is important for two reasons, firstly because it shows how from the beginning of their contact with these people the missionaries had difficulty in seeing beyond this apparent outlandishness to the real men beneath, and secondly because it shows the misunderstanding on the part of a number of the missionaries about Kakungulu's aims. In this article we are given the impression that he went to Bukedi primarily in order to evangelize it, an impression which is very far indeed from the truth, though this extreme notion may be due to the editor rather than to Buckley.[17]

Not quite all the missionaries took this attitude towards the Bakedi, and Crabtree, who was the next to visit the country, was refreshingly free from it.[18] He became considerably more sceptical about Kakungulu's achievements both in the secular and the evangelistic spheres, and too interested in their language to be put off by their strange methods of adornment. His account deserves quoting at length:

> Much might be written about the occupation of the country by the Baganda, however, I hardly like to go into many details on a subject about which there might be a good deal of diverse opinion. They are certainly encouraging people to wear clothes, but they do not seem to understand how to encourage trade, by which alone the people can become able to buy for themselves. I am not aware of any market in the whole of Kakungulu's district. The system of administration is the feudal system so familiar to us in Buganda. I think it is too soon to say what influence the Baganda will have on the direct evangelization of the country. At first I was disappointed, but perhaps unjustly. The Baganda throughout the district are somewhat estranged by their position as rulers, and what one might term the Protectorate Police. As the occupation of the country progresses, the Baganda settle down in gardens or spheres of influence (emitala) allotted to them. Then they make friends with the people, and I think at Nabowa one may see hopeful signs for the future. This is due to a greater similarity of language. The language is Lusoga, a language very like Luganda . . . At Nabowa there are a few people of the place beginning to read. But among the Bakedi the language difficulty comes in; those boys or lads who join the Baganda and learn their language are being taught slowly at Bululu and Kikabukabu the Kago's fort in the Lumogera District. But all the rest of the people are left untaught. The Baganda are slowly learning Lumogera, but then they have been connected with that district for nearly three years. Three years and yet not a Muganda able to teach in the vernacular; this shews our need of patience.[19]

He did, however, in another area find one Muganda who had learnt the local language. Eriya Zagenda who lived at the headquarters of a chief named Masa spoke the local language fluently and had many friends, but he had done no teaching. But how could he, Crabtree asked himself, since he had no books and understood his faith too little to translate 'our adaptations of Christian terms from Luganda into Teso'?[20] So during the visit, Crabtree prepared a Teso version of the *Mateka,* but a few months later he wrote saying he had so far been unable to distribute it as he had intended because of the pressure of work among the Gisu people in the area where he was stationed.[21]

Later in the same year the Rev. W. Chadwick travelled through Bukedi and remarked on the thousands who lived around.[22] But here matters ended for the time being, and in order to understand one part of the reason for this we must go back and look from a somewhat different point of view at what Kakungulu was doing in Bukedi.

3

KAKUNGULU IN BUKEDI

Kakungulu's first contact with Bukedi was in 1895 when he led a sortie into Lango country in an attempt to capture Kabalega.[23] In this he failed, but he returned with 500 head of cattle which he had captured. The disposal of these led to a further quarrel with Apolo Kagwa—there had been previous disagreements—and eventually to Kakungulu's resignation of this chieftaincy of *Kimbugwe*. The British administration was glad, however, to make use of him in the defence of lands recently won from Bunyoro, and he was made chief of Bunyala in the north of what is now Bugerere county in Buganda, and its former chief, Nyamuyonjo, was made subject to him. Nyamuyonjo was a Bito, and his sphere of influence had extended westwards through north Busoga and part of western Teso. At Mudochi in Teso, Osodo, a native of the place, was appointed to collect tribute for the *Mukama* of Bunyoro, and was invested with a drum, stool, and spear as insignia of office to show his relationship with the *Mukama*.[24] Kakungulu built a fort in north Bugerere which he named Galiraya (Galilee), and from there he set out to make his influence felt among the people on the opposite shore of Lake Kyoga. He seems to have done this partly at the instigation of the British who wanted to stop the people of Lango from sheltering Kabalega, and partly in order to secure their friendship for himself. In 1896 he started to build forts on the edges of Lango and Teso country. His first contact with the Teso was at his island fort, Kaweri, and he helped them against the Langi who were raiding them. Although he claimed to have penetrated fairly deeply into Lango and Teso, it seems doubtful whether he did so. His forts clung close to the lake-shore except in Teso.

In coming into this area when he did Kakungulu benefited from the political vacuum left by the defeat of Kabalega. His own chieftaincy in north Bugerere had previously been under a Bito ruler, and the areas in which he now sought to establish himself had previously been under the influence of Bunyoro. One wonders whether this was coincidental or whether it was part of a deliberate policy. He had plenty of reason to know which areas had been under Nyoro influence, and must have known the extent of Nyamuyonjo's rule. Just as Bito chieftaincies had been established around Lake Albert, so they had also been established around Lake Kyoga, using the lake as a highway, not thinking of it as a barrier. The people living around the lake-shore seem to have found their focus on the lake rather than inland, where there was no central authority to bind them.

In 1898 Kakungulu had accompanied an expedition whose purpose was to survey and explore Lake Kyoga, and he was thus able to add further to his knowledge of the area. When in 1898 he mentioned to the sub-commissioner, Grant, his idea of giving up his Bugerere chieftaincy for a chieftaincy in Busoga, was he perhaps looking for a better vantage-point? His call to Mt Elgon in 1900 and his understanding that Johnston would make him *Kabaka* of all the lands from Lango to the mountain would seem to have altered and widened his conception of what he might be able to achieve. Sir John Gray suggests that before he was called to Masaba he was using chieftaincy titles for those whom he established as chiefs, the use of which would suggest that he was already thinking of himself as *Kabaka*.

But with the summons to Masaba in 1900 he entered on a new phase. Prior to this his only foothold in Teso country would seem to have been the fort at Sambwe established in 1899 and placed under a Ganda named Malaki Magongo after some fighting had taken place. Sambwe lies on a peninsula surrounded by marsh and open water, so Kakungulu was still sticking closely to the lake shores. On his march to Masaba in 1900 he passed through Sambwe, and then went on to Gogonyo in Pallisa where he also built a fort, again on a peninsula jutting out into the marshes. Here he was approached by Ijara the son of Omusage of Ngora, who had quarrelled with his father and now sought the aid of the Ganda against him. A fierce battle took place at Opege, a few miles west of Ngora, where the Teso were defeated by a force of some 250 rifles, and here too a fort was established. The Teso took refuge among the granite outcrops by day, emerging at night to salvage what they could of their looted crops and livestock. Not till the following year was there a return to normality, and a county of Ngora was then proclaimed and placed under Jafari Mayanja, one of the Ganda leaders at the battle of

Opege. He was given the title of *Mugema,* but Ijara also held a position of authority and the people of the area were slowly united under his leadership. The Teso of Nyero defeated an attempt to build a fort at Kumi, and on their way back to Palissa the Ganda constructed a fort at Olaicho near Mukongoro instead, garrisoned by fifty men armed with rifles.[25] A further opportunity of the sort offered by Ijara had occurred when Omiat of Usuku had gone to Bululu to ask for help against some of his enemies in 1901. He repeated his request a number of times before it was taken up in 1904.

At about this time the fort at Sambwe was abandoned, and a second county chieftaincy established in Teso based on Serere. This was placed under Kyagirikama who was entitled *Sekibobo.* Although the fort at Bukedea was not built until 1904 a chief named Isaka Nziga and entitled *Pokino* was placed there.

Ganda now swarmed into the area, hearing that estates were to be had for the asking, and they helped themselves to cattle and to women as well as to land. Rumours that the local inhabitants were being misruled and rendered destitute now began to filter through to the British administration. And after enquiries had revealed the truth of this, William Grant arrived at Kakungulu's headquarters which were then at Budaka in early 1902, and required him to evacuate all the posts he had established, and settle on land to be allocated to him at Mbale. Grant toured the country and garrisons of police were left at two places in Teso, Mukongoro and Khomeleko, the latter being south of Ngora. This brought to an end the first period of Ganda rule in Teso. The northern areas of the country had not been affected at all, and at Kumi resistance had been too strong for Kakungulu to achieve what he had wanted. Too short a time had elapsed for any constructive administration to have taken place, and the period was marked by the misbehaviour of some of Kakungulu's followers.

Teso now came under the control of an administrative officer based first at Budaka and then from 1904 onwards at Mbale. At the end of 1903 Kakungulu was given a new lease of life when Colonel Hayes-Sadler the Commissioner reinstated him as a county chief, convinced that he could be of great usefulness to the administration because of the influence he had with some of the local chiefs. At the beginning of 1904 he was sent back to Teso to establish and re-establish administrative posts. Forts were built at Bukedea and at Kumi, the latter being made a new county headquarters in place of Ngora. In 1904 Soroti was also made a county headquarters and placed under Reuben Bitege who had previously been in Kumam; a post was established at Serere, and a number of outposts were set up. This time the administration was better based, and although there were a good number of Ganda, not nearly as many flocked in to acquire land. The British were impressed by the effectiveness of the system, mainly manifested by the fact that there was little resistance and that the people were made to construct an excellent system of roads.

From this account it is possible to see one reason why the beginnings of evangelism noted by the missionaries in 1900 to 1902 did not come to very much. Only in one or two places were forts long enough established and on a sufficiently permanent basis for any catechetical teaching to be possible, let alone successful. Although Kakungulu was not primarily concerned with evangelism, he would have liked to please the missionaries by doing what he could in this respect, as he was a sincerely religious man. At one or two places the missionaries found that something was being done: in 1901, for instance, Crabtree found twelve people at Bululu awaiting baptism,[26] though it is not clear whether they were Ganda or local people. He noticed that in this area the population along the lake shore was very mixed, but that further inland the people were all Bakedi (Langi).[27] The other place at which something was achieved was Sambwe, where in 1901 Crabtree found what he considered would be an excellent centre of evangelism, and its Ganda chief was baptized by Bishop Tucker in July 1903.[28] But the general situation was summed up by Buckley in 1901:

> A very little work has been done among them (the Teso) by Christian Baganda, but as their language is totally different from Luganda it is necessary that books be written in their language.[29]

All they had was the *Mateka* translated by Crabtree and printed at Mengo early in 1901 which had been sent out to some of the Christian Ganda living in the forts in Teso.[30] Buckley went on to describe how he had reached his conclusions about the amount of Christian teaching being given in the forts:

> Shortly after our coming here, Mr Chadwick and myself thought it well that the Rev. Andereya Batulabude, a Muganda, who had been stationed in Bukedi about a year before our arrival, should visit the forts constructed by Kakungulu in Bukedi, and in which Baganda were living. We asked him to keep a diary, and on his return he gave us his diary. His report shewed that very little had been done for the Bakedi. He visited the Teso district, and also the

> other district, Bululu. He reports a country much more densely populated than Uganda. There are some places in which a few Baganda Christians are struggling to teach the Bakedi, but it is hard work. The languages of the Bakedi are very difficult for the Baganda to learn . . .[31]

There were in fact two other difficulties which faced the Ganda catechists in Bukedi which do not figure in Buckley's report.

Firstly, everywhere else in Uganda where Ganda catechists had gone, even in Bunyoro, they had been asked for by local leaders. Whatever degree of political motivation may have crept in, they went primarily as Christian catechists. But in Bukedi Christian teaching was not requested by the people. It is true that on at least two occasions Teso leaders asked the Ganda to help them militarily in local quarrels, but they did not ask for anything else. And secondly, every other place opened up by Ganda catechists had been in one of the interlacustrine Bantu kingdoms where there was a considerable degree of common culture. The difficulty the Ganda faced in Teso was more than just a linguistic difficulty. Instead of being able to fit into the cultural pattern of the area, as they had been able to do elsewhere because of similarities to their own culture, the Ganda in Teso were instrumental in breaking down the existing cultural pattern. As always in occupied territory there were a few who allied themselves with the occupying power and learnt the language of the conquerors, and it was these few who received some Christian teaching in the forts. But such a group would not prove a satisfactory nucleus if it were hoped that Christianity would achieve any real breakthrough in Teso society. The situation was similar to that in Bunyoro, where the real breakthrough of Christianity did not come through Yosia Kitehimbwa and Tomasi Semfuma at Masindi, but through Paulo Byabacwezi and those who had instructed him.

There were many reasons why the mission was unable to take up the opportunities which presented themselves in Bukedi. Firstly, it was already fully committed to opening new missions elsewhere, and could not find the resources to meet the opportunity in Teso. European missionaries had begun work in Bunyoro in 1899 and in Ankole and Bugisu in 1901, and it was hoped that those in Bugisu would supervise work throughout the rest of the area known as Bukedi. Distance, linguistic difficulties, the unsettled state of the area, and shortage of staff after Chadwick had been invalided home and Buckley withdrawn because it was felt he could not be left alone at Budaka made expansion into Teso impossible.[32] Secondly, to begin work in Teso required a gifted linguist, and one was not available. The best person was Kitching, but he was sent in 1904 to Acoli which was a natural extentsion of the mission in Bunyoro for which Bunyoro catechists were available.[33] A third difficulty lay in finding sufficient catechists of good quality. In 1900 to 1902 there were so many calls on the Mengo Church Council for catechists that it had great difficulty in meeting them all. Then in 1905 there was a crisis over the catechists' pay which made matters more difficult still.[34]

4

CHRISTIANITY, CIVILIZATION, COTTON AND CHIEFS

When in 1904 a county headquarters was opened at Kumi in Teso, it came under the spiritual care of the Rev Andereya Batulabude, who was sent to Teso by the Rev. J. B. Purvis, successor to Crabtree at Nabumale.[35] He is said to have become quite proficient in the Teso language.[36] It has been noted that the only reading matter available was the *Mateka* prepared by Crabtree and this Kitching later found to be somewhat inaccurate, which is hardly surprising since it was prepared after only the briefest contact with Teso speakers.[37] Teaching was therefore almost certainly given in Luganda, and only those few Teso who were prepared to accept the new rulers and to learn their language would have benefited from it. From 1906 to 1908 only nine people were baptized in Teso country, six of whom were Teso, the others being Ganda. At Serere one man was baptized, and apart from this, nothing seems to have resulted from the teaching started at Sambwe. The names of those six Teso baptized by Batulabude do not appear in the communicants' register later kept at Ngora, and although great efforts were made to trace them, these proved successful in only two cases. One of the two who were traceable was Yokana Petero Okwaling'a, a youth from Mukongoro who is said to have been an interpreter for the Ganda. When Kakungulu's followers left Olaicho, he went with them to Kumi to learn to read. He never returned to Mukongoro, and nothing further is known of him.[38] It is just possible that Samwiri Opolot is the Z. Opolot who was a catechist at Kalaki,[39] but no further information is available about him, and negative evidence suggests, therefore, that none of the six played any important part in the history of the

Anglican church in Teso. This is most unusual, for the first converts in an area usually played a very significant role. But by acting as servants and interpreters of the Ganda, these men had alienated themselves to some extent from their own people so that they could never have formed a satisfactory nucleus of a Teso church, and there is some suggestion that Okwaling'a left Mukongoro and did not return because he was no longer *persona grata* with the Teso.[40] People have said that when the Ganda left, their Teso interpreters went with them, probably eventually going to Buganda. Kitching considered that the beginning of Christian teaching had no effect at all upon the people outside the forts built by the Ganda.[41]

And indeed, on their arrival in March 1908 the Kitchings had to make a new start. After their withdrawal from Acoli they had gone to Mengo, and then travelled to Teso by way of Iganga and Nabumale. Leaving his wife there, Kitching set out with Buckley to look for a site for the new mission. They went first to Kumi, but decided on Ngora, eleven miles to the west. It had a good water supply, was in a thickly populated area, and was almost in the centre of the country occupied by the Teso people. Here Mrs Kitching joined her husband, and to begin with they lived in the compound of the Ganda agent until a temporary house was ready for them on what was to be the mission compound.[42] Kitching's first task was to learn the language and reduce it to writing. This task was made easier because Batulabude was able to send Kitching two boys to help him who also knew Luganda. These were Ogwang' and Ekusai, both baptized by Kitching a couple of years later.[43] By the following year a *Mateka* had been translated and printed, and work was in progress on St Mark's Gospel and on a few hymns.[44] At the end of the year the Kitchings were joined by H. G. Dillistone who took over the work of building, leaving Kitching free to do language work. The Rev. Andereya Batulabude moved from Kumi to Ngora, and it was probably he who was responsible for teaching some Ganda catechumens, six of whom were baptized in 1910.[45]

Early in 1909 Bishop Tucker and Dr Cook visited Ngora and made a safari through the Teso and Lango districts with a view to making plans about future mission work throughout these areas. They noted the huge population of the area, though they overestimated this, and the amount of sickness, particularly leprosy. They concluded that at least two more mission stations were needed if the whole area was to be effectively reached, and that a hospital ought to be established, as well as a school with a strong agricultural and technical bias for the sons of chiefs.[46] Probably for no other area in Uganda had such a careful survey and summary of needs for effective mission work been made, and a very real effort was made to implement these proposals. In 1909 a second mission station was opened at Kalaki among the Kumam and the Rev. W. G. Innes was sent to work there, but after a series of mishaps which turned the people against the mission, he died of blackwater fever in 1910. No other European missionary followed him, but exceptionally good work was done here and elsewhere in Teso by Petero Lukungu, later to become a Canon of the Diocese of the Upper Nile.[47] A school was also started and in 1910 Mr and Mrs Syson arrived to take charge of it.[48] Dispensary work was started immediately by Mrs Kitching, but it was not until after the war in 1922 that the hospital was opened, whilst the establishment of a mission station in Usuku has never been achieved.[49] Catechists from Buganda and Busoga were sent out in the usual way, and as soon as Teso Christians were trained they also became catechists.[50]

At almost the same time as the mission was started in Teso, cotton was introduced into the district. The Teso took to cultivating it with remarkable speed until their 'progress' became something of a byword in Uganda. By 1910 news about the Teso cotton crop figures as frequently in *Uganda Notes* as does news of evangelism in the area. Lawrance says it was the CMS who introduced cotton into the district, and he credits Syson with introducing the plough and teaching its use at Ngora High School.[51] Mission work, the cultivation of cotton, and the development of government administration went hand in hand. In the schools run by the CMS were trained the chiefs of the future; the mission in Teso as elsewhere set great store on the importance of chiefs and of the Ganda agents brought in to assist them; emphasis was placed on cultivation not only in the school for the sons of chiefs, but also in what was styled the 'missionary college' where catechists were trained, from which, to quote Kitching, 'it is hoped to send out teachers who may in all ways be useful to their chiefs, not merely to teach the three R's.'[52]

As everywhere, the missionaries of the CMS hoped to see as many of the chiefs as possible Protestant Christians because they felt this would further the work of the gospel. Cook, writing after his visit in 1909, was very satisfied with the progress made in this direction:

> . . . the country is administered by the District and Assistant District Commissioners through Baganda agents stationed at every important place. With hardly any exception, these men, who are in a position of considerable authority, are Protestant Christians. The reason of this is interesting: the Government is strictly impartial, and is only anxious to employ the best educated natives.

> These are found in the ranks of the Protestant Baganda. Many of them have their own little private churches, and thus the country is covered already with centres of potential Christian activity.[53]

Later, when Teso began to be appointed as chiefs they were still in the main Protestant Christians.[54] Expounding his principle of training teachers 'who may be in all ways useful to their chiefs' Kitching continues:

> This last principle has been kept in view from the beginning in the Teso District; chiefs have been encouraged to bring to us their damaged cycles and their injured persons, to send us their sick dependents and their lame watches; the aim has always been to get the people to look to us for anything and everything and so be the more ready to accept our religious teaching. As a result we have only once had any difficulty in placing a teacher in a village where we desired to get a foothold.[55]

Although reliance on chiefs had failed in Acoli, Kitching was still continuing to try to use in Teso the method which he felt had been so successful in the Bantu kingdoms. In Teso there was an illusion of success at first, and the missionaries were able to congratulate themselves on 'the extraordinarily rapid progress of the tribe in the arts of civilization, due mainly to the suitability of the district for cotton.'[56]

But in spite of the attempt to use the old methods of reliance upon chiefs and Ganda catechists, it is evident from these extracts that in Teso the missionaries were quite deliberately trying to add something new to the old methods of working. They were consciously trying to 'civilize as well as to evangelize', and it seems as though for them to 'civilize' meant to encourage material progress.

The establishment and work of Ngora High School was one of the most successful of the mission's ventures.[57] It was started in 1909 by H. G. Dillistone, and the following year a start was made on erecting permanent buildings, and W. S. Syson arrived to take charge of the school. By 1911 there were forty-six pupils and two Ganda teachers. In 1912 the school was told by the CMS that there was no money to support it, and that if it were to continue it would have to be self-supporting. Thanks to the possibility of growing cotton, this was quickly achieved. At the same time school fees were introduced. A good many would-be pupils were rejected because they (or their parents) could not pay the fees, yet by 1913 the number of pupils had risen to 150, an indication not only of the growing confidence of the people in the school, but also of the success of the administration in persuading the chiefs and others that they should send their sons to school. The school was eminently successful in educating the chiefs of the future—when Bishop Gresford Jones consecrated a new chapel in 1922 he found forty old boys present at the service, all of whom held chiefly rank of one sort or another.[58] When the first four Teso were appointed to county chieftaincies in 1920 they were all old boys of the school, and so were many of those appointed later.[59] Only the very beginnings of this school fall into the period prior to 1914, and in that year there was still some difficulty over boys running away and their fathers doing nothing about it. Teso parents were far from keen on education to begin with, and many boys attended school in spite of their parents' displeasure.[60] In 1912 Satulo Byantuyo, an old Budonian, was appointed headmaster of the boarding-school, and in that position he wielded an influence for good. He established exceptionally friendly relations with the Teso, and spent much of his life in the area.[61]

Alongside the High School for the sons of chiefs, there was the day school or catechumenate where reading was taught and instruction for baptism and confirmation was given for an hour or two each day. By 1914 the number of baptized was beginning to grow. For the first three years after Kitching's arrival in Teso, there had been only twenty-five baptisms, and only four of these had been of people who were natives of the area. By May 1911 a fair number of Teso had completed their instruction for baptism, and the remainder of 1911 saw thirty-three Teso baptized, as well as a number of Soga who were living in the area. In 1912 the practice of recording a convert's tribe was abandoned because almost all were now local people. By the end of 1914 the total number of baptisms recorded in the Ngora Register was 397. Forty-two of these had been confirmed, and others were under instruction for confirmation. But of those baptized, only sixteen of the adults were women, and only two women had been confirmed.[62] On the whole, however, it looked as though the mission was making good progress, and only in much more recent times has it become apparent that the Christian impact on Teso has been much slighter than was thought, and that few of the baptized make any attempt to practise their religion.[63] It is possible that the superficiality of Christianity in Teso owes something to the new approach which the missionaries introduced. At the time it seemed to them promising, but on further examination it will be seen that in reality it meant that the Christian gospel had little relevance for the people to whom it was preached, and did not sufficiently engage their attention for them to persevere in their Christian profession.

The missionaries were so taken up with 'civilizing' the Teso that they did not come to understand their way of life, nor had they much respect for what they saw of it. There seemed to them so little in Teso culture worthy of appreciation that the only thing to do was to change it altogether. There are some who will maintain that this was the attitude of the missions everywhere, but in fact there are considerable variations in missionary attitudes, and some cultures were much more undervalued than others.

4

THE CHRISTIAN IMPACT

There were a number of reasons why the missionaries of the CMS in Teso adopted different methods of work, and why they underrated Teso culture. Firstly, in the Bantu kingdoms there was a centralized form of monarchical government which the missionaries admired because they could find certain similarities between it and the type of society to which they themselves belonged. There was a very real sense in which the early missionaries felt that the Ganda and members of the other Bantu kingdoms were already civilized. In Teso they had no chance to see the indigenous social structure because in the area where the mission was established it had been radically undermined by the suppression of the initiation ceremonies connected with the age-sets. Even had they arrived early enough to see these in operation, there would have been nothing about the social structure which would have been familiar and comprehensible to them as there had been in Buganda. When they came to Teso, the missionaries saw an apparently superior group of Ganda bringing order out of chaos. The historical reasons for the conflicts between the Teso and their neighbours and between various groups of Teso were unknown to them. When they arrived, they found good roads, an orderly system of administration, and the people living in peace. All this was attributed to the presence of the Ganda, and it seemed to the missionaries an infinite improvement upon the former state of affairs.

Secondly, in the Bantu kingdoms the missionaries had met with people who wore clothes, and who did not, for the most part, practise bodily cicatrization. This had a considerable psychological effect on them, and made it easier for them to recognize the people as possessing a degree of civilization. The Ganda introduced the Teso to the missionaries as the Bakedi – the naked ones – and as has been noted already, the missionaries thought their style of personal adornment barbarous and outlandish. It was easy for the missionaries to feel that they were savage people who needed to be taught to dress and weaned away from such peculiar customs.

Thirdly, the missionaries arrived at virtually the same moment as the introduction of cotton and the hut-tax, and one of their more successful undertakings was the High School under Syson who taught cotton cultivation and the use of the plough to the pupils. The missionaries saw the introduction of cotton as a means of uplifting the Teso, and cotton and Christianity became inextricably confused. This involvement with cotton caused the missionaries to be yet more fully occupied with changing and 'civilizing' the Teso instead of meeting them on their own ground. It must also have obscured from people the real message of Christianity.

Fourthly, there was the emphasis on educating the chiefs of the future. As in Acoli, the chiefs who had been in power before the British came proved resistant to Christianity, and it was felt that the hope for the future lay in their sons. None of those Teso who had risen to chiefly positions before the arrival of the Ganda was converted, and the new system imposed by the British and the Ganda fairly soon demanded men who could adapt more easily to the new regime. It is probable that at the beginning of the twentieth century a new system of leadership was just beginning to emerge among the Teso, but the arrival of the British brought this evolution to an end and imposed a new pattern. A great many of the pupils of the CMS schools, and of Ngora High School in particular, were appointed chiefs, but in Teso the office of a chief does not command the same type of respect that it does in the Bantu kingdoms, though a particular chief may, through his own merits, achieve considerable influence. So the emphasis placed by the mission on gaining the allegiance of the chiefs was out of place in Teso. Even in the Bantu kingdoms the days when a chief could persuade his clients to follow his lead in matters of religion were fast disappearing. In the development of chieftaincy in Teso the CMS through its schools played a not inconsiderable part, though one has to qualify this by adding that the British administration considered many of the chiefs inefficient and constantly replaced them. Some of those who became chiefs modelled themselves successfully on the Ganda pattern which was held up to them to copy, and when meeting some of the older generation, one may today be temporarily deceived into thinking that one is speaking with a Ganda of the old school. But all this has proved in the long run to have had no relevance to the growth of the church, and the emphasis placed by the mission on producing a new and more 'civilized' type of chief has meant that in yet another sphere of activity the missionaries were prevented from meeting the Teso on their own ground.

Fifthly, we must consider the missionaries themselves. Kitching, Syson and Dillistone are remembered with respect and gratitude by many Teso today because of what they did for education and to raise the economic condition of the people, and there is no doubt that they worked with zeal and devotion. But their attitude to the people they had come to evangelize was different from that of many of the earlier CMS missionaries in Uganda, and in the long run it must be regretted. They brought a kind of thinking current in their day, but new to the Uganda mission, for they were imbued with ideas of social evolution which placed the institutions of peoples such as the Teso near the bottom of the evolutionary ladder, and they were wont to talk of the 'child races' of Africa. Given this premiss it was natural that they should see their task in terms of uplifting the people and so helping them to reach a higher rung on the evolutionary ladder.

For all these reasons there was little continuity with the past in Teso. Instead of helping to bridge the gap between the past and the present, the old and the new, Christianity was associated only with the new, and with those forces which widened the gap. In the Bantu kingdoms the institution of kingship survived the introduction of colonial rule (though not of independence), as did something of the old structure of society, and both the people and the missionaries found a common meeting-ground in their respect for and interest in those institutions (the disadvantages of this have been noted). New ideas brought by education and Christianity were used to enhance the old, and whilst this did not always work out satisfactorily, it gave the missionaries something to start from. In Teso Christianity was associated first with the Ganda, and then with the arrival of the Protectorate administration, education, and cotton, and hence with poll-tax. It might provide a clue to the future but it did not have any roots in their past.

It was also important for the future of the church that in the main only youths were converted to Christianity; the older people, and in particular the indigenous leaders of the Teso, did not respond. Christianity therefore became all too easily something one grew out of, and many of those converted in the early years later lost interest, including a number of those who later became chiefs. In the Bantu kingdoms it is noticeable that many of the leaders were committed

Christians, and Christianity therefore became associated with leadership and maturity, as it could not do in Teso.

A further point which must be mentioned is that Christianity probably received too much official encouragement and protection in Teso, or at least, education did, and to a large extent education and Christianity were synonymous in Teso as elsewhere in Uganda. The Protectorate administration wanted literate men whom they could use as chiefs and clerks, and did much to encourage boys to go to school. People were excused certain kinds of labour such as road-making if they were attending church classes.[64] It was also well known that only those who had been to school would be eligible for appointment to chieftaincies, and however new the chieftaincy system was, plenty of Teso were ambitious to become chiefs. Nor did the Christians in Teso ever have the testing that the Christians in Buganda and Acoli had. It is true that some boys were beaten by their parents for going to school, but they stood an equal chance of being beaten by the teachers for staying away.[65]

And lastly Teso was the first place in Uganda to which the missionaries went uninvited by the local people. They were invited in, but by the Ganda, not by the Teso. The Teso were little interested in what the mission had to offer, though eventually, like other peoples throughout East Africa, they took advantage of mission schooling since literacy was essential to progressing under colonial rule.

The weakness of the mission's work in Teso did not become clear for a long time. In 1926 Bishop Gresford-Jones was still able to enthuse about the 'new missionary régime':

> If we take stock of the various missionary experiments that have sprung up within the one Uganda Mission there is none that should more quickly evoke our attention than this in Teso. *Alike in its industrial, its educational, and its moral aspects, it has ideas to contribute to the future training of the African that are of an important kind.*[66]

But today the weaknesses are abundantly clear, and the widespread lack of devotion or even of interest in the church are the despair of local clergy and of missionaries alike. There is a tendency to blame this on the Teso people, indulged in by Teso clergy and expatriate missionaries alike who say that the people lack perseverance, or that in some way the weakness of the church is due to the fact that the Teso are not Bantu. It seems better to seek an explanation for this situation (if the assessment of it is correct) in the way in which

Christianity was introduced into Teso. The missionaries did not succeed in meeting the Teso on their own ground, but always the meeting took place on ground of the missionaries' choosing. This is probably a major reason why Christianity has not succeeded in evoking from any but a few a whole-hearted response. Dr Michael Twaddle has noticed that 'social Darwinianism' was not found among the more fundamentalist CMS missionaries, and that those who were more conservative in their theology were better able to enter into close relationships with Africans than those who held evolutionist views on social development.[67] It also needs to be noted that missionaries holding 'modernist' views, including 'social Darwinianism', came into the mission at a later date when circumstances no longer threw them into the close relationship with Africans achieved by the missionaries before 1900. Then the amenities of European-style living could not be imported and there were still so few missionaries that they could not form a self-contained community among themselves. It may be that circumstances as much as theological views determined the course of development.

Some doubt has been cast on the usual assessment of the church in Teso by recent study by the anthropologist, N. Nagashima. He has suggested that the Teso have been deeply affected by the teaching of the missions, and that those who have come within range of mission influence have moved from a vague deism to a theistic understanding of the world.[68] Some Teso bear this out, and state that the teaching of the mission has radically altered the 'world view' of the Teso, especially their understanding of God as creator. Support for this seems to come from the observation of a number of people that the Christian message has often been heard in East Africa as a message about God, not about Christ.[69] If it be true that the Teso have largely moved from deism to theism, they may have taken a larger step in the direction of Christianity than has been realized. A current recognition among church leaders of the need to gain a better understanding of the traditional religion and the mentality of the people is encouraging, as are efforts by Teso Christians to relate Christianity to Teso life and thinking.[70] Little work has been done on Teso society and religion (apart from Lawrance's study), and the missionaries were not much interested in this. By contrast with writings on Buganda and other of the Bantu kingdoms, the missionaries' writings on Teso have little to say about the traditional religious beliefs of the people. Until more is understood of Teso attitudes to religion and of their 'world view' it will not be possible to make a satisfactory evaluation of the impact of the missions.

Chapter VII

Postscript

Two things remain to be done. The first is to comment on the reasons for the weakening of the impetus which led so many Ugandans to work as teachers and evangelists outside their own area in the years before World War I. The second is to try and evaluate the movement as a whole, and see whether any conclusions can be drawn.

In the places where Ganda catechists had pioneered, there came a time when they were no longer needed. Wherever the church was securely planted, it was able to produce its own catechists within a few years, and it was an essential requirement of healthy growth that it should do so. It has been noted that each area of the country found a sphere of evangelism outside its own borders, so that catechists from Toro went to Ankole, Mboga and Burega; catechists from Bunyoro went to Burega, Acoli and Lango; and catechists from Acoli went to Sudan and Lango. Had we taken the story on beyond 1914 we should have found catechists from Ankole working in Kigezi, and some from Teso working in Karamoja. But for them too the day came when they were no longer needed in large numbers. Ganda catechists were dispensed with the sooner in the Western Kingdoms because they were suspected of having political motives, and freeing themselves from dependence on the Church Council at Mengo was seen in Bunyoro and Toro as connected with their claim to be treated as equals of the kingdom of Buganda. The people of Acoli and Lango did not suspect the Nyoro of the same territorial ambitions, and the Anglican church in Acoli depended on catechists from Bunyoro for so long that the development of an indigenous Christian leadership may have been impeded. The beginnings of the Ganda missionary movement coincided with the height of Buganda's territorial aspirations, and the imposition of colonial rule did not bring these to an end immediately. By 1914 further territorial expansion was out of the question, and even the use of Ganda as political agents in other areas of the country was ending. The Ganda were still happy to exercise influence where they could, however, but increasingly their interests became focused on Mengo rather than on areas outside Buganda. Religion and politics were so closely entwined that this affected their interest in the expansion of the church.

By 1914 the spread of missions from a base in Uganda had virtually ended, and the missions became concerned with consolidation. This change in emphasis coincided with a growing spiritual uncertainty among Christians in the west. The CMS Uganda mission had begun when Christians in Britain felt themelves to be living in an age of spiritual revival.[1] The need to consolidate occurred when undercurrents of doubt and malaise, temporarily submerged in Victorian England, were clearly running strongly and affecting the strength of religious belief throughout Europe. The economic depression following World War I created a further setback for the missions, and all were beset with financial difficulties, though for a time Catholics retained a measure of immunity from the growing climate of agnosticism. Changes of government policy towards colonial education followed the reports of the Phelps-Stokes Commission, and these changes gave missions the chance of entering the educational field in a new way with the assistance of grants-in-aid for schools reaching certain minimum standards of efficiency.[2] The missions were quick to seize this opportunity and the huge increases in church membership which characterized the inter-war years were largely the result of a successful schools policy. But the growing concentration on schools and on teacher-training led to a decline in the standards of training offered to catechists everywhere, and to training for the ministry in the Protestant missions. Catholic missions, with their different theology of the priesthood, and their greater discipline and resources, continued to give priority to the training of priests. The success of the White Fathers, who ordained the first Ugandans and Tanzanians to the priesthood in 1913 and 1917 respectively, stimulated other Catholic missions in Africa to follow their lead.[3] But the White Fathers' training school for catechists suffered severely. It was the one institution which that mission closed down during the war, and although it reopened in 1920, it was turned into a teacher training college within a few years under the influence of the new schools policy.[4] In recent years this has been seen as a mistake. The church in Uganda and elsewhere in Africa is likely to have to rely on catechists for many years to come, and efforts are now being made to rectify the mistakes of the past in this respect.[5] Since World War II one of the most pressing problems of Protestant churches all over Africa has been to overcome the disastrous legacy of an under-educated clergy.

Ugandan Christians were aware that this change of emphasis in mission policy denoted a decline of evangelical fervour among CMS missionaries, and that this was affecting the life of the church. One of the main contentions of those Christians who joined the *Balokole* revival movement was that there was 'coldness' in the church,[6] and an interesting feature of this movement is that through it the place of lay people in evangelism was restored to the Anglican church in Uganda.

The significance of the *Balokole* (Saved Ones) is greater than this, however. We saw in Chapter I that CMS missionaries encouraged Ugandan converts to show their zeal for Christianity by becoming catechists and evangelists, in the same way that the white missionaries themselves showed their zeal by becoming missionaries in foreign lands. Once catechists were no longer needed outside their own home areas, how was their zeal to be demonstrated? We find the missionaries complaining of a decline in zeal among Christians as early as 1906, but they do not seem to have considered the important question of finding positive outlets for Christian commitment. They complained of failure in marriage and of drunkenness, but there is little evidence of positive thinking. The Catholic church has always encouraged people to show personal devotion in a variety of ways. Private devotion was encouraged; regular church-going and attendance at mass on weekdays as well as Sundays were taken to denote religious zeal; great efforts were made to encourage the frequent reception of communion; family life was built up through devotion to the Sacred Heart; and special gatherings for men, women, and children, separately, were held on particular days each month. And finally there were, of course, the religious orders and the vocation to the priesthood. A family with a religious sister or brother or a priest among its members was much praised for its contribution to the life of the church. The CMS encouraged membership of the Mothers' Union to strengthen family life, and encouraged private prayer and bible reading, but offered nothing parallel to the religious orders, or to the full programme which the Catholics provided for people of all ages through regular corporate devotions, all frequently mentioned in the reports of the Roman Catholic missionaries in Uganda. When the *Balokole* movement began to spread in the 1930s it met a serious need by providing a fellowship embracing many aspects of life.

The inter-war years are perhaps the least inspiring period in the history of the church in East Africa. Whilst there was an advance in education, in almost every other respect there was a degree of stagnation. The goal of a self-supporting, self-governing and self-propagating church was largely abandoned in fact if not in theory, and white missionaries seemed to consider themselves a permanently necessary scaffolding. It took World War II, the growth of nationalism, and the changed economic position of the west, which together led to the breakup of most of the old colonial systems, to shake the missions out of their complacency. But by then much damage had been done, and many of the more enterprising African leaders had found scope for their abilities outside rather than inside the church, though they probably remained members of it.

After 1914 only three areas of Uganda remained to be entered by the missions. One was the West Nile District where both Protestant and Catholic missions started work in 1917. The Protestant mission was the Africa Inland Mission (AIM) which already had work in Kenya and Congo (Zaire). A group of missionaries passing through to Congo was struck by the need in West Nile, and work was begun there as a result. Although the AIM is interdenominational in character, by agreement with the Anglican bishop of Uganda those missionaries who came to Uganda were Anglicans.[7] The Verona Fathers began work in the same year.[8] A second area in northern Uganda which the missions entered late was Karamoja. Both the Verona Fathers and the Bible Churchmen's Missionary Society (BCMS) began work there in the 1930s. The BCMS at first used catechists from the Friends' mission at Kaimosi in western Kenya, but later catechists from Teso worked among the people of Karamoja—the languages are closely related.[9] In both these areas the initiative for evangelism was European, not African. The only area where something of the old pattern was followed was Kigezi in the extreme south-west of Uganda. Catechists from Ankole went there about 1910, but were not followed by European missionaries until after the war. The pioneer Catholic catechist was Yohana Kitagana who has already been mentioned in the story of Ankole. In 1910 he went to the area of Kigezi which was administered by the Ganda chief, Yohana Sebalijja. When the White Fathers arrived in 1923, he moved on to pioneer in Bufumbira.[10] The first Protestant catechist to reach Kigezi was Zedekiya Rwamafa and others followed, European missionaries arriving in 1921. The work of the early Anglican catechists has been somewhat undervalued by the Anglican missionaries.[11] The missionaries belong to a branch of CMS which, although technically in association with CMS, is virtually a mission of its own, and not in entire doctrinal agreement with the parent society. This disagreement stems in large part from a fear that the

CMS is not being faithful to evangelical principles, and is insufficiently concerned with individual conversion. This helps to account for an undervaluing of work done by CMS catechists. A further reason for this attitude is to be found in the fact that both missionaries and converts in Kigezi have been strongly influenced by the *Balokole* movement which, like other revivalist movements, disparages any Christian experience prior to the revival experience. There was, besides, no catechist among the Anglicans comparable to Yohana Kitagana. The initial opposition to Christianity in Kigezi was very considerable,[12] and had European missionaries entered the area before Ugandan catechists had done years of quiet pioneering, the story might have been a very different one in the early stages of missionary work in Kigezi. As it was, the missionaries reaped where others had sown, but did not always remember that fact.

For the sake of completeness one other area must be mentioned. Until 1921 a large part of western Kenya was part of the Anglican diocese of Uganda, although it had ceased to be part of the Uganda Protectorate in 1902. Among the Luo people who occupy much of this area, little use was made of Ganda catechists, though a Ganda clergyman, the Rev. Jesse Weraga, and other Ganda worked among the Bantu Luyia people to the north for some years. The Rev. J. J. Willis, who had pioneered in Ankole, dispensed with this method among the Luo. He taught the first group of boys himself at Maseno with only minimal help from the Ganda, and sent the boys straight out to convert their own people.[13] The Luo are closely related to the Acoli and are just as egalitarian and independent, and this method of throwing them on their own resources from the beginning seems to have been the right one. The Mill Hill Fathers started work in Luo country at about the same time as the Anglicans, and numerous other missions now work in the area, including the AIM and the Seventh Day Adventists. In the area south of the Kavirondo Gulf the planting of the Catholic and the Anglican church was assisted by two outstanding Luo catechists. Ezekiel Apindi, who was later ordained, was the Anglican pioneer, and was virtually responsible for the existence of the Anglican church in this area.[14] Andrea Otwande was his Catholic counterpart, who did comparable work for the Catholic church in more or less the same area.[15] Both men established schools and chapels, some of which later became parish centres. Christianity is vigorous among the Luo by contrast with the Acoli, and this is something which requires investigation.

In recent years there has been a reluctance among Ugandans to work for the church outside their own areas, and reluctance among their bishops to let them do so. In the Catholic church many vocations to the priesthood come from among the Ganda, and in recent years a large number of vocations to the Anglican ministry have come from the people of Kigezi. Unless there was a greater willingness to serve outside their own area, and unless the church could make arrangements for this to be done, it seemed unlikely that the Anglican church could absorb all those from Kigezi who felt themselves to have a vocation. At the same time there has been a tendency in both churches to allow the establishment of ethnically based dioceses, sometimes at government instigation. Only with the reduction of foreign missionary personnel in 1971 has there been any real reversal of the tendency for the church in Uganda to be ethnically bound.

How is this indigenous missionary movement to be evaluated? In many parts of Africa expatriate missionaries depended heavily on African catechists, but probably in few areas was there an indigenous expansion of Christianity comparable to that in Uganda between 1890 and 1914. This coincided with Ganda expansion, but it has been shown that peoples from Bunyoro, Toro and Ankole were also involved in large numbers. Motivation was clearly mixed, but we can plainly discern a genuine desire to share a newly found dimension of life with others. It is difficult not to see a parallel with the European missionary movement which has waxed and waned over the last five centuries. In the same way as European missionaries were drawn to areas where their own countries had possessions or influence, so Ganda, Nyoro and Toro missionaries were drawn to those areas with which they had long-standing ties, as was the case with the three Ganda who went to Sukumaland. To write off either movement as 'merely expansionist' would be untrue to the evidence, though this is sometimes done for propaganda reasons. In both movements there is evidence of genuine religious motivation, paternalistic beneficence, and expansionism, which is sometimes (not always) conscious. In both movements there was a sincere belief that one's way of life and religion was good and deserved to be spread. Ideas could not be spread at all without some such driving belief.

The extent of African committal to Christianity shown in this episode of history also gives the lie to the idea that Christianity was more or less forcibly imposed on unwilling subject populations. Ugandan Christians, not expatriate missionaries, were the pace-setters. Nor is it possible to label the adventurous and sometimes turbulent personalities described here as mere 'colonial stooges'. Both missions and government tried and sometimes failed to curb them.

Nuwa Mbaguta has received as fierce a drubbing on this score as any of the leaders mentioned here, yet one of his severest critics, Dr S. Karugire, writes of him:

> Those who saw him late in life readily testify to his personal magnetism . . . If the era of public rallies and exhortations had dawned on Uganda's political scene, Mbaguta would probably have been described as a charismatic leader. His presence was awesome—he exuded confidence and evoked obedience from those around him. His authority and ability as a born leader of men was communicated to those he came into contact with as if by some osmotic process . . .[16]

Karugire goes on to speak of his personal bravery which verged on rashness, and of his inner drive to excel. He finds generosity and kindness combined with political ruthlessness, and moderated by a sense of humour. Yet this vigorous personality became a 'collaborator'. But Karugire cannot dismiss him as a stooge, and rightly sees that he must be evaluated within the context of his times:

> Given the context of colonial administration, Mbaguta was unquestionably a great man for collaborators are not necessarily bad men on account of being collaborators. It can be reasonably argued that the existence of a powerful collaborator such as Mbaguta saved Ankole of the probable ravages of futile resistance to the advance of colonial rule.[17]

To him must also go 'the credit for the laying of a solid foundation for missionary education in Ankole and for inreasing agricultural production as indeed for most other development.'[18]

There were, of course, good, bad, and indifferent missionaries, chiefs and catechists. Among both missionaries and catechists were many who were mediocre, many who were hard-working and faithful without being outstanding, as well as a few who were worthless and a few who were saints. Inevitably it is the bad as well as the excellent who are remembered and by whom the whole group is judged. We have found both expatriate missionaries and Ugandan catechists who have a respectful attitude to cultures which differ from their own, and others who lack this, and in both cases a lack of respect jeopardized their work. Perhaps the most depressing aspect of this account is the regression in European attitudes towards the Ugandan church. African initiatives and capabilities were more highly valued in the 1890s than in the 1920s and after. This growth in colonial mentality seems to be closely related to the missionaries' growing ability to follow a European life-style in Uganda, and to form large enough enclaves to become isolated from their Ugandan fellow-Christians. Both Ugandan and European accounts of the 1880s and 1890s show a comradeship which sadly died away. Probably the most disturbing legacy of colonialism is that too many successful Africans have become almost as isolated from the mass of their people as missionaries and colonial officials were, through imitating the same life-style.

Although this study shows that certain aspects of Christianity have long been indigenized; there is still an urgent need to make the church 'a place to feel at home'.[19] Unfortunately the evidence shows that Ugandan missionaries and clergy were not always more sensitive or more successful than their European counterparts especially when working outside their own ethnic group. Insensitivity to other people's points of view is a basic human failing, though virtually institutionalized by colonialism. In the Western Kingdoms of Uganda resentment which might otherwise have been directed against the British was deflected on to the Ganda because of the way in which they were used as chiefs and political agents, and catechists came in for a share of the same resentment. When Willis was appointed to western Kenya he decided against the use of Ganda catechists amongst the Luo, and his decision may have been reached in part as a result of his experiences in Ankole. European missionaries most sensitive to African opinion often found themselves in difficulties with the mission authorities, and were sometimes eased out of the mission: Maddox, Purvis and Crabtree, none of whom was sufficiently conformist, were all labelled as 'difficult' if not 'impossible' by the mission, and resigned. Purvis had several vigorous disagreements with the Protectorate government, to the extreme annoyance of the CMS. He flatly refused to believe that colonialism was designed to benefit anyone other than the colonial power.[20] Archdeacon Owen, not nearly radical enough for modern African opinion, was far too radical for the mission authorities, and from time to time caused them great embarrassment. The dilemma of Fisher, who was genuinely sympathetic to the people of Bunyoro but also determined to remain acceptable to the mission, is apparent in the chapter dealing with Bunyoro. Apolo Kivebulaya's practice of evangelical poverty is sufficiently contrary to the norms of Ganda society to earn him much adverse criticism even from some theological students of the present generation. Because the Uganda martyrs put obedience to God above obedience to the *Kabaka* some Baganda think they deserve the fate they met and are uncomfortable that they are acclaimed by the universal church. A tension always exists between the need to adapt Christianity to local cultures on the one hand, and the need for all cultures to be judged and transformed by Christianity on the other. Because under colonial rule there was little attempt made to assess African culture at its true value, the pendulum has now swung to the other extreme.

As a result of this swing, it is sometimes difficult for Africans today to accept the testimony of Christians of an earlier generation that for them the coming of Christianity was like new light breaking in—'Now the light is shining', wrote Mika Fataki at the end of his account of how Christianity first came to Bunyoro. Christian commitment and the achievement of some education can be seen in this account to have opened up new vistas for many people. Apolo Kagwa used his literacy to write an account of the *Kabaka*s of Buganda; Ham Mukasa (a county chief who does not figure in this account except as sponsor of Apolo Kivebulaya) used his to write biblical commentaries, now, alas, out of print. A number of the unpublished manuscripts found in Uganda have proved to contain accounts of the impact of Christianity. The modern preoccupation with indigenizing Christianity has led some people to suppose that Christianity was most acceptable when it could most easily be understood in terms of the old religion, and when it caused least disruption to traditional life. There is some evidence which suggests just the opposite: that it was welcomed because it offered something new. If it offered nothing radically different, why bother to change from the old way? To many Ugandans it offered new commitments and opportunities which they gladly accepted. Yet there had to be some point of contact, some common ground on which the missionaries and catechists could meet those to whom they went. The history of Christianity in Teso suggests strongly that where there was no real meeting-place, Christianity did not catch on. In most places there was also a measure of conflict with the traditional religion. In Bunyaruguru, Yohana Kitagana engaged in trials of strength with traditional powers over healing, and he won. In Acoli people recognized a new power which, they felt, challenged their previous beliefs, and it was unwelcome. In Ankole fetishes were burnt or handed over. In none of these cases was the conflict precipitated by European missionaries. In Acoli they were unaware of the conclusions drawn by the people from their cinematograph show. It is impossible to see how such conflicts can be totally avoided. Part of Christian proclamation has always been concerned with turning from one way of life to another, new life. It is possible, however, to discern that in some areas there was cultural disparagement and damage of a kind which was totally unnecessary, whilst where better relations existed, and the colonial mentality was less entrenched, change could be effected without traumatic results. Uganda was fortunate in being saved the kind of conflicts which have beset Kenya.

A study of only five societies cannot provide many answers. It is probably more important that it should raise questions. The incompleteness and inadequacies of this study should be enough to indicate areas of study and research which would repay attention.

NOTES

CHAPTER I

1. Rowe 1969(i), p. 1.
2. Oliver 1952, pp.182–3.
3. Ibid., p.193.
4. It was generally believed by CMS missionaries that in sending his White Fathers to Uganda, Cardinal Lavigerie had as his main purpose the thwarting of the CMS (v. Stock 1899, Vol. III, p.105; Tucker 1911, p.6). Lavigerie was indeed concerned at Protestant domination of the Brussels Conference (v. Oliver 1952, p.74, note 2), but he did not intend his missionaries to enter into open conflict with the Protestants. In dealing with Protestant missions he counselled patience and charity, and he ordered his missionaries not to open a station close to a Protestant station—the distance he ordered them to keep was increased from eight or ten to twenty-five kilometres (v. Lavigerie: *Instructions*, pp.73 and 136). When he heard that acrimonious debates had taken place at *Kabaka* Mutesa's court, he expressed his severe displeasure to the Superior of the Uganda Mission, reminding him of his previous instructions (v. Lavigerie: *Instructions*, pp.144–6). Unfortunately it was impossible for these instructions to be carried out in Buganda, because the *Kabaka* insisted that the missionaries be within a short distance of his capital and he himself prompted the religious debates. However, the CMS missionary, Robert Ashe, noted that 'public denunciation' had ceased, though he knew nothing of the reproof the White Fathers had received (Ashe 1890, p.159), and he was able to state that by 1889 dealings between the two missions 'were of the pleasantest description'.
5. *Died before reaching their destination*: J. Robertson, Dr J. Smith, Bishop Parker, J. V. Dermott, J. W. Dunn, J. W. H. Hill, H. J. Hunt; *Murdered*: Lt Shergold-Smith, T. O'Neill, W. S. Penrose, Bishop Hannington; *Failed to reach their destination because of ill-health or resigned because of it very shortly*: W. M. Robertson, C. T. Wilson, G. Litchfield, J. G. Pearson, J. W. Hall, Dr G. Wright, (all save Pearson served in other missions of the CMS later on). Information from CMS: *A Register*.
6. Low 1968, p.156.
7. I am indebted to Dr J. A. Rowe here who has drawn attention to the importance of the generation struggle in his work on Buganda, and with whom I discussed this chapter.
8. Works dealing with the martyrdoms include Thoonen 1941, Marie-André du Sacré-Coeur 1962, Rowe 1964 (i), Faupel 1965, Low 1968, Kavulu 1969, Pirouet 1969 (i).
9. Rowe 1964 (i); Kiwanuka 1969.
10. A further *bitongole* chiefdom which included a large armed following was that of the chief entitled *Mujasi*, who was also a Muslim at this time.

11. J. Miti, quoted in Faupel, pp.136-7.
12. Gray 1950, p.43, referring to a letter from C. G. Gordon of 25 Oct. 1889, and to letters of Lourdel dating from the same period.
13. Kiwanuka 1969, p.14.
14. Ashe 1894, p.12; v. also Hastings 1969, p.213.
15. Rowe 1969 (i), pp.11 and 13.
16. Low 1957 (i), pp. 9-10.
17. Twaddle 1969 (ii). Throughout this section dealing with the changes in Christianity after the revolution I am indebted to Dr Twaddle, though for the presentation put forward here I must accept full responsibility. V. also Ashe 1894, pp. 119, 122-3; Kiwanuka 1969, pp.13-14; Kasozi, pp.32-4.
18. Faupel, pp.136-7; Hastings 1969, pp.211-12; Taylor, pp.32-4.
19. Hastings 1969, p.209 points out that a change in Catholic personnel took place in 1890.
20. Low 1957 (i), p.11. Emphasis added.
21. Ibid.
22. Welbourn 1965 (ii), pp.6-7.
23. Welbourn 1964, p.17.
24. Only the more recent dissolution of the kingdoms in 1966 revealed the extent of Anglican involvement with institutions which have proved to be not viable in a modern state. An adjustment to changed conditions took the church some time to make, though this would now (1976) seem to be achieved.
25. Tucker 1911, pp.19, 42, 47-9.
26. Rowe 1969 (i), p.11; Ashe 1894, pp.141-2.
27. Taylor, pp.72-3.
28. *BJ*, 6 Aug., 23 Oct., 12, 13, 23, 26 Nov. 1892.
29. Stock, Vol. III, Chapter LXX, pp.24-34.
30. Taylor, pp.43, 47-8, 62.
31. Oliver 1952, pp.176-7.
32. Tucker, letter of 6 Jan. 1891, quoted in *CMI*, May 1891, p.370.
33. Tucker, letter of 21 Jan. 1891, quoted in *CMI*, May 1891, p.372.
34. *BJ*, Easter Sunday 1891.
35. *BJ*, 13 July 1891.
36. Ibid.
37. Kalikuzinga 1965; Taylor, p.267.
38. Dermott to Lang, 1 Mar. 1892, CMSA G3 A5/08.
39. Tucker 1908, Vol. II, pp.164-5 (in this edition only).
40. Low 1957 (ii), pp.393-4.
41. *BJ*, 16 Mar., 20 Apr. 1891; 6 June, 13 July 1892.
42. v. Table II and WF *Mémento chronologique*.
43. WF *Jubilee Book*.
44. For an account of the build up of tension and of the battle itself v. Rowe 1969 (i).

45. Langlands and Namirembe, pp.9 and 11.
46. WF *Histoire Mercui*, entries for 1892 and 1893.
47. WF *Chroniques*, Rubaga Diary, 1 Sept. 1898.
48. *BJ*, 10 June, 13 Sept. 1892; 18 July 1893.
49. *BJ*, 12 May 1892.
50. Tucker 1911, p.117.
51. WF *Mémento chronologique*.
52. Ashe 1894, pp.51-2.
53. *BJ*, 4 Aug. 1892.
54. Baskerville to Wigram, 18 Aug. 1892, CMSA G3 A5/09.
55. Hellberg does not mention this attempt to send catechists to Kiziba, and says that the first attempt was made in 1896. However, he notes that the first contact with evangelical Christianity came through supporters of the Pilkington revival in Buganda, which perhaps suggests that informal evangelism had begun before 1896. On p.86 Hellberg mentions a group of Protestant Christians in Kianja, a chieftaincy adjacent to Kiziba, 'made up for the most part of immigrant Baganda in 1892'. These would be Protestants who moved away from Buddu when that became a Catholic county, and it may be that the catechists sent to Kiziba later in that year joined and merged with this group. On the general position of Kiziba vis-à-vis the Germans and the Ganda, v. Hellberg, p.64.
56. *BJ*, 22 Oct. 1892.
57. *BJ*, 8 Nov. 1892.
58. *BJ*, 8, 12, 13, 15 Nov. 1892; Taylor, p.71.
59. Kieran, p.136 *et seq*.
60. WF *RA*, 1912/13, Villa Maria.
61. CMS *A Register*. Information on some of the men ordained in the 1880s is scanty and may be incomplete, so the percentage of those with a grammar school education and who worked as catechists is likely to err on the side of being too low. The actual numbers are: 9 graduates, 45 students of Fourah Bay, 6 others with grammar school education, 48 catechists.
62. Tucker 1911, p.108.
63. Tucker 1911, p.110.
64. *BJ*, 28 Dec. 1892; 28 Feb. 1893.
65. *BJ*, 28 Feb. 1893.
66. *BJ*, 7 Mar. 1893.
67. e.g. Nansambu, 'an energetic teacher', and Misaka who had organized some two or three hundred catechumens into an orderly school. *BJ*, 25 July 1893.
68. *BJ*, 25 July, 18 Aug. 1893.
69. The information about these men is compiled from *CMI*, May 1891, which contains brief biographies of them based on information in the missionaries' letters, and Taylor, pp.261-6. See also Low 1957 (ii), p.14.
70. Walker to Stockdale, 8 Sept. 1891, CMSA G3 A5/07.

71. Taylor, pp.261-5.
72. Walker, interview with Group III Committee, 22 Nov. 1892, CMSA G3 A5/09.
73. Harford Battersby, p.183.
74. *BJ*, 20 July 1893.
75. Rowe 1964 (ii), p.194.
76. Walker, letter quoted in *CMI*, Mar. 1893, p.200.
77. CMS *A Register*, appropriate entries.
78. Taylor, p.270.
79. Harford Battersby, pp.162-3.
80. Harford Battersby, p.130; Stock, Vol. III, p.437.
81. Stock, Vol. III, p.740; Tucker 1911, pp.110, 128.
82. Tucker 1911, loc. cit.
83. Taylor, p.42. Perhaps the best documentation of the type of conversion experience referred to here is to be found in James, 1901/2, and Knox, 1950.
84. The revival of the 1930s, which has spread from Rwanda and Uganda to Kenya and Tanzania and beyond, and affected a number of Protestant denominations, has not yet been adequately studied from a theological, sociological or historical point of view. The best published study to date in a brief one by M. A. C. Warren entitled *Revival* (London 1954). But v. also Robins.
85. Low 1957 (i), p.11.
86. *BJ*, 8 Dec. 1893. The White Fathers were horrified by Pilkington's embarrassingly uninhibited public accounts of his spiritual experiences and his claims to have received the Holy Spirit. WF *Chroniques*, Rubaga Diary, 10 Dec. 1893.
87. Harford Battersby, pp.221-39; *BJ*, 8 Dec. 1893 and subsequent entries; Tucker 1911, pp.140-1.
88. Fisher, Annual Letter, 1 Jan. 1894, CMSA G3 A5/010.
89. Pilkington, letter dated 1 April 1894, quoted in Harford Battersby, p.231.
90. *BJ*, 16 April 1894; *CMI*, Aug. 1894, p.610.
91. *CMI*, Dec. 1894, p.917.
92. Letter of Mgr J. Hirth, 20 July 1894. WFA (I am grateful to Dr M. Rooyackers for drawing my attention to this letter).
93. Ibid.
94. Guillermain to Lavigerie, 25 Mar. 1895, WFA.
95. MHM *Nsambya Diary*, especially the entries for 19 Dec. 1895; 28 Mar. 7, 8, 9, 10, 13, 17, 27 April, 14, 20 July, 6 Aug. 1896. For Protestants becoming Catholics v. 24 April, 1 May 1896.
96. CMS *AR*, 1894/5, p.96.
97. Philippians 1: 15-18: 'Some indeed preach Christ from envy and rivalry, but others from goodwill. The latter do it out of love, knowing that I am put here for the defence of the gospel; the former proclaim Christ out of partisanship, not sincerely, but thinking to afflict me in my imprisonment. What then? Only that, in every way, whether in

pretence or truth, Christ is proclaimed.' (American Revised Standard Version.)

98. Low 1968, pp.152-4.
99. Katumba and Welbourn 1964; Gee 1958.
100. Low 1957 (i), pp.1-5.
101. M. C. Fallers 1960, pp.74-6.
102. Ibid., Appendix II, Luganda Literature; Rowe 1969 (ii).
103. Rowe 1969 (ii), p.20.
104. e.g. at Ngogwe, Kako, Nakanyonyi.
105. Goody and Watt, pp.313-14.
106. Kalikuzinga (interview). In spite of the date of this interview being recent I believe Kalikuzinga's account represents fairly accurately what transpired. This informant had a phenomenal memory, and in other conversations which can be checked on has shown an amazing degree of accuracy. cf. Wright: *Buganda in the Heroic Age*.
107. Rev. Eriya Aliwali to Canon Daniell, 26 Sept. 1926, MUA.
108. Harford Battersby, pp.192-3.
109. Welbourn 1969 (ii). For a description of the types of chieftaincy mentioned here, v. L. A. Fallers 1964, pp.84-94. For the *bakungu* under colonial rule v. Twaddle 1969 (ii).
110. Low 1960, pp.50, 62-9.
111. Low 1957 (ii), p.284.
112. v. Chapter III, Section 7, below.
113. Warren 1966, pp.129-42 discusses the question of the established Church of England in the colonies, and notices the ambiguities which arose in its relationship with government at the territorial level. Uganda may be a unique case of the Anglican Church becoming unofficially semi-established at the level of subordinated kingdoms.
114. Lavigerie: *Instructions*, pp.69-70, 112-14.
115. Oliver 1952, pp.183-84.
116. Hellberg, pp.75-87. v. especially p.86 for the group which migrated across the border from Buddu.
117. Walker to Baylis, 6 Mar., 30 April 1896; 20 Sept. 1898; 26 Aug. 1899, etc. CMSA G3 A5/011, 012, 013; A7/01.
118. Low 1960, p.36.
119. Low 1957 (i), p.14.
120. Baskerville to Lang, Aug. 1891, CMSA G3 A5/07.
121. Walker to Lang, 5 Aug. 1891, CMSA G3 A5/07. Emphasis added.
122. L. A. Fallers 1964, pp.220-21, 224, 300-01.

CHAPTER II

1. In this account of Toro traditional history, use has been made of the following: WF *Chroniques* and *Rapports Annuels*, 1895-7 (these contain letters and diary extracts written by Achte, and reports based on them); Fisher 1911 (this gives a different account of the reasons for

setting up an independent kingdom in Toro, but this account agrees with others in saying that Kaboyo was a particularly beloved son, that the defection took place during the reign of Mugenyi's predecessor, that his father eventually agreed to Kaboyo's independence in Toro, and that Kaboyo was offered the position of *Mukama* of Bunyoro after his father's death, but that he refused it); Rukiidi; Winyi 1931; Balya 1965 and 1966; accounts collected by Fr R. Chaput, W.F. at Virika Mission, of which he kindly allowed me to take a copy; Low 1963; Taylor and Richards, pp.127-136; Furley, pp.184-198; Ingham 1975; Rukiidi, n.d.

2. This appears to mean that he recognized him as a territorial chief and made him a *mujwarakondo* (crown wearer). It is of interest that the crown or *kondo* worn by the *Mukama* of Toro does not have the 18 eyeless needles which are peculiar to the *kondo* worn by the *Mukama* of Bunyoro. See Roscoe 1923 (i), p.131, and Fisher 1911, photographs of Andereya Duhaga (frontispiece) and Daudi Kasagama (facing p.182).
3. Ashe 1890, p.215; Johnson, pp.56-7.
4. Ibid.
5. Apolo Kivebulaya: *Notebook 1896-1906*, MUA. (This was pointed out by Dr J. A. Rowe.)
6. Perham and Bull, Vol. II, p.201.
7. Ibid.
8. Jaasi-Kiiza (interview); v. also note 11, below.
9. Balya 1966; Rukiidi, pp.33-4.
10. Perham and Bull, pp.410-11.
11. Johnston, p.134.
12. *Bond mss.*, 21 March 1908.
13. Perham and Bull, Vol. II, p.410.
14. Ingham 1965, pp. 53-6; Furley, p. 189; Bacwa. As a youth Bacwa witnessed the fighting between the Nyoro forces and Byakweyamba's men, and fled to the forest with the survivors.
15. Roscoe 1923 (i), pp. 149-50.
16. Furley, pp.190-2.
17. The Finance Committee Minutes for 9 July 1894 record that four catechists went. Bacwa speaks of a group. Achte mentions more than four by name, but some names are incorrect, and probably he includes boys who accompanied the catechists. Tucker, Johnson, Balya and Luck speak of two only. However, Balya was not in Toro in 1894. Kitching 1912 quotes the Rev. Nuwa Nakiwafu writing in *Ebifa*, November 1911, who says he was in Toro from 1894-7. Information collected by M. Nyakazingo in 1966 has the names of four catechists: Petero Nsubuga, Mako Lweimbazi, Nuwa Nakiwafu and Tito Wakibingi. The last named is on Baskerville's list of those baptized before 1888. 'Lweimbazi' = Luganda 'Luyimbazi', a chiefly title (Rukiidi pp.40 and 63 gives 'Luyimbazi').
18. The accepted story of the coming of Christianity to Toro simply states that Lweimbazi and Nsubuga went there in 1894 at the request of Kasagama and Byakweyamba, and that Kasagama was among

those whom they taught. Only Johnson, pp.57–9 records that Nsubuga had taught Byakweyamba in Buganda. Bacwa, who was at Butiti in 1894, did not remember Lweimbazi; Binyomo, who was a child at Kasagama's court, knew of Lweimbazi but not of Nsubuga. Johnson records that Tabaro, *Mukama* of Mboga, visited Kabarole in 1894 and afterwards told Johnson: 'The king and Marko spoke to me that I should read'. The most likely explanation of all this seems to be that teaching was carried on both at Butiti and at Kabarole from the beginning, Nsubuga going to the headquarters of his old pupil.

19. WF *Chroniques*, Bukumbi, 14 Dec. 1894.
20. Ibid., Rubaga, 15 Nov. 1895.
21. Minutes of the Finance Committee, 9 July 1894, CMSA G3 A5/010.
22. Hansen, p.13.
23. *Vi. Di.*, 15 Nov., 4, 18, 30 Dec. 1895; 12 Jan. 1896.
24. The following account of Apolo Kivebulaya is based on Mrs Luck's study of him in which she draws extensively on his diaries. Information drawn from other sources is noted.
25. Leblond, pp.196–7.
26. Furley, pp. 192–3; Komuntale (interview).
27. Bacwa; Balya 1965 (interviews).
28. Balya 1966 (interview).
29. Tucker 1899, p.17.
30. Hansen, p. 9.
31. *Vi. Di.* 24 April 1896.
32. Ibid. 11 May 1896.
33. WF *Chroniques*, Toro, 27–31 May; 1 July 1896.
34. Achte to Lavigerie, December 1895; Toulze to Lavigerie, 8 Jan. 1896; Achte to Lavigerie, 30 April 1896, *Co. Ny. Sept.*, WFA 87.
35. Tucker 1899, p.17.
36. Luck, pp.66–7, quoting Fisher's Diary.
37. Lloyd 1899, p.155; Tucker 1899, pp.22, 31; Johnson, p.149; Luck, pp.66–7. Baptisms took place at Ngoma in 1896 and catechists are known to have gone there early, and in view of the interest of the *Nyina Omukama* it seems safe to assume that this was one of the seven districts, in spite of its proximity to Kabarole. Kyaka (Kitagweta) appears from Tucker's account to have been an afterthought.
38. Lloyd 1906, p.87; Tucker to Baylis, 3 June 1899, CMSA G3 A7/01.
39. Kisoro (interview).
40. Tucker 1899, p.22.
41. Luck, p.67.
42. Balya 1966 (interview); *Bu. Bap. Reg.*
43. Walker to Baylis, 16 Aug. 1897, CMSA G3 A5/013; Maddox in *Men/Ug. Notes*, June 1901, p.58; Balya 1966. I am grateful to Mr Andrew Wheeler for information on Kyerre, the immediate successor of Byakweyamba.
44. *Vi. Di.*, 29 June, 3 and 5 July, 3 Aug. 1896.
45. Furley, p.193; Low 1965, p.70.

46. *Vi. Di.*, 16 July, 31 Aug. 1896.
47. Low 1957 (i), p.491; Furley, pp.191–3.
48. Tucker 1899, p.31.
49. Ibid.
50. Lloyd 1899, p.273.
51. Walker to Baylis, 20 Sept. 1898, CMSA G3 A7/01.
52. Roscoe to Baylis, 12 April 1899, CMSA G3 A7/01.
53. Roscoe to Baylis, 26 Sept. 1898; 12 April 1899, CMSA G3 A7/01; *Ka. Ch. Co. Mins*, 31 Dec. 1898.
54. Balya 1966 (interview).
55. Binyomo (interview).
56. Balya 1965 (interview).
57. Mukidi (letter); Balya 1966 (interview).
58. Balya 1966; Binyomo; Byabusakuzi; Schofield (interviews).
59. Information about these last three men came from Binyomo and Kisoro (interviews).
60. Tucker: 'A Memorandum concerning the language to be used in elementary teaching in Toro', 16 Feb. 1900, CMSA G3 A7/01.
61. Walker to Baylis, 1 June 1900, CMSA G3 A7/01.
62. Balya 1966 (interview).
63. Low 1957 (ii), p.507–8. Kabwegyere argues that the Ganda did not intend to 'acculturate the rest of the Protectorate in Kiganda ways with the aim of Buganda spreading its rule outwards', and that Ganda political agents and others worked for themselves as individuals, not for 'Buganda as a political entity'. See pp. 80–1. He would clear them of the charge of collaboration. However, in the early period discussed here, the evidence seems to contradict Kabwegyere's claim. Maddox to Baylis, 4 Dec. 1899, CMSA G3 A7/01.
64. Enclosure in Walker to Baylis, 26 Sept. 1901, CMSA G3 A7/03.
65. CMS *AR*, 1902/3, p.134.
66. Maddox to Baylis, 4 Dec. 1899, CMSA G3 A7/01.
67. Roscoe to Baylis, 22 June and 4 Aug. 1900, CMSA G3 A7/01.
68. *Ka. Ch. Co. Mins*, 20 Aug. 1900.
69. *COU Record Bk*; Byabusakuzi (interview).
70. CMS *AR*, 1901/2 (cf. Table III); Hurditch to Jenkins, 16 Feb. 1902, CMSA G3 A7/03.
71. Rukiidi, pp.24, 30; Komuntale (interview).
72. *Toro W.T.Rec.*; Komuntale (interview).
73. Typescript life of Mother Mechtilde kept at Bwanda Convent; WF *RA*, 1903, General Report by Mgr Streicher, and Report on Villa Maria.
74. WF *RA*, 1903, Virika.
75. *Vi. Di.*, 7 Oct. 1910.
76. *Kat. Ju. Bk.*
77. In Tanzania the Universities' Mission to Central Africa, which represents the 'high' Anglican section of the Church of England, has

religious sisters among its missionaries and has started an indigenous order which has grown slowly. The 'low' church CMS tended to look on religious orders as dangerously close to Roman Catholicism.

78. Lloyd 1899, p.172; Leblond, p.197.
79. Maddox to Baylis, 13 Jan. 1900, CMSA G3 A7/01.
80. *Men/Ug. Notes*, June 1903, p.30.
81. *Bond mss.*, May 1905; 28 Aug. 1908.
82. *Vi. Di.* eight safaris of eight days each were made during the first six months of 1913, for instance: Rwakahumire.
83. WF*RA*, 1903, 1908/9, Virika.
84. Bacwa (interview).
85. Roscoe to Baylis, 22 June 1900, CMSA G3 A7/02.
86. Maddox in *Men/Ug. Notes*, June 1901, p.58.
87. Luck, p.94.
88. Maddox, loc. cit.
89. CMA *AR* 1902/3, p. 134.
90. Kitching was sent to open the new mission at Keyo in Acoli; v. Chapter V below.
91. *Bond mss.*, May 1905.
92. Balya 1966 (interview).
93. *Toro W.T. Rec.* In 1896 the Church Council at Mengo began issuing catechists with letters of introduction to the Christian congregations to whom they were sent. Later a letter came to mean a certificate that a catechist or teacher had undergone a course of training. A 'first letter teacher' had usually undergone a few months' to a year's training and was qualified to give only the most elementary instruction in reading and catechism. His training was unlikely to have been full time. Those who showed promise as catechists might be chosen to work for their second 'letter'. In districts outside Buganda this was generally done in the local vernacular. For the third 'letter', which would qualify a man to give instruction for confirmation, training was usually done at Mukono and was in Luganda.
94. Tucker 1899, p.34.
95. *Men/Ug. Notes*, April 1902, pp.27-9 gives an account in English of an address given by Yasoni Kironde, a Ganda catechist, to a meeting at Mengo at which he described his work in Toro.
96. *Toro W. T. Rec.; Ka. Ch. Co. Mins.; Ka. Bap. Reg.*
97. *Bond mss.*, Aug. 1909.
98. Ngoma is now usually known as Rwengoma, but the old form of the name is retained here to avoid confusion when contemporary records are referred to.
99. Johnson, p.88.
100. CMS *AR*, 1901/2, p.139.
101. *Bond mss.*, May 1905.
102. *Toro W. T. Rec.*; *Ka. Ch. Co. Mins*; Balya 1965; Komuntale.
103. Tucker 1899, p.32.
104. *Men/Ug. Notes*, April 1902, p.28.

105. Ibid., pp.27-9, CMS *AR*, 1901/2, p.142.
106. *Ka. Ch. Co. Mins*, 22 June 1901.
107. *Men/Ug. Notes*, April 1902, p.29.
108. *Toro W.T. Rec.*; *Ka. Bap. Reg.*
109. *Bond mss.*, Aug. 1909.
110. *Ka. Bap. Reg.*; *Bond mss.*, Aug. 1909; Balya 1965; Rwakahumire.
111. Research carried out by the Rev. (now Bishop) Cyprian Bamwoze on leadership in Nakanyonyi Church of Uganda Parish is illuminating on this point. He believes that the chief's influence was far more important to the missions in connection with the acquisition of land than because of the influence they were able to exercise over their clients.
112. Nyakazingo, whose informants on this point were his father, Samusoni Rwakabugili, Binyomo and Kamuhiigi.
113. *Bond mss.*, 21 March 1908.
114. Ingham 1975, p.104 and notes 32 and 33, p.175.
115. *Bond mss.*, loc. cit.; Rukiidi, p.53. The chiefs' head-dresses were not ready in time for the *empango*.
116. v. Chapter III, Section 7, below.
117. *Bond mss.*, loc. cit.
118. *Men/Ug. Notes,* May 1908, p.71.
119. Ibid., p.72.
120. Pirouet 1966, where the whole of Mrs Bond's letter is quoted.
121. Jones, p.74.
122. e.g. the life of Mika Sematimba by J. A. Rowe in *UJ* 28, 2, 1964, pp.179-200.
123. These things were condemned, not because they were African, but because the missionaries thought they were sinful. It needs to be remembered that many evangelical missionaries thought that abstention from dancing, smoking, drinking, going to the threatre, and many other pleasures was essential to the practice of Christian holiness, and they refrained from these things in their own society. The condemnation of such 'worldly' pleasures is today misunderstood as being racist in origin, but this does not seem to be so. There appears to be some measure of corelation between rigid fundamentalism and racism, so the confusion is the more easily understood.
124. e.g. Rwakahumire and Byabusakuzi (Anglican catechists); Balya, Binyomo and Kamuhiigi (Anglican clergy).

CHAPTER III

1. KW, p.67, v. also introductory section to Chapter II, above.
2. Dunbar, p.81.
3. Not all of what is now known as Toro was included in the area over which Kaboyo made himself Mukama; v. Map 2.
4. Roscoe 1923 (i), pp.194-7; Beattie 1960 (i), p.103.

5. Kiiza, confirmed in conversation by Nyakatura (interviews).
6. KW, p.66.
7. Whether this is a true derivation or not matters little. It is the association of ideas which is important.
8. Since this research was carried out Dr G. N. Uzoigwe has also worked on the *barusura*. In the main his conclusions and mine are in agreement.
9. This account of events in Bunyoro is based on the following: Dunbar, pp.81-96; Low 1957 (ii); Gray 1971; Lanning, esp. pp.120-33.
10. Beattie 1960 (ii), p.21; Hemphill, pp.407-8, 422; Burke, p.79.
11. WF *Chroniques*, 16 July 1894.
12. Low 1957 (ii), p.378; Dunbar, pp.88-9.
13. Information about Lubaale, otherwise known as Fataki, is based on his own articles in the *Bu. Ch. Mag.* pp.65-7, 96, and an interview with S. Fataki and A. Lukayi, two of his surviving sons.
14. The name is said to mean gunpowder in Swahili, and he was given it because of his skill as a marksman according to most informants. Fisher says it was given because of his lively temperament. *Fisher mss.*, X A, p.38.
15. Fataki gives the date as 1894, but he makes other minor mistakes over dates, and I have therefore presumed that he went to Toro with the other *barusura* in early 1895, v. note 12, above. In this sentence Fataki refers to Mako Kironde, but two paragraphs further on he calls him Mako Kironde, Rweimbazi. 'Rweimbazi' = Luganda 'Luyimbazi' and is a chieftaincy title.
16. *Fisher mss.*, XA, pp.34, 46.
17. Fisher to Baylis, 26 May 1896, CMSA G3 A5/012; *Fisher mss.*, VI, pp.4-5; X A, p.35.
18. Fataki dated the visit February 1896, three months later than it really was. He was perhaps confused with Fisher's second arrival in February 1899.
19. Fataki, p.65.
20. *Fisher mss.*, VI, p.6.
21. *Masindi Bap. Reg.* 20 Aug. 1899; *Fisher mss.*, VIII, p.16; X A, p.36; Kakumba (interview).
22. *Namirembe Bap. Reg.*
23. Tucker 199, p.244.
24. *Fisher mss.*, VI, p.7; X A, p.31.
25. Dunbar, p.88: quoting Gregory, p.212; Mrs Lloyd in *Men/Ug. Notes*, Nov. 1901, p.86: 'We hear that an attempt has been made to get at the number of the inhabitants, and the opinion of the best able to judge is, that the whole of Unyoro does not contain more than one hundred thousand . . . The people are miserably poor and very dirty, the number who are afflicted with itch is simply astounding.' Scabies, also noted in Toro, is commonly found where the living conditions are very poor.
26. Beattie 1960 (ii), p.22.
27. *Fisher mss.*, X A, p.36.

28. Thruston, pp.126–9, 209, 218, 222.
29. Everyone in Bunyoro whom I have questioned is agreed that the *barusura* raided and plundered in Bunyoro itself, living off the country. v. Lloyd 1906, p.17 and Uziogwe, pp.14–16.
30. Information given by the mother of my interpreter, Mr A. Kandumba. v. also Stafford in *UJ*, 1955, p.208.
31. *Ladbury mss.*, numerous entries; Beattie 1960 (ii), p.4.
32. *Fisher mss.*, X A, p.34; XV, 'Death of an Historical Character'.
33. Thruston, p.191.
34. Lloyd 1906, pp.33, 34.
35. Fataki, p.66; Bikundi (interview); *Fisher mss.*, XV, loc. cit.
36. *Fisher mss.*, XV, loc. cit.
37. K.W., p.67; *Bu. Ch. Mag.*, anon., 1932, pp.68–9.
38. Hemphill, p.405; Uzoigwe, pp.16–17.
39. *Fisher mss.*, X A, p.47; S. Fataki and A. Lukayi. In 1896 Ternan had been entrusted with setting up an administration in Bunyoro. Kabalega had been driven out, and Ternan put no one in his place because of the rivalry between Byabacwezi and Rwabudongo, both of whom seemed to him to be claiming the position of *Mukama*. It seems that he misunderstood the nature of the quarrel. Low 1957 (ii), p.382.
40. Low 1957 (ii), pp.502–3. But Low seems to be incorrect in accepting that Rwabudongo had been Kabalega's *katikiro* (first minister), although this is certainly how Evatt understood the situation.
41. *Bamuroga*, the chief religious functionary in Bunyoro, was probably the most powerful person other than the *Mukama*. His position would have made him unacceptable to the British, however, even had they recognized his importance. Roscoe 1923 (i), pp.107, 120.
42. S. Mbabi-Katana, personal communication; Kyopaali (interview).
43. cf. Uzoigwe, p.32. The arrogation of royal prerogatives was too widely agreed upon by my Nyoro informants to be discounted.
44. Lloyd 1906, p.33.
45. Tucker 1911, p.244.
46. *Fisher mss.*, X A, p.34.
47. S. Mbabi-Katana 1953, and personal communication.
48. Tucker 1911, p. 245.
49. *Masindi Bap. Reg.; Fisher mss.*, XII, p.12.
50. *Masindi Mar. Reg.*, 21 Oct. 1899. Like some others, Byabacwezi took the opportunity offered by becoming a Christian and having to get rid of all but one wife, to choose an entirely new partner.
51. *Empango* Celebrations Committee 1967, p.6.
52. *Fisher mss.*, XA, p.42; XI, p.14. 11 May 1899; XII, pp. 3, 12, 13.
53. Dunbar, p.106.
54. *Fisher mss.*, Bunyoro Notes 7, p.14; 8, p.30; XI, p.31; XII, pp.9, 12
55. Roscoe to Baylis, 22 June 1900, CMSA G3 A7/02.
56. Lloyd 1906, p.31. Sub-title.
57. *Fisher mss.*, Bunyoro Notes 7, p.19.

58. Beattie 1960 (ii), p.4.
59. Ibid., p.23.
60. Hastings 1969, pp. 225-6.
61. Anon. *Bu. Ch. Mag.* p.77.
62. *Ladbury mss.*, Letter Book, 21 Jan. 1907; Sept. 1905.
63. *Fisher mss.*, XIII, 2 Oct. 1899; Beattie 1960 (ii), p.23.
64. Dunbar, p.108, note 17.
65. For Sira Dongo: Lawrence. pp.6-7. For Mika Fataki: S. Fataki and A. Lukayi. For Yafesi Isingoma: Kabuliiteka. For Leo Kaboha: P. Kaboha. For Z. Kyopaali and A. Mutunzi; their own oral information. For Y. Wamala: Bikundi. For F. Kyaherwa: his own oral information (interviews).
66. The extent of Kabalega's influence over Kitagwenda, Busongora, Buhwezu, and Buzimba is open to some question, as it is also said that they were paying tribute to Ntare V of Ankole. However, Kabalega's troops certainly raided into Busongora.
67. v. Chapter II, Section 4, above.
68. *Bu. Ch. Mag.* Anon., pp.68-9. KW, p.67.
69. Kiiza and Nyakatura (interviews).
70. Dwakaikara and Muherya (mss).
71. *Masindi Bap. Reg.*
72. Kyaherwa (interview).
73. WF *RA*, 1903, Hoima. The following figures are given:

Catholics	*Anglicans*
650 baptized	300 baptized
3,500 catechumens	2,500 catechumens

74. CMS *AR*, 1901/2, p.144.
75. *Masindi Bap. Reg.*; *Hoima Bap. Reg.*
76. Lloyd in *CMI*, Sept. 1901, p.713.
77. Lloyd, quoted in Walker to Baylis, 26 Sept. 1901, CMSA G3 A7/03.
78. S. Mbabi-Katana, personal communication.
79. Ecob to Hattersley, 14 Aug. 1901, CMSA G3 A7/02 gives a particularly outspoken expression of this point of view.
80. *CMI*, Oct. 1902, p. 775, quoting a letter from the Rev. N. Nakiwafu, dated 4 April 1902.
81. WF *RA*, 1903, Hoima.
82. Kabuliiteka (interview).
83. Mrs Lloyd in *Men/Ug. Notes*, April 1901, p.47.
84. Dunbar, p.121.
85. Lloyd 1906, pp.33-4.
86. Mrs Lloyd, loc. cit. p. 44.
87. Dunbar, p.108.
88. Fisher, letter of February 1905, quoted in *CMI*, June 1905, p.460.
89. Fataki, pp.66-7, 96; Farthing, in *Men/Ug. Notes*, Oct. 1902, p.66. *Masindi Serv. Bk.*; *COU Teachers' Record*; Kyopaali (interview).

90. CMS *AR*, 1904/5, pp.120–3; L. Kakumba (interview).
91. *COU Record Bk*; *Fisher mss.*, XVIII, Annual letter, 5 Dec. 1912; *Hoima Serv. Bk.*; Masa (interview).
92. Farthing in *Men/Ug. Notes*, Oct. 1902, p.66.
93. *Masindi Bap. Reg.*; *Gulu Serv. Bk.*; *Hoima Serv. Bk.*; *Ladbury mss.*, 3 Feb. 1908; *Mins of the Theol. Bd.*, 2 May 1917; Kyopaali and L. Kakumba (interviews).
94. *Masindi Bap. Reg.*; Kyopaali (interview).
95. Kabuliiteka (interview).
96. *Ladbury mss.*, 14, 18, 20, 21, 27 Oct., 11 Nov. 1906; 21, 23 Jan., 5 Feb. 1908.
97. *Fisher mss.*, XVIII, Annual letter, 30 Nov. 1905.
98. *Fisher mss.*, Bunyoro Notes 7, p.31, 14 Dec. 1899; 8, p.15, 7 Jan. 1900.
99. Nyamayarwa and Kaparaga (interviews).
100. *Ladbury mss.*, Mrs Ladbury, 3 Nov. 1906.
101. *COU Record Bk.*; *Fisher mss.*, XVIII, Annual letter, 5 Dec. 1912; *Hoima Serv. Bk.*; Masa (interview).
102. Masa (interview).
103. *Mins of the Theol. Bd.*, 16 May 1918.
104. Tegart to Fisher, 26 Sept. 1902, CMSA G3 A7/03.
105. The story as told here depends on a ms account written down by the Rev. A. Muherya of his father's recollections. Muherya's father was Dwakaikara.
106. From Tegart's point of view the catechists were sent, not by Kitehimbwa, but by himself and the church in Bunyoro. However, they would undoubtedly have got the approval of the *Mukama* for the undertaking.
107. From the Belgian point of view the catechists were representatives of the British Empire, apparently.
108. Nyamayarwa and Kibumbirire (interviews).
109. Dunbar, p.107; *Ladbury mss.*, Letter Book, 1 Jan. 1907.
110. Tegart to Fisher, Sept., and 15 Oct. 1902, CMSA G3 A7/03.
111. *Ladbury mss.*, 6 Nov, 1905; 2, 9, 11 March 1906.
112. *Fisher mss.*, XVIII, Annual letter, 9 Dec. 1907. The late H. B. Thomas, OBE, who collated these papers for CMS has noted in the margin that Fisher seems to have gone to Burega about Christmas, 1907. The Bugoma Baptism Register was lost when the catechist's house was destroyed by fire, so no check is available. This is the only Baptism Register I have found to be missing.
113. *Uganda Atlas* 1962, p.75; Kaliisa (interview).
114. Nakiwafu, letter dated 4 April 1902, quoted in *CMI*, Oct. 1902, p.775.
115. *Fisher mss.*, XVIII, Annual letter, 9 Dec. 1907.
116. Nakiwafu, loc. cit.
117. Lloyd 1906, p.89.

118. Nakiwafu, loc. cit., p.774; Lloyd, letter of 9 Nov. 1902, quoted in *Men/Ug. Notes*, Jan. 1903. Lloyd says they were Alur, but they were teaching in the Palwo area, and at this time there was much confusion about the Lwoo peoples. The catechists were Sirwano Ndyanabo and Yoasi Nkonge.
119. For a fuller account of this, v. Chapter V, below.
120. *Fisher mss.*, XVI, Fisher to Tucker, Nov. 1905; Odurkene, Enin, Ogwal, Obura, Oluol (interviews).
121. Roscoe to Baylis, 11 May, 25 Aug. 1905, CMSA G3 A7/04.
122. *Fisher mss.*, XVI, Fisher to Tucker, 8, 12 June, 20 Nov., 4 Dec. 1905.
123. *Fisher mss.*, XV, 'The Rise of the Uganda Church', n.d.; *Bu. Ch. Co. Mins,* 30 June 1906.
124. *Fisher mss.*, loc. cit.; XVIII, Annual letter, 5 Dec. 1912.
125. Dunbar, p.110.
126. Roberts 1962 (ii), p.445.
127. Dunbar, pp.144-5; *Ladbury mss.*, 31 Jan. 1904.
128. Fisher to Baylis, 11 May 1907, CMSA G3 A7/05.
129. Fisher to Baylis, 12 July 1907, enclosing a copy of this letter, CMSA G3 A7/05.
130. Fisher to Tucker, 25 May 1907, CMSA G3 A7/05.
131. *Ladbury mss.*, 19 May 1907; Mrs Ladbury, 27 April 1907, quoting a letter from Miss Chadwick, a CMS missionary at Hoima.
132. *Empango* Celebrations Committee 1967, p.7.
133. Fisher to Tucker, 20, 25 May 1907, CMSA G3 A7/05.
134. *Hoima Di.*, 16 May 1907.
135. *Hoima Di.*, 16, 27, 30 May, 24 June, 18-20 Dec. 1907; 10 Jan. 1908.
136. *Men/Ug. Notes*, Oct. 1908, pp.149-52.
137. Dr Michael Twaddle, personal communication.
138. *Fisher mss.*, Fisher to Bardsley, 30 Nov. 1910.
139. WF *RA*, Hoima, 1908/9, 1910/11, 1911/12.
140. *Hoima Di.*, 31 March, 15 June 1911; 14 Feb., 3 June 1912.
141. *Hoima Di.*, 3 June 1912.
142. *Hoima Di.*, 31 Dec. 1911; 26-7 May, 3 June 1912.

CHAPTER IV

1. Karugire 1970, 1971.
2. Morris 1962, 1964; Oberg; Roscoe 1923 (ii); Stenning 1960; B. K. Taylor; Karugire 1970, 1971, 1973.
3. Stenning 1960, p.149. Karugire 1973, p.39 points out that the office of *katikiro*, the Luganda term by which the British called the *enganzi*, did not exist in Ankole before the arrival of the British.
4. Morris 1964. War and cattle are the themes of all these recitations.
5. Stenning 1960, pp.151-2.

6. Oliver 1952, p.183.
7. Morris 1962, p.14. The Ganda had backed Ntare's rival in the struggle for the succession.
8. F. L. Williams, p.126. This area was later annexed by Buganda, so that the prophecy of Kiboga that trouble would follow if the Ganda were allowed to settle was fulfilled.
9. There may have been other reasons as well why Ntare refused to see, not only Stanley, but any European:
   (i) There was a belief that if two rulers of the status of the *Mugabe* were to meet, one of them would die or suffer serious disaster. v. Ntare School History Society in *UJ* 29, 2, 1965, p. 189: 'Ntare regarded Stanley as one of his own rank.'
   (ii) The people had taken Stanley and his companions as Cwezi or Nyabingi, v. Stanley 1890, Vol. II, pp. 317, 335. Did Ntare fear losing his power to them? Would this add weight to (i)?
10. F. L. Williams, pp.126-7.
11. Morris 1962, p.7.
12. F. L. Williams, p.131.
13. Morris 1960, pp.32-3.
14. Buningwire 1965 (interview).
15. Roscoe, letter dated 29 Aug. 1894, in *CMI*, Dec. 1894, p.917.
16. There is a puzzling reference in a letter of the Rev. H. Clayton of 4 Sept. 1904: 'We had a sermon today from a visitor named Firipo Muwanga. He was the head teacher in Koki when I first went there, and just about seven years ago Leakey and Pilkington sent him here as an envoy to visit Kahaya's father, and ask if he would allow teachers to be sent, but he refused.' It is not clear whether this refers to 1894 or to 1897. If to 1894, then 'seven years ago' is not correct; if to 1897, then 'Kahaya's father' is not correct, as he had died in 1895. This is quoted from a *copy* of an original letter, the copy having been made by Clayton himself in 1964. It would be very convenient if we could suppose a small copying error and read: 'This man was the head teacher in Koki when I first went there seven years ago, and Leakey and Pilkington sent him here . . .' This would then refer to the 1894 occasion when Pilkington and Leakey were together at Mengo, and Pilkington was the moving spirit behind the evangelistic outreach that year when we know the Church Council considered the possibility of evangelizing Ankole.
17. *Clayton mss.*, 8 July 1897.
18. Tucker 1911, p.271.
19. Buningwire 1965 (interview).
20. The account here is based primarily on the *Clayton mss.* Information from additional sources is referenced.
21. The names of the catechists were supplied by Buningwire.
22. Buningwire 1965; Katunji; Katoomizi (interviews); Tucker 1911 writes, 'At length another great chief, the *Mugema*, came forward and craved permission of the Church Council for two of his own followers to go to Ankole . . . On this occasion, however, they did not go alone. Clayton who . . . had long had his eyes on Ankole . . . at once

embraced the opportunity of seeing for himself what prospects there were for the planting of the cross, and arranged to accompany the two Baganda evangelists. Kahaya received the party kindly, if not cordially, and at once acceded to Clayton's request for permission to preach and teach.' There are difficulties in Tucker's account:

(i) Clayton, writing contemporarily, gives no hint that these men were sent by the *Mugema*.

(ii) Bungingwire denies categorically that they were. He is able to name them, and if the names given are correct, then the men would not seem to have had any connection with the *Mugema*.

(iii) Tucker is not correct in saying that Kahaya acceded at once to Clayton's request.

23. *Clayton mss.*, 25 May 1899.
24. Ibid., 24 May 1899.
25. Buningwire attributes this failure largely to a lack of suitable food; Tucker to heathern opposition. Tucker gives the date of their appearance before the Church Council as May; but they had their first interview with Kahaya as late as 25 May, so must have returned to Mengo in June.
26. *Clayton mss.*, Sept. 1899.
27. Buningwire 1965 (interview) supplied the full names of the catechists, and these were subsequently confirmed from the *Willis mss.*, 'Visit to Uganda 1933'.
28. Tucker 1911, p.274.
29. A. R. Cook, Journal letter, 3 Dec. 1899, CMSA G3 A7/01.
30. Buningwire 1964 (interview).
31. Tucker 1911, p.278; *Clayton mss.*, 3 Sept. 1899; Clayton in *Men/Ug. Notes*, Nov. 1900.
32. Buningwire 1964, 1965 (interviews). He says that the catechists arrived one week later, and is emphatic about this. Cook and Tucker say they remained at Rushasha. The contradiction can be resolved by supposing that they were left behind by the missionaries, but that they left immediately for Koki to fetch food, returning one week later.
33. T. S. M. Williams, p.172 has a note on the shortage of food in Ankole. He brings evidence to show that there was a genuine shortage of food and that Kahaya was not just making excuses. To this evidence must be added that of the *Willis mss.* which was not available to Williams; e.g. 7 Jan. 1901, concerning the choice of Mbarara as capital: 'They seem to have chosen the one place in Ankole where you have to march a whole day or two days in every direction before you come to any cultivation worth the name.'
34. Some dissatisfaction with the traditional religion is reflected in the fact that before the arrival of Europeans the people of Ankole had started to accept new cults from outside, such as the Nyabingi cult from Karagwe. People were willing to pay a high price for initiation into these when their own cults seemed to be doing little good. I am indebted to Rev. Y. K. Bamunoba and Dr M. Mushanga for information on this point.
35. Morris 1962, p.33.

36. Gray 1960, p.172.
37. *Rurembo*—royal kraal. Usually translated 'palace', but this seems so misleading when used for *rurembo* at this date that it seems better to retain the vernacular term. It was during this year that the *rurembo* was moved from Rushasha to Kamukuzi, where the missionaries found it when they arrived in 1901.
38. The following account is taken almost verbatim from interviews with Buningwire in 1894 and 1965, translated for me by Y. K. Bamunoba.
39. *Clayton mss.*, 24 April 1900.
40. Buningwire 1964 (interview).
41. *Clayton mss.*, 21 Sept. 1900.
42. *CMI*, May 1901, p.391, based on Baskerville, says that the *Mugabe* also burnt his fetishes; v. also the letter quoted in Johnson 1908, p.189. But Clayton and Willis both record the burning of the *Mugabe*'s fetishes in June 1901. Tucker is derivative. The confusion over the *Mugabe*'s charms being burnt possibly arose because Mbaguta burnt his in the *rurembo*.
43. *Willis mss.*, 13 Jan. 1901.
44. Oliver 1952, p.193.
45. *Willis mss.*, 30 July 1901.
46. Buningwire 1965 (interview).
47. *Willis mss.*, 6 Jan., 1 Feb. 1901.
48. It was customary in Ankole for rich Hima to divide their cattle into several herds, each numbering, perhaps, a thousand head. With each herd some sheep were kept, partly for sacrificial reasons, and partly because it was believed that cattle disease would be diverted into the sheep, and the cows would be protected. This explanation was offered by L. Kamugungunu, one of the richest cattle-owners in Ankole; but see also *UJ* 13, 1, 1949, p.113 for a veterinary officer's comments. I have also been told that in a mixed herd the sheep will always bring up the rear, and the herdsmen know that when the sheep appear, no more cattle are likely to be straying behind (M. Doornbos, personal communication). It has already been noted that disease had greatly reduced the numbers of cattle in Ankole in the years preceding 1900. Willis makes a further reference in 1901 to the severe losses still being sustained by Mbaguta. When disease struck the cattle, several herds would be amalgamated. The owner would then find himself with more sheep than he required, and the surplus would be useless to him since there was a taboo on the eating of mutton or the wearing of sheepskin by the Hima. This explains why Mbaguta was able to be so generous with sheep. I am grateful to Y. K. Bamunoba and M. Mushanga for this information.
49. *Willis mss.*, 7 Jan., 19 June, 23 June 1901; 16 Feb. 1902.
50. Balya and Binyomo (interviews).
51. Kacibala (interview).
52. *Willis mss.*, 8 April 1902.
53. Kamugungunu (interview).
54. CMS *AR*, 1905/6, p.97; Kacibala (interview).

55. Except where otherwise stated, the information in this paragraph and the preceding one was given by Kacibala.
56. *Willis mss.*, 13 Jan., 23 June 1901.
57. *Willis mss.*, 2 Jan. 1902.
58. Bamunoba and Welbourn, p.17.
59. *Willis mss.*, 10 Aug. 1902.
60. *Mbarara Di.*, introductory paragraphs in Vol. I; *Willis mss.*, 9 Jan. 1901.
61. *Mbarara Di.*, loc. cit.
62. Ibid., 7 Dec. 1902; *Ank. Bap. Reg.*
63. *Willis mss.*, 1 Sept., 8 Nov. 1902; *Clayton mss.*, 11 Dec. 1902.
64. *Willis mss.*, 8 Nov. 1902; Kacibala (interview).
65. *Clayton mss.*, 11 Dec. 1902.
66. Katunji (interview).
67. *Mbarara Di.*, 3, 10 Oct., 9 Dec. 1903; 22 Feb. 1904.
68. *Willis mss.*, 12 April 1902.
69. Gray 1960, p.167; Morris 1962, p.8.
70. Gray 1960, pp.170–3.
71. Ibid., p.174.
71. *Willis mss.*, 13 Jan., 12, 13, 14 April 1901.
73. Ibid., 26 June 1901.
74. Ibid., 4 July, 18 Sept. 1901.
75. Gray 1960, p.174 gives the date of her death as 1903, but Willis mentions it in a letter dated October 1902, and says that it had occurred 'recently'.
76. Buningwire 1965 (interview).
77. *Clayton mss.*, 22 May 1903.
78. Gray 1960, p.174 says she handed her charms to the *Mugabe*, and gives the date of her baptism as 29 September. He gives as his reference Nganwa: *Abakozire eby'okutangaza omuri Ankole*, Nairobi 1948, Chapter VIII; but I have followed the contemporary record, and the date of her baptism has been checked with the Baptism Register.
79. Buningwire 1965 (interview).
80. *Willis mss.*, 1 Nov. 1901.
81. Ibid., 29 April 1901.
82. *Willis mss.*, 22 June, Nov. 1901; 2 Jan., 26 Feb., 14 April, 2 May 1902.
83. Of the four, only two were, strictly speaking, the products of the Ankole mission. One had been taken to Bunyoro as a child and had been taught to read there, and one came from Buganda. The two others were natives of Ankole of about fourteen years of age. *Willis mss.*, 2 May 1902.
84. *Willis mss.*, 12, 18 Aug. 1902.
85. Morris 1962, p.40 gives the date of his death as 1901, but *Willis mss.*, 24 Aug. 1902 states that Kaihura had died since Willis's last visit in May 1902.

86. Another son, Macaca, was even more eager to read, and was baptized with his two other brothers some months before Kasigano in February 1903 (v. *Ank. Bap. Reg.*). Willis was greatly impressed with Macaca's eagerness. Local opinion has it that this was mainly due to his desire to marry Malyamu Kacibala, which he did on 15 June 1903. It was a great shock to Willis when for a time before his baptism Macaca toyed with the idea of receiving religious instruction from the White Fathers, but Mbaguta persuaded him against this. *Willis mss.*, 15, 20 Sept. 1902.
87. Morris 1962, p.40. He spent many years in Toro, returning to Ankole about 1920 and living near Kyagaju, but taking no active part in affairs (Kamugungunu (interview)).
88. Buningwire 1965 (interview).
89. Langlands and Namirembe, p.24.
90. Morris 1962, p.39.
91. *Willis mss.*, 12 Oct. 1902.
92. Karugire 1970, p.245.
93. This is Willis' rough translation of the letter.
94. *Willis mss.,* 30 July, 2 Sept. 1901: 16 Feb., 27 April, 2 Sept., 12, 21 Oct. 1902.
95. Kamuhiigi (interview).
96. *Willis mss.*, 27 April 1902; 'They are far ahead of our teachers.'
97. *Clayton mss.,* 22 May 1903; *Ka Ch. Co. Mins.*, 28 March 1903.
98. Gray 1960, pp.174-6; Morris 1960.
99. Low 1965, p.85, fn. 4 as well as my own findings.
100. Morris 1960, p.16.
101. Karugire 1973, pp.41-54; *Mbarara Di.*, 9 Nov., 22 Dec. 1903.
102. Karugire 1973, p.57; *Mbarara Di.*, general entry, 1905.
103. *Mbarara Di.*, loc. cit.; Gray 1960, p.166.
104. *Mbarara Di.*, loc. cit.
105. Morris 1960, pp.3-4.
106. *Mbarara Di.*, loc. cit. At this point only a typescript copy of the original diary remains. The original was damaged by white ants. The typist was unfamiliar with Ugandan names, and has sometimes mistranscribed Gorju's handwriting. 'Kahaya' appears as 'Rawaga', for instance. 'K' might easily be mistaken for 'R' in Gorju's handwriting, and 'y' for 'g'. 'Kahaya' was sometimes spelt as 'Kawaya' by Europeans. Some further difficulties arise because of vernacular words and phrases intermingled with Gorju's French and which also seem to be mistranscribed in some intances, and because of gaps in the text, but these seem to be small. However, the diary clearly states:

    > Mr Knowles et Mbaguta vont voir Gumira, . . . tous les deux échappent à un assassinat. Les Bahima (Bahinda) et Rawaga avaient décidé de les tuer, de kusuane même. Depuis quelques jours les paquets de . . . arrivaient chez Gumira. À peine le sous-commissaire (de) retour que Rawaga se rendre chez Gumira, son oncle, l'auteur du complot. Ayant manqué leur coup, ils attendent à ce moment là que Mr Galt vient à Nkole.

The remainder of the lengthy text relevant to this incident expresses surprise that the British did not divine the extent of the plot and Kahaya's own involvement. Morris 1960, p. 15 records a 'legend' about the presence of a White Father at Ibanda the day before Galt arrived, but notes that the presence of the White Father may well be fact, not legend.

107. *Mbarara Di.*, loc. cit.
108. Morris 1960, p.5.
109. Morris 1960, pp.11-12.
110. *Mbarara Di.*, 7 Dec. 1905. A. Katate and L. Kamugungunu: *Abagabe b'Ankole*, Kampala 1953, devotes little space to this incident, which is not surprising since Katate is the son of Ruhara at whose home the revellings took place, and who is mentioned, along with Igumira, Ryamugwizi, and Bucunku, as one of the authors of an earlier plot against Mbaguta. v. *Mbarara Di.*, 3 Nov. 1903.
111. *Willis mss.*, 3 Sept. 1901.
112. Ibid., 3 Sept. 1901; 27 April, 12 Oct. 1902.
113. *Mbarara Di.*, 31 Oct. 1908; Aug., Oct. 1910; WF *RA*, 1909/10, Bunyaruguru; Nicolet: *Yohana Kitagana*.
114. *Willis mss.*, 8 April 1902; v. also Chapter II, Section V.
115. Katunji; Buningwire 1965; Rugungura (interviews).
116. CMS *AR*, 1906/7, p.94; Kacibala (interview).
117. CMS *AR*, 1914/15, p.72.
118. Buningwire 1965 (interview).
119. CMS *AR*, 1906/7, p.94.
120. Shalita; Katunji; Buningwire 1965 (interviews).
121. Buningwire 1965; Katunji; Rugungura (interviews).
122. Buningwire 1965, 1966; Kamugungunu (interviews).
123. Buningwire 1965; Kashenya; Rwabite (interviews).
124. Taken almost verbatim from Kamugungunu (interview).
125. Gray 1960, p.175; Buningwire 1964, 1965 (interviews).
126. Rwabite (interview).
127. Buningwire 1965; Kamugungunu; Katunji; Ragungura (interviews).
128. CMS *AR*, 1908/9, pp.69-70.
129. CMS *AR*, 1904-9.
130. CMS *AR*, 1907-9; Kamugunugunu; Rwabite (interviews).
131. As note 130 and *Ank. Bap. Reg.*
132. CMS *AR*, 1910/11.

CHAPTER V

1. CMS *AR*, 1904/5, p.124.
2. Lloyd 1906, p.206.
3. Crazzolara, pp.481-2.
4. v. also Chapter III, Section 5, above.

5. Ogot 1967, pp.40–1; Webster and Onyango-ku-Odongo, pp.6–8.
6. Crazzolara, pp.240–1; Atkinson, pp.2–3.
7. Crazzolara, p.240.
8. Gray 1951; Atkinson.
9. Okot p'Bitek 1963; idem. 1965, pp.85, 87, 91–2.
10. In the Bantu areas the missionaries had no difficulty in finding a vernacular term which they felt they could use for the Christian God. In Acoli the Protestant missionaries could find no such term, and used a word which may have been imported. A discussion of this can be found in Southall 1956, pp.371–2, note 1; Ogot 1961; Okot p'Bitek 1963. Mbiti 1969, speaking of the traditional ideas and beliefs of nearly 300 African peoples including the Acoli, states: 'In all these societies, without a single exception, people have a notion of God as the Supreme Being.' v. also Mbiti 1970. For a conflicting point of view, v. M. Singleton in Singer and Street 1971. A comparison with the beliefs of the Dinka and the Nuer suggests that the Acoli may once have had a concept similar to that possessed by the Nuer today, but this is by no means sure. The possibility of Semitic influence on the more northerly of the Lwoo groups cannot be ruled out.
11. Bere 1946.
12. Lloyd 1906, p.192; Cook, p.192; Okech, p.21; Bishop and Ruffell, p.12; Girling, pp.152–3. Girling alone is unimpressed by the kinship claims of the Acoli with the Bito.
13. Cook, p.192.
14. Lloyd 1906, p.193. It was some time before the name Gang' or Ganyi, by which the Nyoro knew the Acoli, dropped out of use.
15. *Keyo mss.*
16. Lloyd 1906, p.207.
17. Russell, pp.4–6, 93–5.
18. Lloyd 1906, p.149.
19. Except where otherwise stated this account of Sira Dongo is based on Lawrence and Latigo.
20. An Alur name suggesting the meaning 'Although I am born, yet I shall die'. Latigo (interview).
21. Lawrence gives the name as Anyuza on p.5. Crazzolara, 1954, Part III, p.414, mentions an Alur clan called Ang'uzza in the Erusi area, on the border between what is now the West Nile District of Uganda, and Zaire. Latigo, who has worked over the history of Sira Dongo extensively, confirms that Dongo was born in this area.
22. Lucira Dongo. Lawrence, p.6, records that a brother of Bakarunga called Aduboker actually captured Dongo; that Bakarunga, seeing how intelligent Dongo was, took him as his gun-bearer, whilst Aduboker kept Katuku. But Lucira Dongo insists that Bakarunga married Katuku, and since he became a chief and his children by her are still alive, this must be correct, though it does not rule out the possibility that she was someone else's wife first. Neither Lucira Dongo nor any Acoli informants were able to throw light on who Aduboker was: they suggested that the name might be a corruption of the Arabic Abu Bakr, as there were Arabs in Bunyoro at the time. However, Dr

Anne Sutton who was working on the Alur came across the following information: Abok, son of Kinobe, was an Alur chief who died about 1885, supposedly as a result of magic practised against him by Kabalega because he had stopped tribute payments to Bunyoro from his own people and others. He was succeeded by his son Okelo. Kabalega sent a band of *barusura* to capture Okelo and his brother Odubuker, and they were held for a time at Kikobe near Masindi. There was rivalry between the brothers, but Odubuker did not contest the chieftaincy which passed to Okelo's child, Ombidi. When Ombidi died in 1940 thirteen clans gathered for the funeral, including the Jopadubuker. Odubuker is almost certainly Lawrence's Aduboker, and Dongo's capture incidental to this incident. Okelo of Panyimur is mentioned by Emin Pasha and Ternan.

23. Bishop and Ruffell, p.18, have conflated two incidents here.
24. Theoretically it was not mission practice to send out men as catechists until they had been confirmed. The bad state of some of the teaching in Bunyoro of which Ladbury complains must have been due in part to this lowering of standards.
25. Lawrence, p.9, gives her name as Kasemera. Lucira Dongo herself says her names are Lucira Farwenyo Karungi, and that her husband gave her the third name, which means 'good'. Christians in this part of Uganda sometimes changed their African names if these expressed a fatalism felt to be at variance with Christianity, and 'Farwenyo' conveys the sense of being lost. Lawrence's mistake arose because he thought she had been baptized at Masindi, and the only Lucira in the Masindi Baptism Register was Lucira Kasemera. But the baptismal registration number given on her marriage certificate refers to an entry in the Hoima Register, and this has been checked.
26. This account of Lloyd's journey is based on Lloyd 1906, pp.193–224, checked against the 1:250,000 Ordnance Survey Map.
27. Lloyd's account of his arrival at Ojigi's village is puzzling. Two of Awic's sons, *Rwot* Yasoni Lugaca and Suleman Omagi, both insist that this was the same Ojigi who had led the delegation to Hoima, yet Lloyd writes as though he was meeting him for the first time.
28. Lloyd 1906, p.221. The account continues: '. . . all of which helped to gain the confidence of these wild yet simple folk.' Did Western medicine and magic-lantern shows really help to gain their confidence? That they excited their curiosity is easier to accept. And 'wild yet simple folk' seems a curiously inept description of the Acoli! In most places Lloyd found the people friendly, though in one village almost everyone fled from his approach.
29. v. Crazzolara, p.241, note, where it is explained that a *ladom* acting for a chief might easily be mistaken by foreigners as important in his own right. But a *ladom* might achieve status or pass it on: Obwona Acoli's son, Ali, was elected *Rwot*. Crazzolara, p.254.
30. Cook, p.189.
31. Ibid., pp.192–9.
32. Latigo, transcribed verbatim (interview).
33. Cook, quoted in Lloyd 1906, p.253.

34. Tucker to Baylis, 30 Dec. 1904, CMSA G3 A7/03.
35. Tucker to Baylis, 10 May 1905, CMSA G3 A7/03.
36. Transferred from Belgian rule to British in 1910 when it became part of the Sudan. Transferred to Uganda in 1914. *Uganda Atlas*, pp.74–5.
37. Oral information from his son, Mr A. B. Adimola. The sorry tale about a slave whose life was endangered is recorded by Bishop and Ruffell, p.14, who take it to be correct.
38. Okech 1953, p.25. In spite of his name, I found no evidence that Yohana had been one of the *barusura*.
39. CMS *AR*, 1906/7, p.100.
40. Okech 1953, p.25.
41. CMS *AR*, 1906/7, p.100.
42. Enin (interview).
43. CMS *AR*, 1904/5, pp.125–6; Rev. L. Ashley, Secretary of the British and Foreign Bible Society in Nairobi in 1964. Personal communication based on the Society's records.
44. CMS *AR*, 1904/5, p.126.
45. Roman Catholics use the variant form *Rubanga*.
46. Okot p'Bitek 1963, pp.24–5, and 1966, pp.111–32; but v. also Southall 1956, p.93.
47. CMS *AR*, 1904/5, p.126 (quoting Kitching).
48. CMS *AR*, 1906/7, p.100 (quoting Kitching).
49. *Gulu Bap. Reg.*
50. Latigo (interview).
51. The actual date was 26 Nov. 1905. *Gulu Bap. Reg.*
52. CMS *AR*, 1905/6, p.94.
53. Ibid., p.93.
54. Olal and Okech 1964 (interviews).
55. *Gulu Bap. Reg.*; *Keyo mss.*
56. Tucker to Baylis, 24 May 1905, CMSA G3 A7/03.
57. Roscoe to Pleydell, 12 May 1905, CMSA G3 A7/03.
58. CMS *AR*, 1907/8, p.78.
59. Executive Committee Minutes, 7 March, 8 April, 27 Aug. 1907, CMSA G3 A7/05.
60. Minutes of a Special Meeting of the Executive Committee of the Uganda Mission held on 27 Dec. 1908, CMSA G3 A7/06.
61. *Keyo mss.*; Russell, pp.22–4.
62. *Tipo* means: (i) shadow: that which is caused by light falling on an opaque object.
   (ii) picture (also called *cal* – likeness).
   (iii) ghost.

   On this occasion when the phrase *mako tipo* was used, all three meanings are synchronized into one event. (Okot p'Bitek, personal communication).
64. CMS *AR*, 1907/8, p.78; 1908/9, p.73.
65. CMS *AR*, 1908/9, p.73.

66. *Keyo mss.*
67. Aluku (interview).
68. Komakec (interview).
69. CMS *AR*, 1908/9, p.74, says that no catechist was left at all in Acoli when the missionaries departed. Acoli informants are unanimous that someone remained, though they are confused as to who it was. Okech 1953 says that Nyuta remained, though not at Keyo; v. p.27. Okech is usually reliable and his information, which is more circumstantial than any other, has been accepted.
70. To say that a man is sociable and active is to praise him very highly. To be sociable is to be generous and hospitable and able to get on well with all kinds of people. An active man is mentally alert as well as physically vigorous.
71. Olal (interview).
72. *Gulu Serv. Bk.*; Latigo (interview). Jaganda stayed in Acoli until 1926 when Lawrence took him to Lango to help open the station at Boroboro near Lira.
73. Lawrence, p.13.
74. Okech 1953, p.57.
75. *Gulu Ch. Co. Mins*, where their names occur constantly as present at meetings.
76. *Gulu Serv. Bk.*; Latigo (interview).
77. Lawrence, p.14.
78. *Gulu Bap. Reg.*
79. Aluku (interview).
80. *Gulu Serv. Bk.*
81. Aluku (interview).
82. Katyanka and Bulera, p.59.
83. Okech 1953, p.27.
84. Okech 1964 (interview).
85. Latigo (interview).
86. Dellagiacoma, pp.1 and 2.
87. CMS *AR*, 1913/14, p.17.
88. Dellagiacoma, pp.2–3.
89. Adimola, personal communication.
90. Dellagiacoma, p.3
91. Okech 1964; Olal (interviews).
92. Aluku (interview).
93. *Gulu Bap. Reg.*
94. Russell, pp.28–9; Aluku (interview).
95. Sangree, p.131; Nicolet: *Yohana Kitagana*, episodes in Bunyaruguru; Pirouet 1969 (ii).
96. e.g. P'Bitek Okot's *Song of Lawino*.
97. *Gulu Bap. Reg.* Note written against his name.
98. Latigo (interview).
99. *Keyo mss.*

100. Omagi (interview).
101. Bishop and Ruffell, p.19.
102. Obi (interview).
103. Otim; Obi (interviews).
104. Latigo; Obi; Ogwang'gujji (interviews).
105. Komakec (interview).
106. *Gulu Serv. Bk.*

CHAPTER VI

1. Webster 1973, pp.xx-xxiii.
2. Ogot 1967, p.114; Uganda Atlas 1962, p.37; Ong'ola (interview).
3. Ogot 1967, p.113 et seq.; Lawrance, p.9; Webster 1973.
4. Ong'ola (interview).
5. Lawrance, pp.72-3.
6. Webster 1970, pp.53-4.
7. Ibid., pp.56-7.
8. Emwanu, p.172; Emulu; Ong'ola (interviews).
9. Webster 1973, pp.23-4; Emulu (interview).
10. Webster 1973, p.63.
11. Ogot 1967, pp.116-17; Ong'ola (interview). It should be noted that the Lwoo are remarkably good at assimilating other people into their clans, and their language seems to be learnt by others fairly easily. Large numbers of Alur are not Lwoo in origin but have been assimilated into Lwoo clans, and in western Kenya the Luhya are easily assimilated by the Luo.
12. The meaning and derivation of the word have been variously explained, but the missionaries of the time generally accepted a Ganda explanation of Bakedi as meaning 'the naked ones'.
13. Crabtree to Buckley, 25 Jan. 1901, quoted in *CMI*, May 1901.
14. Here and throughout this chapter Bukedi means, not the modern district of that name, but the whole area north and east of the Nile referred to above, which was known as Bukedi at the beginning of the colonial period.
15. *CMI*, July 1900, p.527.
16. Roscoe to Baylis, 31 March 1900, CMSA G3 A7/02.
17. *CMG*, May 1901, pp.66-8.
18. Crabtree was one of the more fundamentalist missionaries, whom Dr Twaddle (personal communication) finds less imbued with social Darwinianism than those holding modernist views, and better able to establish good relations with Africans, because they saw all men as equally sinful and in need of grace, and equally potential citizens of heaven. It is more common to find a correlation between fundamentalism and racism, but the CMS missionaries to whom Twaddle is referring are better described as conservative evangelicals than as fundamentalists. It seems more likely that the older missionaries were

of a generation less imbued with these ideas, and that the doctrinal standpoint is coincidental.

19. *Men/Ug. Notes*, June 1901, Supplement, p.58.
20. Ibid.
21. Crabtree to Roscoe, Masaba, 4 June 1901, quoted in *CMI*, Nov. 1901, p.860.
22. *Men/Ug. Notes*, Oct. 1901, p.79.
23. This account of Kakungulu is based on the following, except where otherwise stated: Lawrance, pp.17-22 and 24; Gray 1963; Emwanu 1967; Emulu (interview). Twaddle 1967 was also consulted. On the question of Kakungulu's objectives in moving into areas recently under Nyoro rule, I have reached slightly different conclusions from Twaddle.
24. K.W. pp.66-7; Ong'ola: Kato; Oguti (interviews).
25. This fort may still be seen about two miles from the *etem* headquarters at Mukongoro. It is rectangular and covers about an acre of ground. The ditch surrounding it was originally deeper than it is now, and was sheer-sided. A gap in the ditch where the gate was is clearly visible. Many of the Ganda lived outside the fort.
26. Crabtree to Buckley, 25 Jan. 1901, quoted in *CMI*, May 1901, p.369.
27. Crabtree in *Men/Ug. Notes*, May 1901, p.51.
28. Crabtree to Buckley, 25 Jan. 1901, quoted in *CMI*, May 1901, p.370; Tucker: 'A Journey to Mount Elgon and the Bukedi Country', *CMI*, April 1904, p.261.
29. Buckley, quoted in *CMI*, March 1902, p.191.
30. Crabtree, quoted in *CMI*, March 1902, p.182.
31. Buckley, quoted in *CMI*, March 1902, p.191.
32. Tucker, op. cit., p.258.
33. CMS *AR*, 1904/5, p.125.
34. Roscoe to Baylis, 11 May and 25 Aug. 1905, CMSA G3 A7/05.
35. Kitching in *Men/Ug. Notes*, Nov. 1913, p.154; Ong'ola; Bishop and Ruffell, p.21.
36. Kitching 1912, p.65; Bishop and Ruffell, p.21; Ong'ola.
37. Kitching, op. cit., p.254.
38. Emunyele; Okwaling'a and Okerinyang' (interviews). The Ngora Baptism Register gives the names of the first two Teso to be baptized as Karinga and Gwangi. Bishop and Ruffell give the names correctly as Okwaling'a and Ogwang'. They say that the former originally came from Mukongoro. An effort was therefore made to trace Ogwang' in this area, but no one had any knowledge of him. In every other area of Uganda the first converts were well known, so this was surprising. However, three informants were found who knew of Okwaling'a, and who said that three Teso youths, Okwaling'a, Namuseke, and a third nicknamed Muwereza, became interpreters for the Ganda at Olaicho, and that when Kakungulu's men left and went to Kumi, these three went with them to read. Bishop and Ruffell are not correct in saying that it was this Ogwang', whose baptismal name they give as Musa, who helped Kitching to learn the language. They have confused him

with Isaka Ogwang' who was baptized at the same time as Andereya Ekusai, who also, in 1910, helped Kitching to learn the language.

39. Bishop and Ruffell, p.24.
40. Okwaling'a; Okerinyang'; Emunyele (interviews).
41. In *Men/Ug. Notes*, Nov. 1913, p.254.
42. Kitching 1912, pp.58-61.
43. *Ngora Bap. Reg.*; Kitching 1912, p.65; Bishop and Ruffell, p.21 (but see note 40).
44. *Men/Ug. Notes*, April 1909, p.62.
45. *Ngora Bap. Reg.*; Bishop and Ruffell, p.21.
46. Tucker and Cook: 'A Cry from Central Africa', *CMI*, June 1909, pp.363-6; Cook 1948, pp.260-6.
47. Bishop and Ruffell, p.24; Lukungu (interview).
48. Kitching in *Men/Ug. Notes*, Nov. 1913, p.254.
49. Kitching, op. cit., p.255; Thomas and Scott, p.331.
40. Kitching, loc. cit.
51. Lawrance, p.25; v. also Jones, p.121; Bishop and Ruffell, p.22.
52. Kitching, loc. cit.
53. Tucker and Cook, op. cit., p.365.
54. Burke, p.154.
55. Kitching, loc. cit.
56. Ibid.
57. The passage on Ngora High School is based on *Men/Ug. Notes*, Nov. 1913, pp.262-3; Nov. 1914, p.239.
58. Jones, p.127.
59. These were Nasanaeri Ipuruket (Kumi), Enoka Epaku (Soroti), Yonosani Oumo (Serere), Eriya Ocom (Usuku). Emwanu, confirmed by Oguti, Okwerede, Odiit (interviews).
60. Emeetai; Emulu; Odiit (interviews).
61. *Men/Ug. Notes*, Nov. 1914, p.239; Oguti.
62. *Ngora Bap. Reg.*; Ngora Communicants Register.
63. Some Catholic priests have expressed doubts as to how deeply rooted Christianity is in Teso, but there are a number of religious sisters and priests, and they praise the devotion of these.
64. Odiit (interview). Confirmed by Dr T. Watson, personal communication.
65. Odiit; Emeetai; Emulu (interview).
66. Jones, pp.115-16, italics added.
67. Dr M. Twaddle, personal communication.
68. Dr N. Nagashima, personal communication.
69. This remark was made by a number of seminary teachers. A group of students in the Department of Religious Studies, Makerere University, argued vigorously against the proposition that Christian teaching and preaching should be Christocentric. They insisted that Christianity was a religion about God (sic).

70. In 1971 the staff of Ngora Hospital started a project to relate Christianity and health teaching which the hospital was undertaking more closely to local life and felt needs.

CHAPTER VII

1. Vidler, p.248; Chadwick, p.219.
2. Oliver 1952, pp.263-84.
3. Pirouet 1970, p.5.
4. Pirouet 1970, pp. 20-1; Nolan in Shorter and Kataża, p. 25.
5. v. Shorter and Kataza pp.ix-x.
6. Hewitt, p.228.
7. Dobson, p.7 gives the date as 1917; Richardson, p.189 as 1918.
8. Dellagiacoma, p.4.
9. Hooton and Stafford Wright, p.60.
10. Sebalijja in Denoon, p.198.
11. Guillebaud, p.17.
12. Nicolet in Denoon, p.233.
13. Ogot 1966, especially pp.24-5.
14. Oguti (interview).
15. Bernadette Ouma, daughter of Otwande, oral information, 1971.
16. Karugire 1973, p.68.
17. Ibid., pp.86-7.
18. Ibid., p.86.
19. Welbourn and Ogot, 1966, title.

Bibliography and List of Sources

1

ORAL INFORMANTS

Aluku, Andereya (Acoli). Son of Muca Ali, the first Christian convert in Acoli. Interviewed 1 September 1964.

Bacwa, Samwiri (Toro). A 'boy' of the Rev. (later bishop) A. L. Kitching from 1902 to 1904. Lived near Butiti all his life. Interviewed 16 September 1965.

Balya, Rt Rev. Aberi K. (Toro). Born c. 1880. The first East African to be consecrated a bishop of the Anglican Church. Well known for his historical knowledge. Interviewed 15 September 1965, 26 February 1966.

Bikundi, Isaya (Bunyoro). He says: 'Samuel Baker came to see Kamurasi in 1861, and in 1867 he came to see Kabalega for the first time. That was the year I was born.' So he celebrated his 100th birthday in 1967. Baker actually saw Kamurasi for the first time in 1862, and Kabalega in 1872 but we did not feel it fair to disabuse Bikundi of this cherished notion. Baptized 1901, a sub-county chief from 1902–8, and a county chief 1915–21. Interviewed near Biiži, Masindi. Apart from the error over the date of his own birth, he was a reliable informant who gave correctly a number of dates which could be checked. Interviewed 15 and 20 June 1967.

Binyomo, Rev. Ezekieri (Toro). Born about 1880. Brought up in Kasagama's enclosure. Worked as a catechist and was later ordained. Interviewed 9 September 1965.

Buningwire, Rev. Canon Yoweri (Ankole). Born c. 1881. Came to Kahaya's court in 1896. One of the early converts to Christianity in Ankole. Interviewed 4 and 5 August 1964, 1 March 1965.

Byabusakuzi, Paulo (Toro). A Mukonjo originally from the Lake Katwe area. Has worked as a catechist all his life, qualifying as a third letter catechist. Still at work in the early 1970s near Fort Portal. Father of Timothy Bazzarabuza, first Ugandan High Commissioner in London. Interviewed 14 September 1965.

Dongo, Lucira (Acoli). Widow of Canon Sira Dongo. Interviewed for me by Dr T. Watson, December 1964.

Emeetai, Tomasi (Teso). Probably born c. 1904. Baptized 1917, and has worked as a catechist ever since. Interviewed 27 September 1968.

Emulu (Teso). Born near Ngora c. 1890 and has lived in the area all his life. Interviewed 26 September 1968.

Emunyele (Teso). An adult when the Ganda first came to Mukongoro and has lived there all his life. Interviewed 3 April 1968.

Enin, Petero (Lango). Son of *Rwot* Odora of Lango and author of a ms. account of his father's life which is now in Makerere University Archives. Interviewed 4 September 1964.

Fataki, Suleiman (Bunyoro). Eldest son of Mika Fataki. Interviewed 3 August 1967.

Jaasi-Kiiza, Isaac (Toro). Tutor, Bishop Stuart College, Mbarara, who has made a study of the customs of his people. Interviewed 28 June 1967.

Jawe, Zakayo (Bunyoro). Son of Paulo Byabacwezi who later became a county chief. Interviewed 1 August 1967.

Kaboha, Pancras (Toro). Lecturer, Makerere University. Grandson of Leo Kaboha. After consulting with his family, he supplied details of his grandfather's life. Interviewed 8 November 1967.

Kabuliiteka, Abiri (Bunyoro). Son of Yafesi Isingoma and himself a catechist for many years. Born c. 1903. Interviewed 26 July 1967.

Kacibala, Malyamu (Ankole). Niece of Nuwa Mbaguta. Baptized 1902. Has worked for the church all her life. Interviewed 23 February 1965.

Kagwa, Canon Kezekia (Buganda). Ordained 1909, died 1967. Interviewed by the (Rt) Rev. Cyprian Bamwoze, June 1965. Material used with permission.

Kakumba, Lilian (Bunyoro). Born c. 1900. Trained as a catechist. Married Samwiri Kakumba, also a catechist, and both have worked for the church all their lives. Interviewed 27 July 1967.

Kaliisa, Andereya (Bunyoro). Born c. 1895. Retired catechist. Interviewed 29 July 1967.

Kalikuzinga, Simeoni (Buganda). Remembers the martyrdoms which took place when he was very young. In 1888 he accompanied the missionaries to Usukuma where he returned as a catechist in 1891. He was then thought by the missionaries to be 16 to 18 years of age. Subsequently employed by the Protectorate administration as an interpreter, and his name appears as such on the Ankole Agreement. Interviewed by me and the (Rt) Rev. C. Bamwoze in 1965. Also extensively used as an informant by M. Wright and J. Rowe (q.v. in Bibliography).

Kamugisha, F. (Ankole). Primary school teacher in the Kabwohe (Kitoju) area. Interviewed 11 August 1965.

Kamugungunu, Owek. Lazaro (Ankole). Born about 1880. Baptized 1903. Formerly an *Enganzi* (Chief Minister) of Ankole. Interviewed 24 February 1965 and 10 August 1966.

Kamuhiigi, Rev. Yosiya (Toro). Born c. 1880. Ordained deacon 1907, priest 1909. Interviewed 21 January 1964.

Kamujanduzi, Rev. Edward (Ankole). Parish priest of Kinoni. Born c. 1895. Interviewed 27 February 1965.

Kanyiki, Erifase (Buganda). Nephew of Rev. Tomasi Semfuma.

Interviewed by the (Rt) Rev. C. Bamwoze in June 1965. Material used with permission.

Kaparaga, John (Bunyoro). Born in Buyaga c. 1879. Became a Catholic catechist and worked at Bugoma in the first two decades of this century. Then moved to Munteme parish. Interviewed 31 July 1967.

Kasaija, Eriya (Bunyoro). Born c. 1902, and has lived in the Masindi area all his life. As a child he lived with his mother on the church *mailo* land at Masindi. Interviewed 17 June 1967.

Kashenya, Canon Samuel (Ankole). Parish priest of Masheruka. Born about 1895. Interviewed 27 February 1965.

Kato (Teso). A Ganda who has lived at Bugondo for ?40 years. He was born in north Bugerere when that area was under the rule of the Mubito, Nyamuyonjo. He knew Nyamuyonjo and Osodo, a Teso who was subject to Nyamuyonjo at Mudochi near Bugondo, and who held a drum, stool and spear from the *Mukama* of Bunyoro. Interviewed 9 April 1968.

Katoomizi, Tefiro (Ankole). Born c. 1900. Baptized 1916. Has lived at Kinoni. Interviewed 25 February 1965.

Katunji, Owek. Erenesiti (Ankole). Born c. 1890. Has been a county chief and *Enganzi* of Ankole. Brother of the Most Rev. E. Sabiti. Interviewed 25 February 1965.

Kibumbirire, Tomasi (Bunyoro). Born c. 1890. Retired catechist. Interviewed 22 June 1967.

Kisoro, Sedulaka (Toro). Baptized 1897. He was taught for baptism by Nuwa Nakiwafu. Has worked as a clerk to the *Rukurato* (chiefs' assembly). Interviewed 15 September 1965.

Kiiza, Elifasi (Bunyoro). In his youth a page at the court of Andereya Duhaga. Subsequently an employee of the Bunyoro Kingdom Government. Interviewed 2 August 1967.

Komakec, Ven. Y. (Acoli). Archdeacon of the Diocese of Northern Uganda (since divided). Interviewed 31 August 1964.

Komuntale, Ruth (Toro). Daughter of the *Mukama* Daudi Kasagama and *Batebe* (royal sister) of his successor, *Mukama* George Rukiidi. Interviewed 18 September 1965.

Kyaherwa, Franswa (Bunyoro). Born about 1885 (says he was a grown man when Kabalega was captured by the British). His father was a *murusura*. Baptized by Fr Baudouin in 1909. Became a Catholic catechist. Interviewed 24 July 1967.

Kyopaali, Zakariya (Bunyoro). Born c. 1885. Taught to read and write and trained as a general carpenter and handyman by Tegart. Interviewed 16 June 1967.

Latigo, Canon Alipayo (Acoli). Born c. 1900 to 1905. Author of several vernacular ms. accounts of folk-lore and history, some of which have been photocopied and placed in Makerere University

Archives. Interviewed 26 August 1964.

Lugaca, Rwot Yasoni (Acoli). Son of Rwot Iburahim Awac and an early convert to Christianity. Interviewed 27 August 1964.

Lukayi, A. (Bunyoro). Son of Mika Fataki. Educated at Budo. Interviewed 3 August 1967.

Lukungu, Canon Petero (Teso; Busoga). Worked in the Upper Nile Diocese, mainly in Teso, from 1911–47, when he retired to Busoga. Interviewed by (Rt) Rev. C. Bamwoze 16 June 1966. Material used with permission.

Masa, Musa (Teso). Born c. 1900. A resident of Bugoma all his life. Interviewed 1 November 1967.

Mbabi-Katana, S. (Bunyoro). Lecturer, Makerere University. Son of Daudi Mbabi. In conversation he amplified several points made in his obituary of his father (v. Mbabi-Katana: 'Death of Daudi Mbabi, Grand Old Man of Bunyoro', *Uganda Herald*, 25 July 1953. Interviewed December 1967.

Muherya, Rev. H. D. (Bunyoro). Son of Rev. Andereya Dwakaikara. Interviewed 28 July 1967.

Mukidi, E. M. (Toro). Granddaughter of Petero Tigwezire. Letter of September 1967 in which, in answer to questions, she gave details of her grandfather's life.

Mutunzi, Aloni (Bunyoro). Born c. 1885. Son of Buhanga, a servant of Kabalega who carried the *Mukama*'s spear. For a time catechist at Masindi. Interviewed 16 June 1967.

Nyakabwa, Eseri (Toro). Born c. 1888. Became a catechist in 1902 and remained active for over 60 years. Interviewed 18 September 1965.

Obaya, Rev. Fesito (Bunyoro). Parish priest of Kigaya which now includes Bugoma. Accompanied me on a visit to Bugoma, and interpreted during an interview with Musa Masa (q.v.). 31 October 1967.

Oguti, Mikaeri (Teso). Ex-*etem* (sub-county) chief, and one of the early pupils of Ngora High School. Has lived at Kyere most of his life, except 1927–41 when he was chief at Bugondo. Interviewed 9 April 1968.

Okech, Rwot Lacito (Acoli). Retired county chief, and an early convert to Christianity. Author of *Tekwaro ki Ker Lobo Acoli*. Interviewed 25 August 1964.

Okerinyang', Yakobo and Okwaling'a, Andereya (Teso). Brothers, both from Mukongoro where they have lived all their lives. Interviewed together 3 April 1968.

Okwerede, Yakobo (Teso). Ex-county chief and one of the early converts in Teso, and an active church member and member of synod for many years. Interviewed 10 April 1968.

Olal, Rwot Andereya (Acoli). Son of Okellomwaka. An early convert in Acoli, baptized 1906. Ex-county chief. Interviewed 17 August 1964.

Oluol, Rwot Elieza (Lango). An early convert in the Aduku area. Interviewed 4 April 1968.

Omagi, Suleiman (Acoli). Son of *Rwot* Iburahim Awic. Now retired and living near Ocekocot. Interviewed 20 August 1964.

Ong'ola, Canon Samwiri (Teso). Born c. 1905. One of the first two Teso to be ordained. Has a more exhaustive knowledge of Teso history than is common. Interviewed 23 February 1968.

Opi, Jebedayo Bitek and Cerina (Acoli). Converts to Christianity after the return of the mission in 1913. Jebedayo was born about 1890. Interviewed 27 August 1964.

Otim, Thomas (Lango). Agricultural officer, Lira. Remembers Sira Dongo when the latter worked in Lira. Interviewed 4 September 1964.

Rugungura, Andereya (Ankole). Retired minor chief. Interviewed 25 February 1965.

Rwabite, Petero (Ankole). Catechist in Kabwohe area. Interviewed 11 August 1965.

Rwakahumire, Andereya (Toro). Retired catechist of Kibumbi, Kitagwenda. Born in the reign of Kabalega. Interviewed 13 September 1965.

Schofield, A. T. Wife of Dr Schofield who spent some years in Toro in the 1920s and 1930s. Interviewed 15 August 1967.

Shalita, The Rt. Rev. Kosiya (Ankole). Bishop of Ankole-Kigezi (the diocese has now been divided). Interviewed August 1965. Read through the chapter on Ankole and made suggestions.

Tibanagwa, Dina (Bunyoro). Was brought up as a child by the missionaries, especially Miss Wright at Hoima. Trained as a catechist by Miss Pike in Toro, and by Hana Kageye. Interviewed 29 July 1967.

2

ARCHIVAL SOURCES

With abbreviations as used in references.

1. *Church Missionary Society, London* (CMSA)

   Archives G3 A5, G3 A7. 1890–1914 (CMSA G3 A5 etc.)

   Papers of the Rev. A. B. Fisher (*Fisher mss*)

   (these were read on microfilm in Makerere University Library).

2. *Church of Uganda* (COU)

   Items indicated by an asterisk are available on microfilm or photostat in Makerere University. Others are located locally.

   *Ankole Baptism Register (*Ank. Bap. Reg.*), 1902–8.

   Butiti Baptism Register (*Bu. Bap. Reg.*), 1900.

*Gulu Documents. These consist of the Keyo Jubilee File (*Keyo mss*), Gulu Baptism Register (*Gulu Bap. Reg.*), Gulu Service Book (*Gulu Serv. Bk.*), Gulu Accounts Book, Church Council Minutes (*Gulu Ch. Co. Mins*). These were deposited in Makerere University by the Rt Rev. J. K. Russell.

*Hoima Baptism Register (*Hoima Bap. Reg.*), 1900–17.

Hoima Service Book (*Hoima Serv. Bk.*), 1909.

Kabarole Baptism Register (*Ka. Bap. Reg.*), 1896–1908.

*Kabarole Church Council Minutes Book (*Ka. Ch. Co. Mins*), 1898–1903.

Masindi Baptism Register (*Masindi Bap. Reg.*), 1899–1930.

Masindi Marriage Register (*Masindi Mar. Reg.*), 1900–14.

Masindi Service Book (*Masindi Serv. Bk.*), 1909–16.

Minutes of the Bunyoro Church Council (*Bu. Ch. Co. Mins*), 1898–1912.

Minutes of the Theological Board (*Mins of the Theol. Bd.*), 1909–26.

Namirembe Baptism Register (*Namirembe Bap. Reg.*), 1900.

Ngora Baptism Register (*Ngora Bap. Reg.*), 1906–21.

Ngora Communicants Register, 1911–27.

Record Book (*COU Record Bk.*), Archbishop's Office Namirembe.

Teachers' Record 1898–1902 (*Teachers' Rec. Bk.*). In the handwriting of the Rev. R. H. Walker, and kept in Namirembe Cathedral.

*Toro Women Teachers' Record (*Toro W.T. Rec.*), 1902–22. In the handwriting of Miss Pike.

3. *Makerere University Archives* (MUA)

Journals of the Rev. J. K. Baskerville, 1891–1900 (*BJ*).

The Letters of Mrs Ashton Bond, 1901–8 (*Bond mss*). Xerox copies in MUA by courtesy of her daughter, Miss Margaret Bond.

The Letters of the Rev. H. and Mrs Clayton, 1897–1904 (*Clayton mss*). Copy handwritten by the Rev. H. Clayton and given to MUA by the writer.

Notebooks of the Rev. Apolo Kivebulaya, 1896–1906. Xerox copies.

The Journals and Letterbooks of the Rev. H. B. and Mrs Ladbury, 1904–54 (*Ladbury mss*). Originals donated to MUA by CMS, Nairobi.

Papers of the Rt. Rev. J. J. Willis, including his Journal of 1901–2 (*Willis mss*). Xerox copies made available by courtesy of the Ven. Archdeacon Cobham of Durham.

4. *Archives of St Joseph's Foreign Missionary Society, Mill Hill,*

London (MHM)

Nsambya Mission Diary, 1895–8 (*Nsambya Diary*).

5. *Archives of the White Fathers Mission, via Aurelia, Rome* (WFA)

Correspondances: Nyanza Septentrional (*Co. Ny. Sept.*).

Diary of Hoima Mission (*Hoima Di.*).

Diary of Mbarara Mission (*Mbarara Di.*).

Diary of Virika Mission (*Vi. Di.*).

Histoire Mercui. Xerox copy made available by M. Rooyackers (WF *Histoire Mercui*).

Also Jubilee Book (WF *Jubilee Book*) made for Mgr Streicher and kept at Katigondo National Seminary, near Villa Maria, Uganda.

3

PERIODICAL AND SERIAL PUBLICATION

**Annual Reports* of the Church Missionary Society (CMS *AR*)

**Bunyoro Church Magazine* (*Bu. Ch. Mag.*) In Runyoro, 1931–40. The only known copy was donated to MUA by the Rev. H. D. Muherya.

Chroniques Trimestrielles of the White Fathers (WF *Chroniques*).

**Church Missionary Intelligencer*, CMS (*CMI*), until 1906.

**Church Missionary Review*, CMS (*CMR*), after 1906.

**Church Missionary Gleaner*, CMS (*CMG*).

**Mengo Notes* 1900–January 1902; *Uganda Notes* 1902–13 (*Men/Ug. Notes*) CMS Uganda Mission publication. The only complete run known to exist is in Makerere University.

Rapports Annuels (*RA*) of the White Fathers Mission.

4

PRINTED MATERIAL: PRIVATE OR LIMITED CIRCULATION

*Church Missionary Society: *A Register of Missionaries and Native Clergy 1804–1904*. London 1905 (*A Register*).

Cardinal C-M. A. Lavigerie: *Instructions aux Missionaires*. Namur 1950.

*White Fathers Mission: *Mémento Chronologique*, Algers, 1900.

5

TYPESCRIPTS, MIMEOGRAPHED PAPERS, UNPUBLISHED THESES, HISTORIES AND MEMOIRS

R. A. Atkinson: 'Adaptation and Change in Acholi 1850–1900', Seminar paper, Dept of History, Makerere University, 1971.

(Bannabikira Sisters, Bwanda Convent, Uganda): 'The Life of Mother Mechtilde', n.d., n.a.

A. M. Bishop and D. Ruffell: 'A History of the Upper Nile Diocese', n.d. typescript in MUA.

V. Dellagiacoma, FSCJ: 'The Catholic Church in Northern Uganda 1910–1969', mimeographed, 1969.

A. Dwakaikara and H. D. Muherya: 'The Life of Andereya Dwakaikara', n.d., photocopy and translation in MUA.

Petero Enin: 'The Life of *Rwot* Daudi Odora', typescript, n.d., photocopy and translation in MUA.

H. W. Hansen: 'British Administration and Religious Liberty in Uganda 1890–1900', EAISR Conference Paper, mimeographed, January 1966.

C. J. Hellberg and A. Kajerero: 'Andereya Kajerero: The Man and His Church', typescript, n.d., in MUA.

A. B. Kasozi: 'The Spread of Islam in Uganda', seminar paper, Dept of History, Makerere University, 1969.

J. A. P. Kieran: 'The Holy Ghost Fathers in East Africa 1863–1914', unpublished PhD thesis, University of London 1966.

D. A. Low: 'The British and Uganda, 1862–1957', unpublished PhD thesis, University of Oxford, 1957. (Low 1957 (ii)).

J. N. Odurkene: material on the early days of Christianity in Lango, collected by the writer when a third year undergraduate at Makerere University; typescript, 1967.

Reuben Ogwal: 'The Coming of Christianity to Lango', n.d. typescript and translation in MUA.

Okalany-Ocuna: 'The Western Migration of the Iteso during the Pre-colonial Period', seminar paper, Dept of History, Makerere University, 1972.

Moses Nyakazingo: graduating essay on the life of Daudi Kasagama of Toro, typescript, Makerere University, 1966.

B. H. L. Nyeko: 'The Acholi of Nothern Uganda during the 19th century', seminar paper, Dept of History, 1970.

M. Louise Pirouet: 'Catechists in Western Uganda', mimeographed paper for Gaba-AMECEA-FERES research project on catechists, Gaba Publications, 1970.

C. E. Robins: '*Tukutendereza*: A Study of Social Change and Sectarian Withdrawal in the *Balokole* Revival of Uganda', unpublished PhD thesis, Columbia University, 1975.

George Kamrasi Rukiidi III: *The Kings of Toro*, (trans. J. R. Muchope). Makerere University, History Department, n.d.

D. J. Stenning: 'Some Preliminary Observations on the Balokole Movement particularly among the Hima in Ankole District', EAISR Conference Paper No 87, Makerere University, 1957.

M. J. Twaddle: 'Politics in Bukedi 1900–1939: an historical study of administrative change among the segmentary peoples of Eastern Uganda under the impact of British Colonial Rule', unpublished PhD thesis, University of London, 1967.

— —'The Muslim Revolution in Buganda', seminar paper, Dept of History, Makerere University, 1969 (Twaddle 1969 (ii)).

J. B. Webster: 'The Iteso during the Asonya', seminar paper, Dept of History, Makerere University, 1969.

— —and Onyango-ku-Odongo: 'A Tentative Chronology for the Lwo', seminar paper, Dept of History, Makerere University, 1971.

F. B. Welbourn: 'The Idea of a High God in Three East African Societies', paper for the Conference on the High God in Africa, Ibadan, 1964.

T. S. M. Williams: 'The Protestant Church in Nkondo', unpublished MA thesis, University of East Africa, 1965.

6

BOOKS AND ARTICLES

Abbreviations:

Journal of African History *JAH*
Uganda Journal *UJ*

A. B. Adimola: 'The Lamogi Rebellion', *UJ*, XVIII, 2 (1954), pp. 166–77.

R. S. Anywar: 'The Life of Rwot Iburahim Awic', *UJ*, XII, 1 (1948), pp. 72–81.

D. E. Apter: *The Political Kingdom in Uganda*, Princeton 1961.

R. P. Ashe: *Two Kings of Uganda*, London 1890.

— —*Chronicles of Uganda*, London 1894.

D. Attwater: *The White Fathers in Africa*, London 1937.

C. G. Baeta: *Christianity in Tropical Africa*, London 1968.

S. J. K. Baker: 'Bunyoro: A Regional Appreciation', *UJ*, XVIII, 2 (1954), pp. 101–12.

— —'The Geographical Background of Western Uganda', *UJ*, XXII, 1 (1958), pp. 1–10.

Sir S. W. Baker: *The Albert N'yanza*, London 1866.

— —*Ismailia*, London 1874.

J. K. Bamunoba and F. B. Welbourn: 'Emandwa Initiation in Ankole', *UJ*, XXIX, 2 (1965), pp. 13–25.

S. N. Bax: 'The Early Church Missionary Society's Missions at Buzilima and Usambiro in the Mwanza District', *Tanganyika Notes and Records*, VII (1939), pp. 39–55.

J. H. M. Beattie: 'The Nyoro', Chapter IV in East African Chiefs, ed.

A. I. Richards, London 1960 (Beattie 1960 (i)).

— —*Bunyoro: An African Kingdom*, New York 1960 (Beattie 1960 (ii)).

T. A. Beetham: *Christianity and the New Africa*, London 1967.

George Bennett: 'Christianity and African Nationalism', *Mawazo*, I 3 (1968), pp. 63–9.

R. M. Bere: 'Awich—A Biographical Note and a Chapter of Acholi History', *UJ*, X, 2 (1946), pp. 76–8.

J. Bouniol: *The White Fathers and Their Missions*, London 1929.

F. G. Burke: *Local Government and Politics in Uganda*, Syracuse, USA 1964.

W. Burridge: *Destiny Africa*, London 1965.

G. Casati: *Ten Years in Equatoria*, London 1891.

Catholic Directory of Eastern Africa, editions of 1965, 1969, TMP, Tabora, Tanzania.

Owen Chadwick: *The Victorian Church*, 2 vols., London 1969 and 1970.

J. E. Church: *Awake, Uganda!* Kampala, n.d.

H. Colvile: *Land of the Nile Springs*, London 1895.

A. R. Cook: *Uganda Memories*, Entebbe 1945.

R. Coupland: *The Exploitation of East Africa 1856–1890*, London 1939.

J. P. Crazzolara: *The Lwoo*, 3 vols., Verona 1950–4.

J. Cussac: *L'Apôtre de l'Ouganda, le Père Lourdel*, Paris 1944.

— —*Evêque et pionnier—Monseigneur Streicher*, Paris 1955.

E. C. Dawson: *James Hannington: A History of His Life and Work 1847–1885*, London 1887.

— —*The Last Journals of James Hannington*, London 1888.

J. Ddiba: *Eddini mu Buganda*, 2 vols., Masaka 1965 and 1967.

J. H. Dobson: *Daybreak in West Nile*, London 1964.

M. Doornbos: *Regalia Galore*, Nairobi 1975.

J. H. Driberg: *The Lango*, London 1923.

A. R. Dunbar: *A History of Bunyoro Kitara*, Nairobi 1965.

Empango Celebrations Committee 1967: *Omurwa Bwabajwarakondo ba Bunyoro-Kitara*, published in Runyoro and English, Kampala 1967.

G. Emwanu: 'The Reception of Alien Rule in Teso', *UJ*, XXXI, 2 (1967), pp. 171–82.

L. A. Fallers (ed): *The King's Men*, London 1964.

M. C. Fallers: *The Eastern Lacustrine Bantu*, Ethnographic Survey of Africa; East Central Africa, Part IX, London 1960.

J. P. Faupel: *African Holocaust*, London 1962.

Mika Fataki: 'Okuija okwo Bukristayo mu Bunyoro', *Bunyoro Church Magazine*, pp. 65-7; 96. (This periodical was published from 1931-40 and the pages are numbered from 1-487 up to 1937. It is not possible to discover where one issue ends and another begins.)

R. Fisher: *On the Borders of Pygmyland*, London 1905.

— —*Twilight Tales of the Black Baganda*, London 1911.

M. Fortes and E. E. Evans-Pritchard (eds): *African Political Systems*, London 1960.

W. D. Foster: *The Early History of Scientific Medicine in Uganda*, Nairobi, Dar es Salaam and Kampala 1970.

O. W. Furley: 'Kasagama of Toro', *UJ*, XXV, 2 (1961), pp. 184-98.

H. P. Gale: *Uganda and the Mill Hill Fathers*, London 1959.

A. Gaulet: *Sur les rives du Victoria*, Paris 1944.

T. W. Gee: 'A Century of Muhammadan Influence in Buganda, 1852-1951', *UJ*, XXII, 2 (1958), pp. 139-50.

F. K. Girling: *The Acholi of Uganda*, London 1960.

J. E. Goldthorpe and F. B. Wilson: *Tribal Maps of East Africa and Zanzibar*, EAISR Kampala 1960.

J. Goody and I. Watt: 'The Consequences of Literacy', *Comparative Studies in Society and History* V (1962/3), pp. 304-45.

J. L. Gorju: *Entre le Victoria, l'Albert et l'Edouard*, Rennes 1920.

J. M. Gray: 'Correspondence Relating to the Death of Bishop Hannington', *UJ* XIII, 1 (1949), pp. 1-22.

— —'The Year of the Three Kings of Buganda', *UJ*, XIV, 1 (1950), pp. 15-52.

— —'Acholi History 1860-1901', *UJ*, XV, 2 (1951), pp. 121-40.

— —'In Memoriam—Archbishop Henri Streicher, CBE', *UJ*, XVII, 1 (1953), pp. 63-7.

— —'Mackay's Canoe Voyage along the Western Shore of Lake Victoria', *UJ*, XVIII, 1 (1954), pp. 13-20.

— —'A History of Ibanda, Saza of Mitoma, Ankole', *UJ*, XXIV, 2 (1960), pp. 166-82.

— —'Kakunguru in Bukedi', *UJ*, XXVII, 1 (1963), pp. 31-60.

— —'Kabarega and the C.M.S.', *UJ*, XXXV, 1 (1971), pp. 79-80.

C. P. Groves: *The Planting of Christianity in Africa,* Vols. 3 and 4, London 1955 and 1958.

L. Guillebaud: *A Grain of Mustard Seed*, London 1959.

C. F. Harford Battersby: *Pilkington of Uganda*, London 1898.

V. Harlow and E. M. Chilver (eds): *A History of East Africa,* Vol. II Oxford 1965.

Adrian Hastings: *Church and Mission in Modern Africa*, London 1968.

——'From Mission to Church in Buganda', *Zeitschrift für Missionswissenschaft und Religionswissenschaft*, LIII (1969), pp. 206–28.

C. J. Hellberg: *Missions on a Colonial Frontier West of Lake Victoria,* Uppsala 1965.

M. de K. Hemphill: 'The British Sphere 1884–94', Chapter XI in R. Oliver and G. Mathew: *A History of East Africa*, Vol. I, Oxford 1963.

G. Hewitt: *The Problems of Success: A History of the Church Missionary Society 1910–1942*, Vol. I, London 1971.

W. S. Hooton and J. Stafford-Wright: *The First Twenty-Five Years of the Bible Churchmen's Missionary Society*, London 1947.

J. G. Huddle: 'The Life of Yakobo Adoko of Lango District', *UJ*, XXI, 2 (1957), pp. 184–90.

L. S. Hunter (ed): *The English Church: A New Look*, London 1966.

K. Ingham: *A History of East Africa*, London 1952.

——'The Amasagani of the Abakama of Bunyoro', *UJ*, XVII, 2 (1953), pp. 138–45.

——'Some Aspects of the History of Western Uganda', *UJ*, XXI, 2 (1957), pp. 131–49.

——*The Making of Modern Uganda*, London, 3rd edn, 1965.

——*The Kingdom of Toro in Uganda*, London 1975.

William James: *The Varieties of Religious Experience*, Gifford Lectures for 1901/2, London, edn of 1928.

T. B. Johnson: *Tramps Round the Mountains of the Moon*, London 1908.

H. H. Johnston: *The Uganda Protectorate*, 2 vols., London 1902.

H. Gresford Jones: *Uganda in Transformation*, London 1926.

T. B. Kabwegyere: *The Politics of State Formation: The Nature and Effects of Colonialism in Uganda*, Nairobi 1974.

J. Kahimbaara and B. W. Langlands: *The Human Factor in the Changing Ecology of Mwenge*, Occasional Paper No 16, Dept of Geography, Makerere University, 1970.

S. Karugire: 'Relations between the Bairu and the Bahima in Nineteenth Century Nkore', *Tarikh,* III, 2 (1970), pp. 22–33,

——*A History of the Kingdom of Nkore in Western Uganda to 1896*, London 1971.

——*Nuwa Mbaguta*, Nairobi 1973.

J. S. Kasirye: *Obulamu bwa Stanislaus Mugwanya*, London and Kampala 1963.

I. K. Katoke: 'Karagwe (Kafuro) and the Founding of the Nyanza Mission (CMS)', *Tanganyika Notes and Records*, LXVI (1966), pp. 155–63.

A. Katumba and F. B. Welbourn: 'Muslim Martyrs of Buganda', *UJ*, XXVIII, 2 (1964), pp. 151-64.

L. O. Katyanku and S. Bulera: *Obwomezi bw'Omukama Duhaga II*, Nairobi 1950.

D. Kavulu: *The Uganda Martyrs*, Kampala 1969.

N. Q. King: *Christian and Muslim in Africa*, New York 1971.

A. L. Kitching: *On the Backwaters of the Nile*, London 1912.

— —*From Darkness to Light*, London 1935.

G. D. Kittler: *The White Fathers*, London 1957.

M. S. M. Kiwanuka: *Muteesa of Uganda*, Nairobi, Dar es Salaam and Kampala 1967.

— —'Kabaka Mwanga and His Political Parties', *UJ*, XXXIII, 1 (1969), pp. 1, 17.

— —*The Kings of Buganda*, Nairobi, Dar es Salaam and Kampala 1971.

R. V. Knox: *Enthusiasm*, Oxford 1950.

N. F. M. Kusambiza: 'Mother Kevin', *UJ*, XI, 2 (1947), p. 123.

K. W. (Sir Tito Winyi, based on information given him by his father Kabalega. The initials stand for Kabalega and Winyi): 'Abakama ba Bunyoro-Kitara', *UJ*, III, 2 (1935), pp. 149-60; IV, 1 (1936), pp. 65-83; V, 2 (1937), pp. 53-67. An anonymous first draft of this material is published under the title 'Habusinge Bw'Omukama Kabalega nabanyoro abali abamasa namasaza gabu, nenganda zabu nebyaro byabu', in *Bu. Ch. Mag.* 1931, pp. 68-9, 77-81. Although published anonymously, it is clear on internal evidence that the writer is Sir Tito Winyi. In some respects the information in these articles is fuller than that in *UJ*.

B. W. Langlands: *Sleeping Sickness in Uganda*, Occasional Paper No 1, Dept of Geography, Makerere University 1971.

— —and G. Namirembe: *Studies in the Geography of Religion in Uganda*, Occasional Paper No 4, Dept of Geography, Makerere University 1967.

E. C. Lanning: 'Kikukule, Guardian of South Eastern Bunyoro', *UJ*, XXXII, 2 (1968), pp. 119-48.

J. C. D. Lawrance: *The Iteso: Forty Years of Change in a Nilo-Hamitic Tribe of Uganda*, London 1957.

T. E. Lawrence: *Kwo pa Ladit Canon Sira Dongo, Won Acoli ki Lango i Nying Yesu Kristo*, Kampala, n.d., n.a., but Canon Lawrence's authorship is confirmed by Mrs Lawrence.

G. Leblond: *Le Père Auguste Achte*, Paris, 1906.

A. B. Lloyd: *In Dwarf Land and Cannibal Country*, London 1899.

— —*Uganda to Khartoum*, London 1906.

Sister M. Louis: *Love is the Answer*, Dublin 1964.

D. A. Low: 'British Public Opinion and the Uganda Question: October-December 1892', *UJ*, XVIII, 2 (1954), pp. 81-100.

— —*Religion and Society in Uganda 1875-1900*, Kampala 1957 (Low 1957 (i)).

— —'The Northern Interior 1840-1900', Chapter IX of R. Oliver and G. Mathew: *History of East Africa*, Vol. 1, Oxford 1963, pp. 297-351.

— —'Uganda: The Establishment of the Protectorate 1894-1919', Chapter II of V. Harlow and E. Chilver: *History of East Africa*, Vol. II, Oxford 1965, pp. 57-122.

— —'Converts and Martyrs in Buganda', Chapter VI in C. G. Baeta: *Christianity in Tropical Africa*, London 1968, pp. 150-64.

— —*Buganda in Modern History*, London 1971.

— —*The Mind of Buganda*, London 1971.

— —*Lion Rampant*, London 1973.

— —and R. C. Pratt: *Buganda and British Overrule*, London 1960.

A. Luck: *African Saint: The Life of Apolo Kivebulaya*, London 1963.

J. R. L. Macdonald: *Soldiering and Surveying in British East Africa*, London 1897.

G. P. McGregor: *King's College Budo: The First Sixty Years*, Nairobi and London 1967.

A. M. Mackay: Pioneer Missionary of the Church Missionary Society to Uganda, by his sister, London 1890.

Soeur Marie-André du Sacré-Coeur: *Ouganda, terre de martyrs*, Castermann, Belgium 1963.

E. M. Matheson: *An Enterprise So Perilous,* Dublin, n.d.

F. Maxse: *Seymour Vandeleur*, London 1906.

S. Mbabi-Katana: 'Death of Daudi Mbabi, Grand Old Man of Bunyoro', *Uganda Herald*, 25 July 1953.

J. S. Mbiti: *African Religions and Philosophy*, London 1969.

— —*Concepts of God in Africa*, London 1970.

H. F. Morris: 'The Making of Ankole', *UJ*, XXI, 1 (1957), pp. 1-15.

— —'The Murder of H. St. G. Galt', *UJ*, XXIV, 1 (1960), pp. 1-15.

— —*Heroic Recitations of the Bahima of Ankole*, London 1964.

S. Neill: *A History of Christian Missions*, London 1964.

K. K. Nganwa: *Abakozire eby'okutangaza omuri Ankole*, Nairobi 1948.

J. Nicolet: *Yohana Kitagana*, Paris 1947.

A. Nicq: *Vie de Père Siméon Lourdel,* Paris 1896.

Ntare School History Society: 'H.M. Stanley's Journey Through Ankole in 1899', *UJ*, XXIX, 2 (1965), pp. 185-92.

K. Oberg: 'The Kingdom of Ankole in Uganda', in M. Fortes and E. E. Evans-Pritchard: *African Political Systems*, London 1960.

B. A. Ogot: *History of the southern Luo*, Nairobi 1967.

——'The Concept of Jok', *African Studies*, XX, 2 (1961), pp. 123-30.

L. Okech: *Tekwaro kiker Lobo Acholi*, Nairobi 1953.

Okot p'Bitek: 'The Concept of Jok among the Acholi and Langi', *UJ*, XXVII, 1 (1963), pp. 15-29.

——'Acholi Concept of Fate—Woko, Wilobo and Run-Piny', *UJ*, XXIX, 1 (1965), pp. 85-94.

——*Song of Lawino*, Nairobi 1966.

——*Religion of the Central Luo*, Nairobi 1971.

R. Oliver: *The Missionary Factor in East Africa*, London 1952.

——'A Question about the Bacwezi', *UJ*, XVII, 2 (1953), pp. 135-7.

——and A. Atmore: *Africa Since 1800*, Cambridge 1967.

——and G. Mathew: *History of East Africa*, Vol. I, Oxford 1963.

M. Perham: *The Years of Adventure*, London 1956.

——and M. Bull (eds): *The Diaries of Lord Lugard*, 4 vols, London 1959.

R. D. Pierpont: *In Uganda for Christ: The Life Story of the Rev. J. S. Callis*, London 1898.

M. L. Pirouet: 'The Coronation of the Omukama of Toro', *Makerere Journal*, XII (1966), pp. 16-24.

——'The Spread of Christianity in and around Uganda', *UJ*, XXXII, 1 (1968), pp. 82-6.

——*Strong in the Faith*, Kampala 1969. (Pirouet 1969 (i)).

——*A Dictionary of Christianity in Uganda*, Dept of Religious Studies, Makerere University 1969.

——'A Comparison of the Response of Three Societies to Christianity (Toro, Teso, Kikuyu)', University Social Sciences Conference, Kampala 1969.

——'The First World War—An Opportunity Missed by the Missions', University Social Sciences Conference, Nairobi 1970.

Sir Gerald Portal: *The British Mission to Uganda in 1893*, London 1894.

J. Poulton: 'Like Father, Like Son', *International Review of Missions*, July 1961.

T. Price: 'The Church as a Landholder in Eastern Africa', *Bulletin of the Society for African Church History*, I, 1 (1964), pp. 8-13.

J. B. Purvis: *Through Uganda to Mount Elgon*, London 1909.

T. O. Ranger: 'The Church in an Age of African Revolution', review article on A. Hastings: *Church and Mission in Modern Africa*, in *East African Journal*, V, 8 (1968), pp. 11-16.

A. I. Richards (ed): *East African Chiefs*, London 1959.

E. Richards: *Fifty Years in Nyanza*, Nairobi 1950.

K. Richardson: *Garden of Miracles*, London and Eastbourne 1968.

A. D. Roberts: 'The Lost Counties of Bunyoro', *UJ*, XXVI, 2 (1962), pp. 194–9. (Roberts 1962 (i)).

——'The Sub-imperialism of the Baganda', *JAH*, III, (1962), pp. 435–50. (Roberts 1962 (ii)).

R. Robinson and J. Gallagher: *Africa and the Victorians*, London 1963.

J. Roscoe: *The Baganda*, London 1911.

——*The Northern Bantu*, Cambridge 1915.

——*Twenty Five Years in East Africa*, Cambridge 1921.

——*The Bakitara*, Cambridge 1923 (Roscoe 1923 (i)).

——*The Banyankole*, Cambridge 1923 (Roscoe 1923 (ii)).

J. A. Rowe: 'The Purge of Christians at Mwanga's Court', *JAH*, V, 1 (1964), pp. 55–72 (Rowe 1964 (i)).

——'Mika Sematimba', *UJ*. XXVIII, 2 (1964), pp. 179–200 (Rowe 1964 (ii)).

——*Lugard at Kampala*, Makerere History Papers 3, Kampala 1969 (Rowe 1969 (ii)).

——'Myth, Memoir and Moral Admonition: Luganda Historical Writing 1893–1969', *UJ*, XXXI, 1 (1969), pp. 17–40 (Rowe 1969 (ii)).

G. Rukiidi (trans. J. R. Muchope): *The Kings of Tooro*, Dept of History, Makerere University, cyclostyled, n.d.

J. K. Russell: *Men Without God?*, London 1966.

W. H. Sangree: *Age, Prayer and Politics in Tiriki, Kenya*, London 1966.

C. Sebuliba: 'The Late Ham Mukasa', *UJ*, XXIII, 2 (1959), pp. 184–5.

A. Shorter and E. Kataza: *Missionaries to Yourselves*, London 1972.

M. Singleton: in A. Singer and B. V. Street: *Zande Themes*, Oxford 1972.

S. R. Skeens: 'Reminiscences of Busoga and its Chiefs', *UJ*, IV, 3 (1937), pp. 185–96.

A. W. Southall: 'The Alur Legend of Sir Samuel Baker and Mukama Kabarega', *UJ*, XV, 2 (1951), pp. 187–90.

——*Alur Society*, London 1956.

D. N. Stafford: 'Bunyoro Grain Pits', *UJ*, XIX, 2 (1955), p. 208.

——'The Burial of Kabarega', *UJ*, XIX, 2 (1955), p. 208.

H. M. Stanley: *In Darkest Africa*, London 1890.

D. J. Stenning: 'The Nyankole', in B. K. Taylor and A. I. Richards: *East African Chiefs*, London 1960, pp. 146–73.

Eugene Stock: *History of the Church Missionary Society*, Vol. III, London 1899; Vol. IV, London 1916.

B. G. M. Sundkler: *The Christian Ministry in Africa*, London 1960.

B. K. Taylor: *The Western Lacustrine Bantu*, Ethnographic Survey of Africa, East Central Africa, Part XIII, London 1962 (B. K. Taylor).

J. V. Taylor: *The Growth of the Church in Buganda,* London 1958 (Taylor).

H. B. Thomas: 'Capax Imperii—The Story of Simei Kakunguru', *UJ,* VI, 2 (1939), pp. 125-36.

——'The Baganda Martyrs 1885-1887', *UJ*, XV, 1 (1951), pp. 84-91.

——'J. J. Uganda: Bishop Willis', *UJ*, XIX, 1 (1955), pp. 103-4.

——'The Rev. A. B. Fisher in Uganda: A Memoir', *UJ,* XXI,1 (1957), pp. 107-10.

——'The Wilsons of Early Uganda', *UJ*, XXI, 2 (1957), pp. 232-3.

——and R. Scott: *Uganda*, London 1935.

J. Thoonen: *Black Martyrs*, London 1941.

A. B. Thruston: *African Incidents*, London 1900.

J. S. Trimingham: *Islam in East Africa*, Oxford 1964.

A. R. Tucker: Toro: *Visits to Ruwenzori*, London 1899.

——*Eighteen Years in Uganda and East Africa*, London, 1st edn in 2 vols, 1908; 2nd edn in 1 vol. London 1911.

M. Twaddle: 'The *Bakungu* Chiefs of Buganda under British Colonial Rule 1900-1930', *JAH*, X, 2 (1969), pp. 309-22 (Twaddle 1969 (ii)).

Uganda Lands and Surveys Department: *Uganda Atlas*, Kampala 1962.

G. N. Uzoigwe: *Revolution and Revolt in Bunyoro-Kitara*, Makerere History Papers, 5, Kampala 1970.

S. Vandeleur: *Campaigning on the Upper Nile and Niger*, London 1898.

M. A. C. Warren: *The Missionary Movement from Britain in Modern History,* London 1965.

——'The Church of England as by Law Established—Unfit for Export?', in L. S. Hunter: *The English Church: A New Look*, London 1966.

J. B. Webster: 'Pioneers of Teso', *Tarikh*, III, 2 (1970), pp. 47-58.

——et al: *The Iteso During the Asonya*, Nairobi 1973.

——and Onyango-ku-Odongo: *The Central Luo During the Aconya*, Nairobi 1976.

F. B. Welbourn: 'Speke and Stanley at the Court of Mutesa', *UJ*, XXV, 2 (1961), pp. 220-3.

——*East African Rebels*, London 1961 (Welbourn 1961 (ii)).

——*East African Christian*, London 1965.

——*Religion and Politics in Uganda 1951–1962*, London 1965 (Welbourn 1965 (ii)).

——and B. A. Ogot: *A Place to Feel at Home*, London 1966.

White Fathers: 'A l'assaut des pays nègres', *Journal des missionaires d'Algers dans l'Afrique équatoriale*, Paris 1884.

——*Vers les grands lacs*, Namur, France, n.d.

F. L. Williams: 'Nuwa Mbaguta, Nganzi of Ankole', *UJ*, X, 2 (1946), pp. 124–35.

C. T. Wilson and R. W. Felkin: *Uganda and the Egyptian Soudan*, London 1882.

E. H. Winter: *Beyond the Mountains of the Moon*, London 1959.

Sir Tito Winyi: v. K.W.

M. J. Wright: 'The Early Life of Rwot Isaya Ogwanggujji, M.B.E.', *UJ*, XXII, 2 (1958), pp. 131–8.

——*Buganda in the Heroic Age*, Nairobi 1971.

C. C. Wrigley: 'Some Thoughts on the Bachwezi', *UJ*, XXII, 1 (1958), pp. 11–17.

Index